ABOUT CHORD CRASH COURSE

MW01011466

Our brains are wired to learn by patterns – finally, a music book that teaches that way.

Meridee Winters is an accomplished author, educator, musician, school director and pioneer in the world of creativity and music education. Her more than 50 music books and learning resources have sold tens of thousands of copies and earned her a devoted global following of teachers, students and musicians.

Chord Crash Course is the first and most popular of Meridee's books, known for its playful attitude and trailblazing "learn by pattern and shape" approach – which doesn't require reading music. It's this unique approach that allows learners to **play famous chord progressions within their first few hours of learning and lead sheets to their favorite songs within just a few chapters**.

Chord Crash Course has become a hit with self-taught musicians, with music teachers looking to boost progress and with professional performers expanding their skillset. (This makes sense, given the book's recording studio origins. Meridee initially developed this method to empower recording artists who were unable to accompany themselves.) Through simple diagrams and step-by-step instruction, you will learn music's most powerful and universal patterns, including chords, arpeggios, intervals, Alberti bass, rock rhythms, pop progressions and so much more. Students can then graduate to Chord Crash Course Book 2 for higher level chord theory, including seventh chords and sus chords.

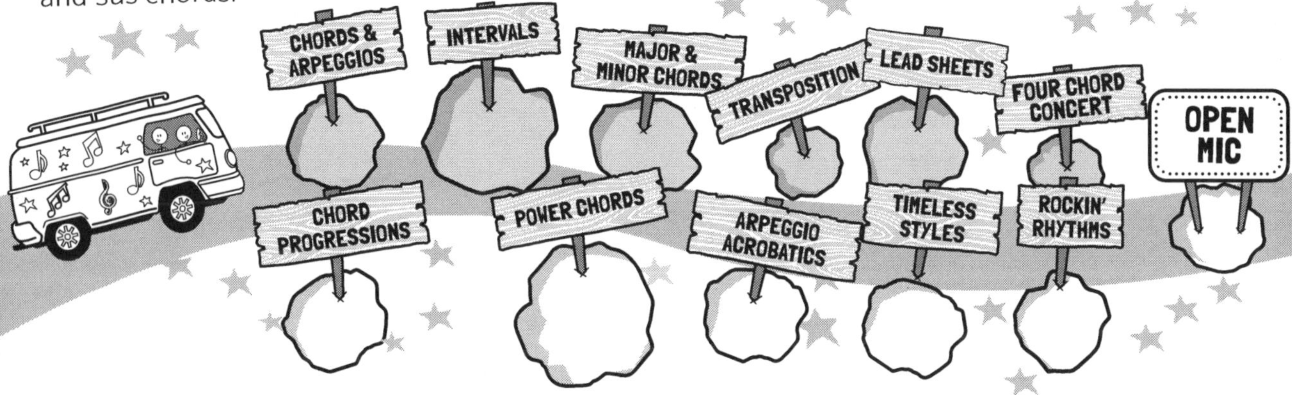

You don't have to read music. (We're serious)

The ability to read music is an incredible skill, and we're all for it. (Our Note Quest Game Book was created to specifically build that skill). This book is designed to work for all levels, however, including those who can and can't read music. Music, including chords and arpeggios, is largely a beautiful combination of patterns. By learning and applying these patterns, anyone can play and write music. For those who can read music, this book works as a great supplement, adding chord theory and comping skills to your existing skillset.

CHORD CRASH COURSE BOOK 1

CHAPTER 1: CHORDS & ARPEGGIOS

Exercise:

CHAPTER 2: CHORD PROGRESSIONS

Exercise:

CHAPTER 3: INTERVALS

Exercise:

CHAPTER 4: POWER CHORDS: FIFTHS

Exercise:

CHAPTER 5: MAJOR & MINOR CHORDS

Exercise:

CHAPTER 6: ARPEGGIO ACROBATICS

Exercise:

Alberti

Klezmer

MERIDEE WINTERS™ CHORD CRASH COURSE BOOK 1

Meridee Winters Publishing • 63 W. Lancaster Ave. #7 • Ardmore, PA 19003
www.MerideeWintersMusicMethod.com
ISBN: 978-1-943821-00-6 • Library of Congress Catalog Control Number: 2016911933

Meridee Winters: Music Composer, Author, and Art Director
Krysta Bernhardt: Graphic Design and Illustrations; Kate Capps: Editor, Creative Consultant
Armand Alidio: Cover Design and Additional Design; Monica Schaffer: Proofreading
Gabriel Rhopers: Additional design; Sean Miller: Graphic design

CHORDS & ARPEGGIOS
OPEN MIC
MERIDEE WINTERS
CHORD PROGRESSIONS
Your harmonic adventure begins!
INTERVALS
POWER CHORDS
FOUR CHORD CONCERT
MAJOR & MINOR CHORDS
ARPEGGIO ACROBATICS
ROCKIN' RHYTHMS
LEAD SHEETS
TIMELESS STYLES
TRANSPOSITION

CHAPTER 1

CHORDS and ARPEGGIOS

Chords and arpeggios are the power patterns used in most songs.

They are used in all types of music - from rock to classical, and everything in between.

Once you've learned to play these basic patterns, you will have the tools to compose or accompany yourself on countless songs.

Let's get started!

Every time you listen to the radio or watch a movie with an oh-so-stirring soundtrack, you are hearing chords and arpeggios. Chords and arpeggios are made of combinations of notes, and give music a foundation known as harmony.

Almost all of the world's music from the past to the present uses harmony. From harp to organ, choirs to mariachi bands, or rock bands to orchestras, harmony is everywhere in our musical world. In this chapter you will learn how to play chords and arpeggios, and you will find that they are not only easy – but fun!

To find out more about our creative community of music teachers and students, visit www.merideewintersmusicmethod.com

WHAT IS AN ARPEGGIO?

1. TRY A RIGHT HAND ARPEGGIO

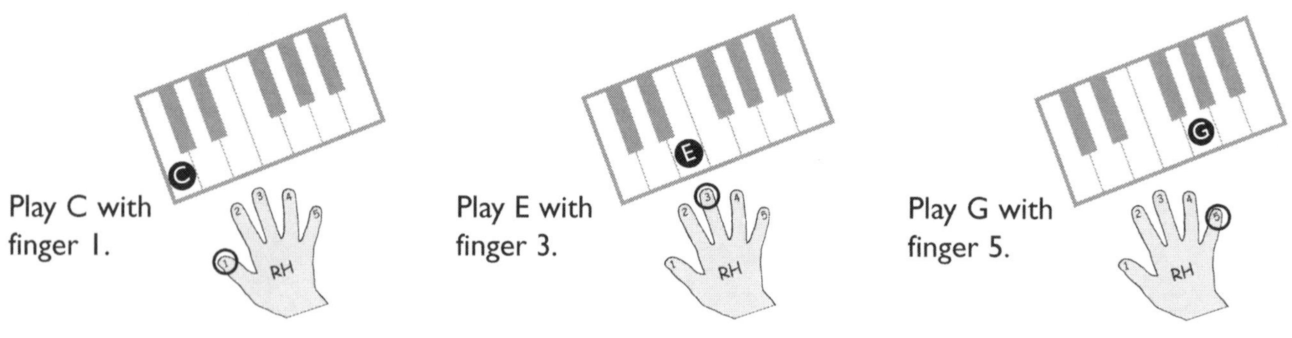

Play C with finger 1.

Play E with finger 3.

Play G with finger 5.

2. TRY A LEFT HAND ARPEGGIO

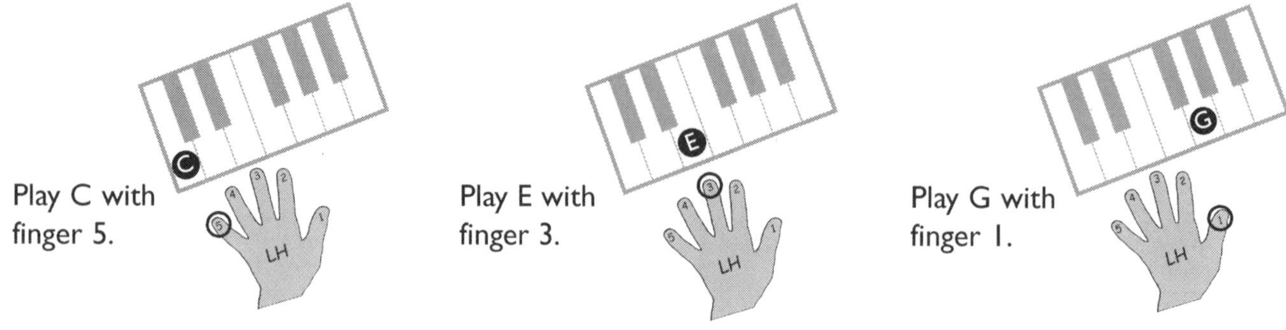

Play C with finger 5.

Play E with finger 3.

Play G with finger 1.

3. LOOK AT THE SHAPE ON THE KEYBOARD AND THE STAFF

Here is what the pattern looks like on the keyboard.

Here is what the pattern looks like on the staff.

Here is what the pattern looks like on the keyboard.

Here is what the pattern looks like on the staff.

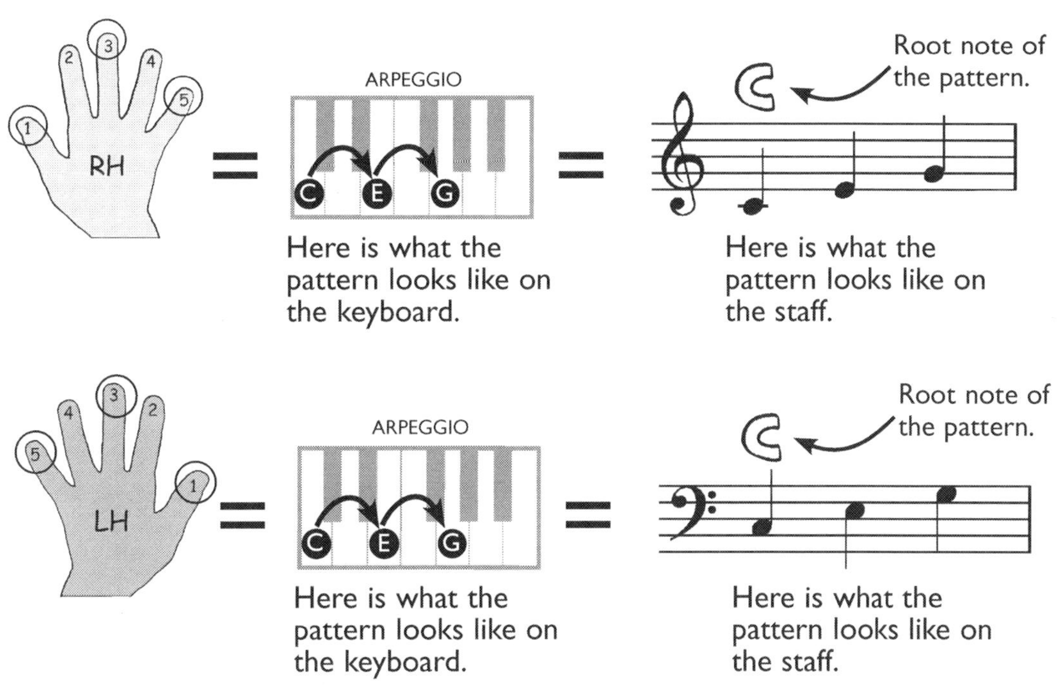

4. NOW PRACTICE

RIGHT HAND

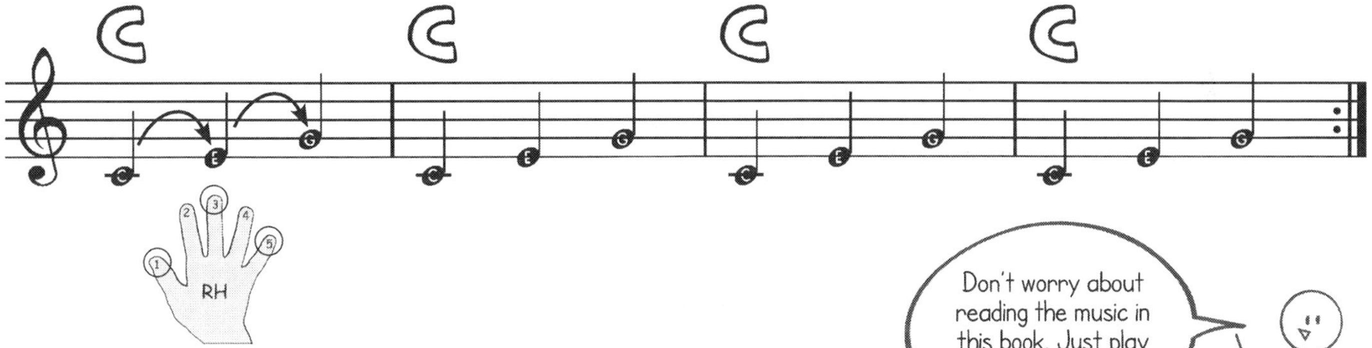

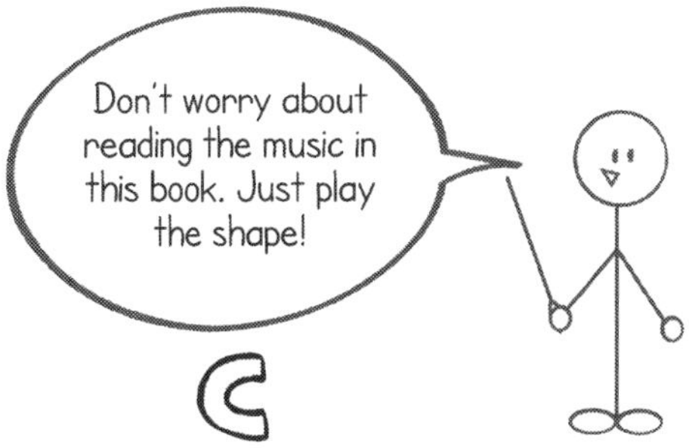

LEFT HAND

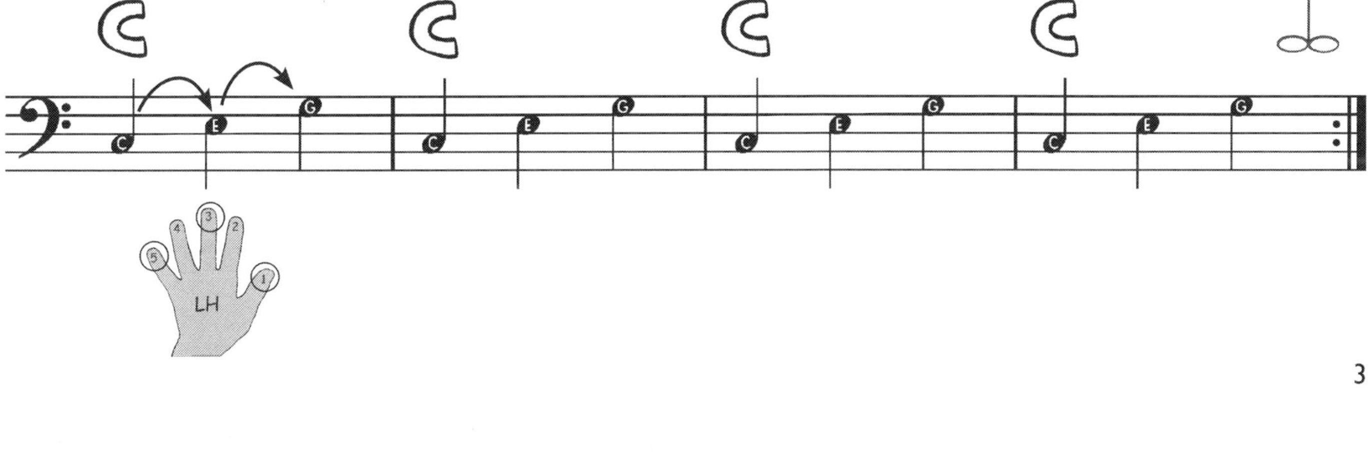

RIGHT HAND CLIMB

Use arpeggios to slowly creep your right hand up the keys. No need to read – just play the shape!

ARPEGGIO
C E G
RH
ARPEGGIO
D F A
RH
ARPEGGIO
E G B
RH
Think of the arpeggio as a "spider" shape.

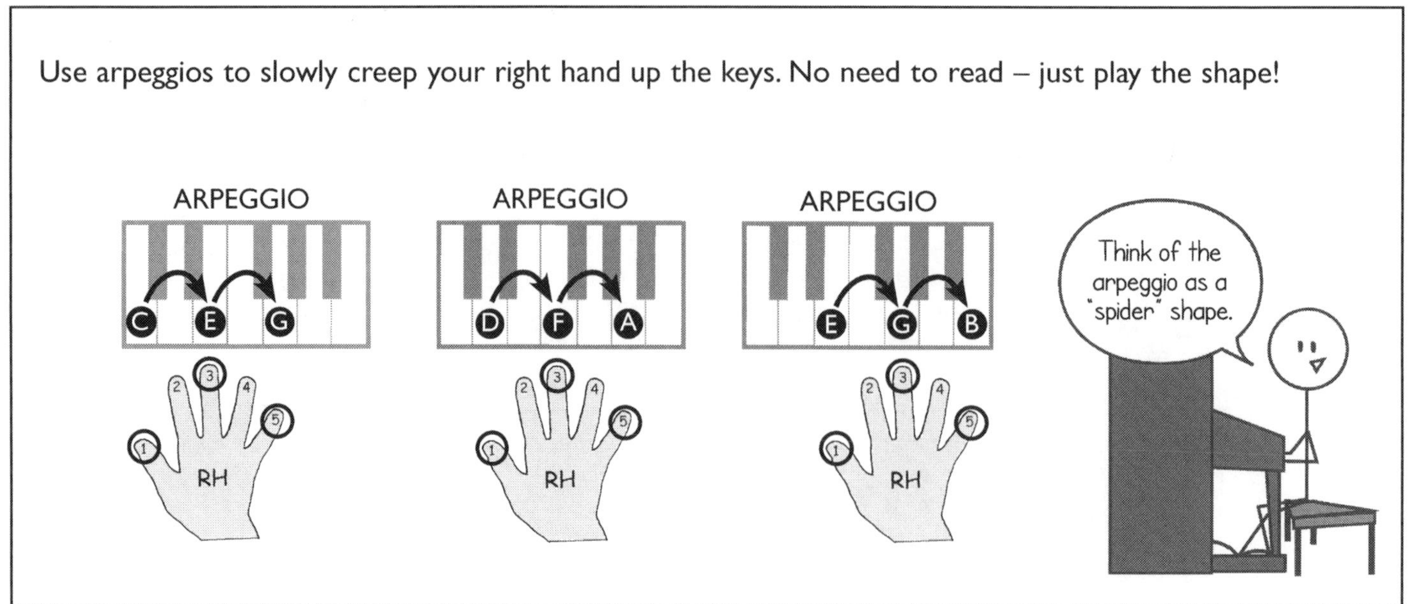

#1. RIGHT HAND CLIMB

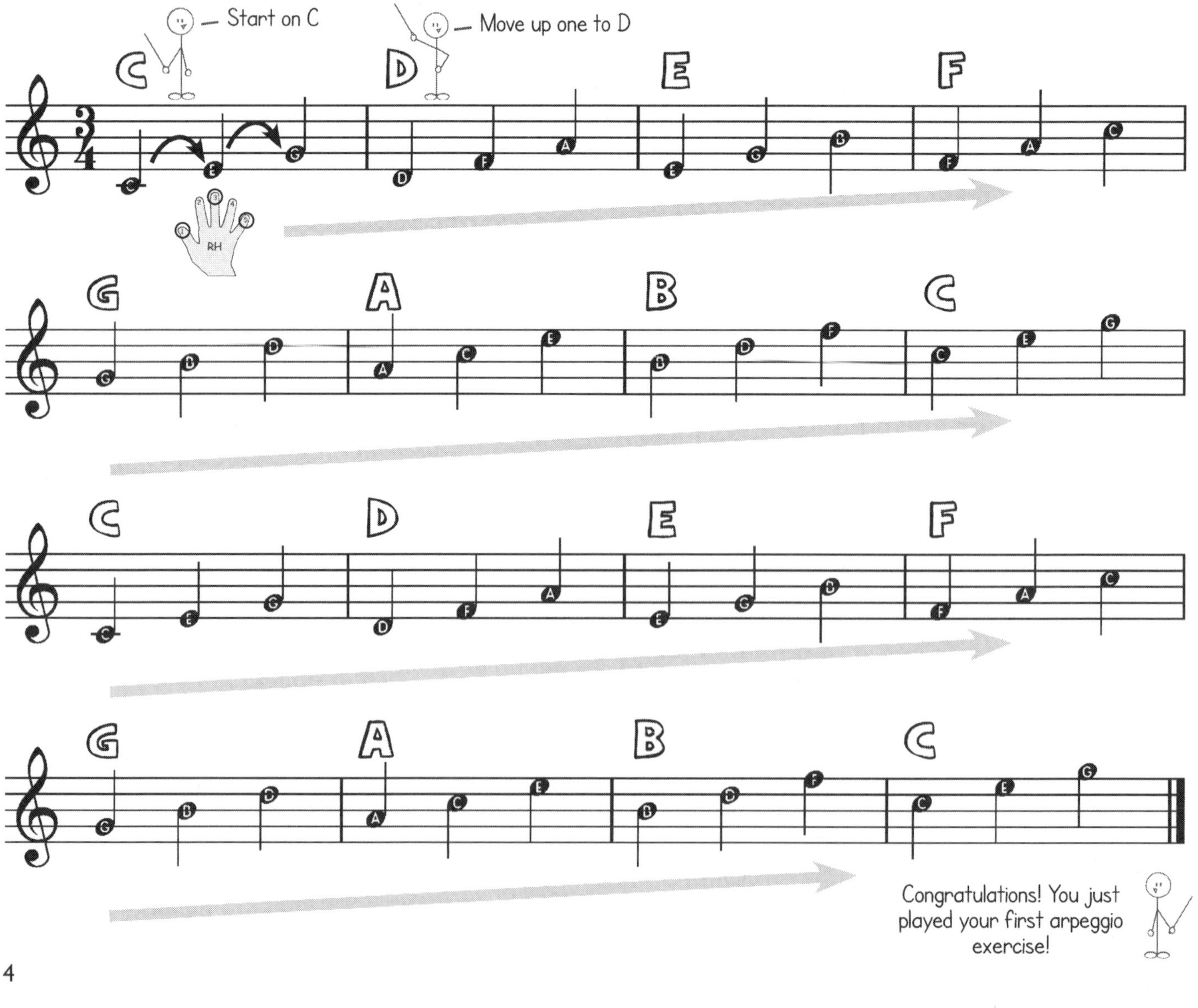

Start on C
Move up one to D
C
D
E
F
G
A
B
C
C
D
E
F
G
A
B
C
Congratulations! You just played your first arpeggio exercise!

LEFT HAND CLIMB

Use arpeggios to slowly creep your left hand up the keys. Just play the shape and climb!

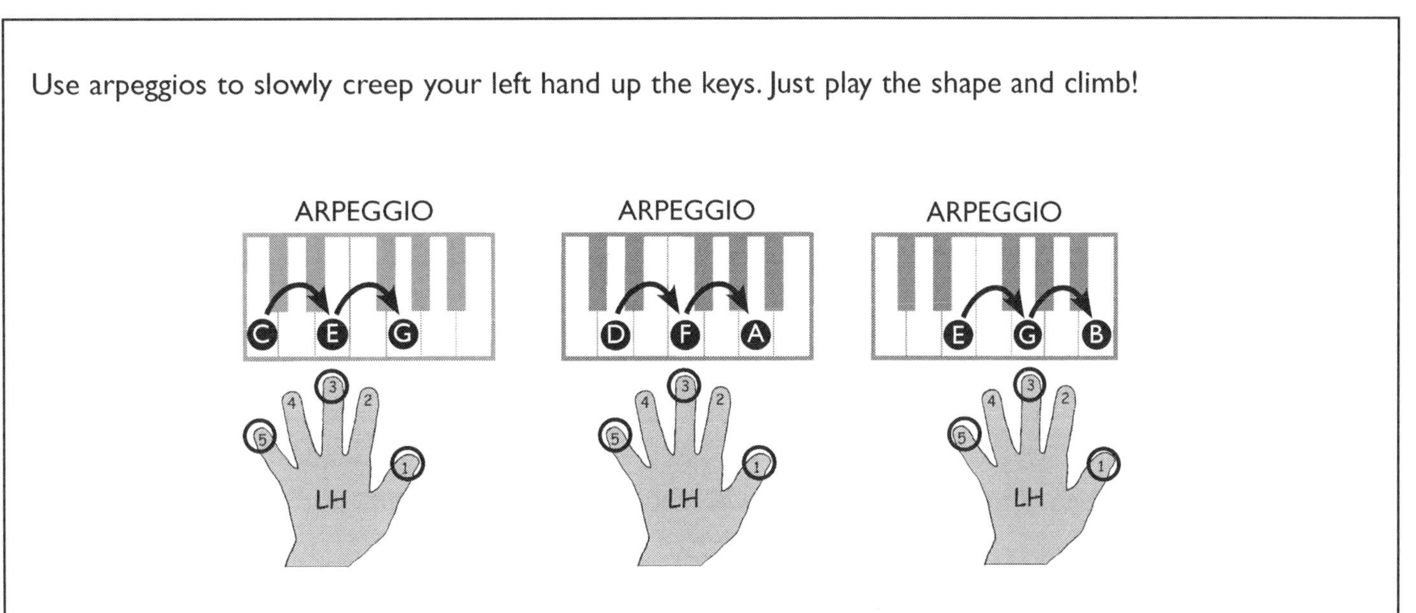

#2. LEFT HAND CLIMB

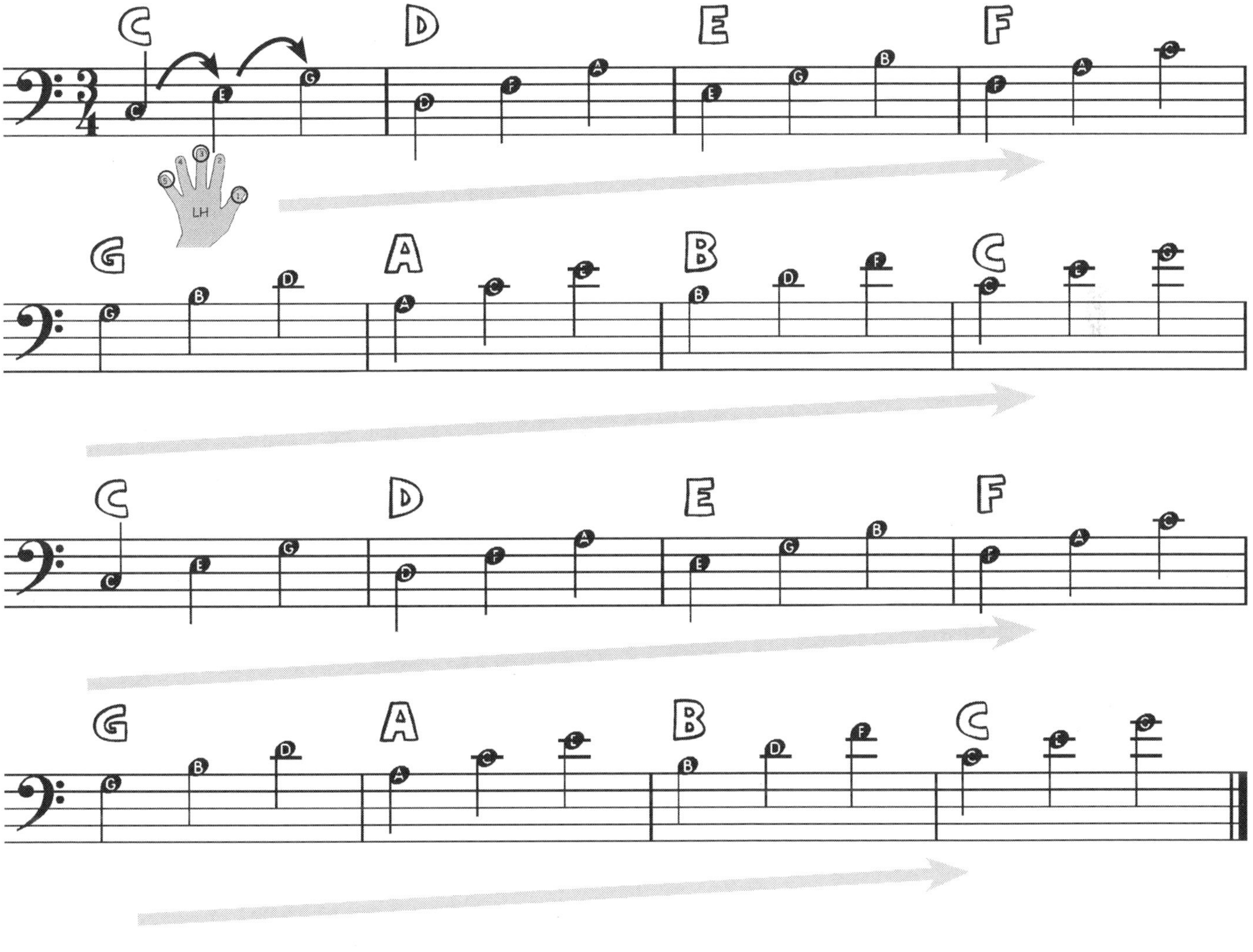

C D E F
G A B C
C D E F
G A B C

ARPEGGIO ACROBAT

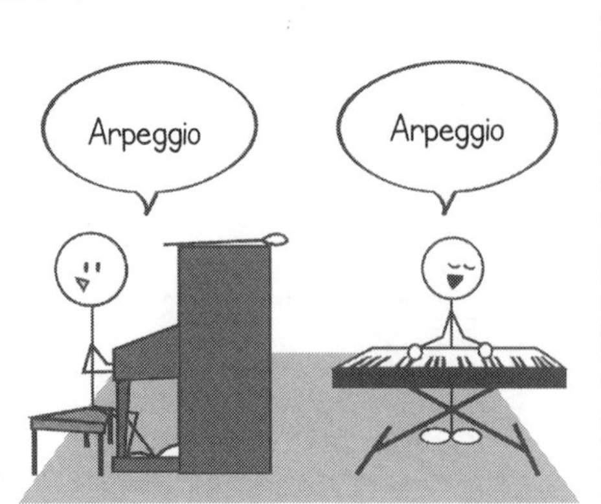

PREPARE: PLACE HANDS

- Place your left hand pinky (finger 5) on bass C and your right hand thumb (finger 1) on middle C. This position is called "C position."
- Play a C arpeggio with your left hand.
- Follow that with a C arpeggio in your right hand.
- Move both hands up one key to D position and keep going.

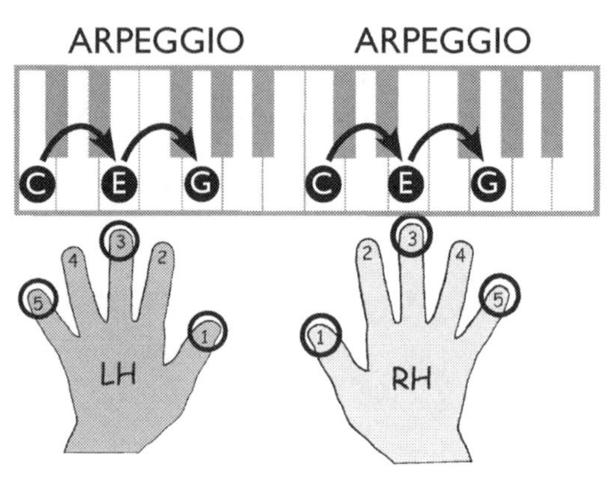

#3. ARPEGGIO ACROBAT

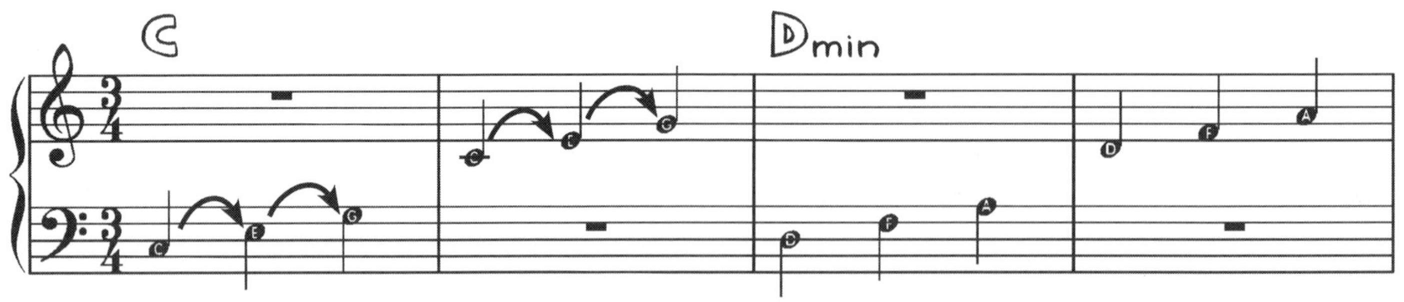

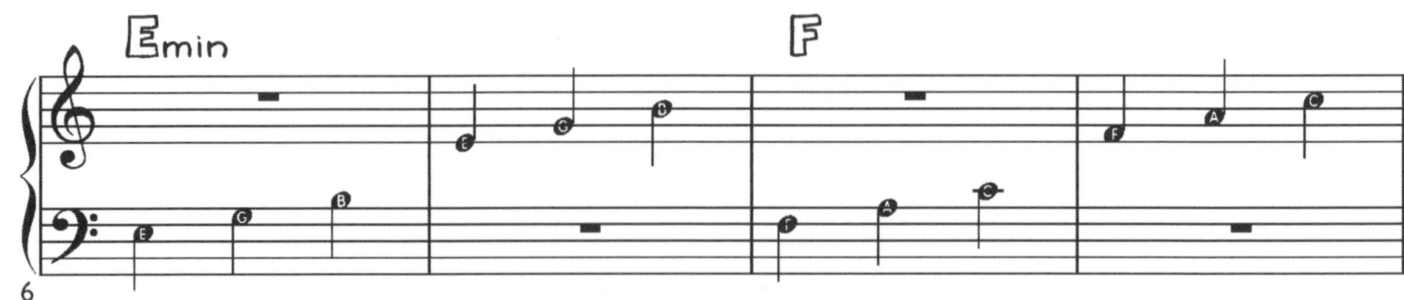

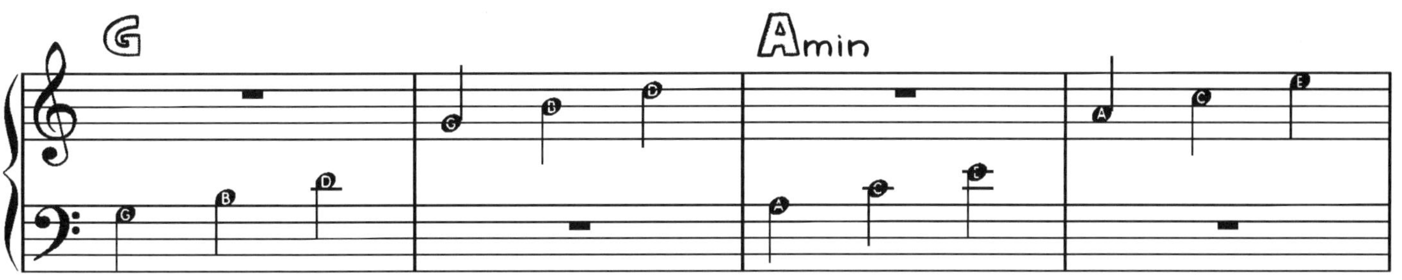

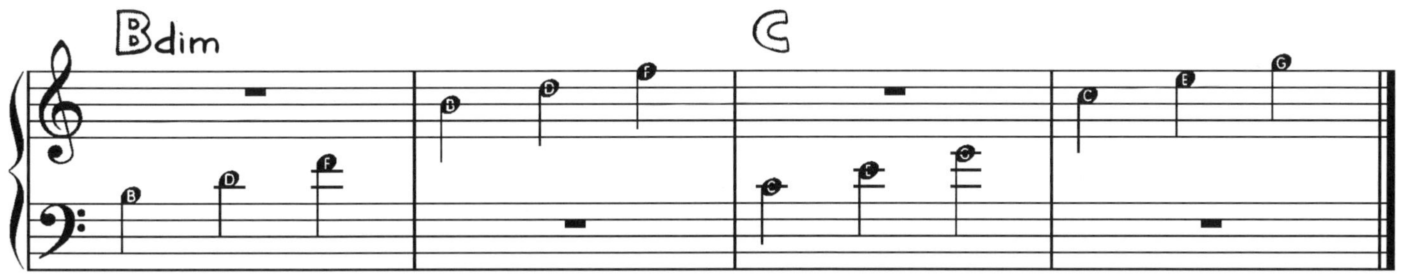

CHORD SYMBOLS

The capital letters you see above the staff are called "Chord Symbols." They're named after the root note and help you quickly find what chord you're playing.

Certain types of chords are called "minor" chords. These are noted in the chord symbol, too (like the D minor chord below). There are a few ways to notate this: Dmin, Dm, or even with a minus sign: D-

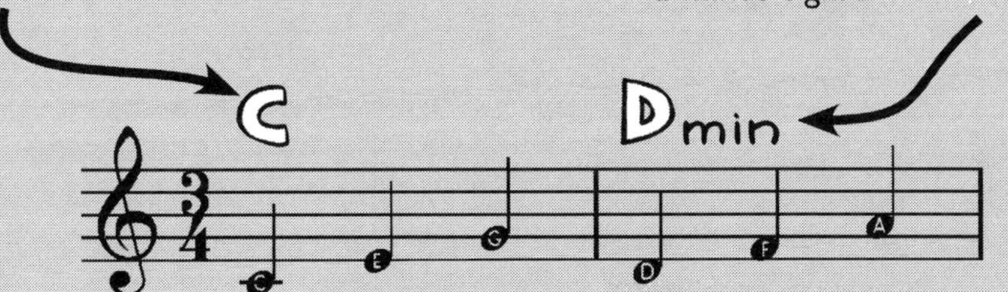

You'll learn more about minor (and major) chords in Chapter 5.

Note: we call it a "chord" symbol, but it applies to chords or arpeggios. You'll learn about chords next!

ROOT TRICK

Think of a plant with a root at the bottom. The other notes in the chord are flowers!

WHAT IS A CHORD?

1. TRY IT...

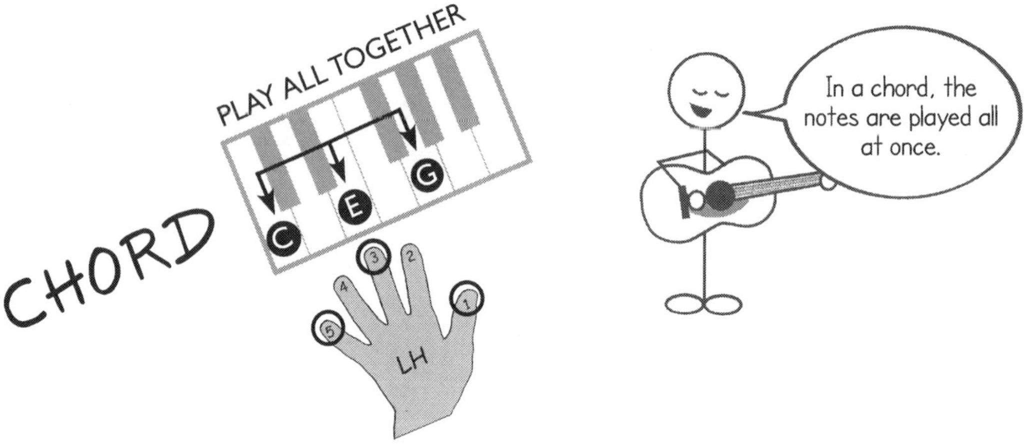

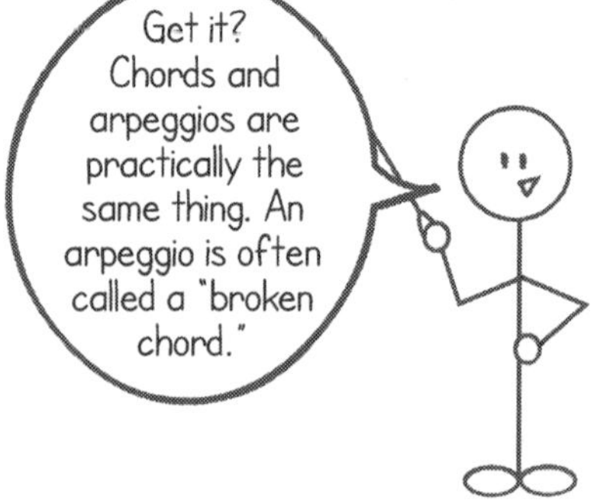

2. LOOK AT THE SHAPE ON THE KEYBOARD AND THE STAFF

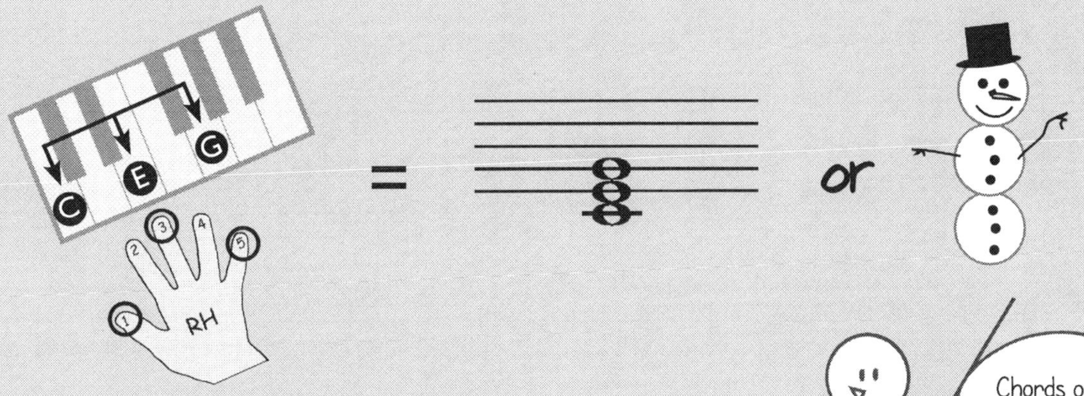

C E G

RH

= or

Chords on the staff look like a snowman!

Notes of the chord are stacked one above the other on the staff, which means you play them at the same time. For the basic chords we're learning, they are either line-line-line or space-space-space.

3. PRACTICE right hand arpeggios and chords until they are smooth.

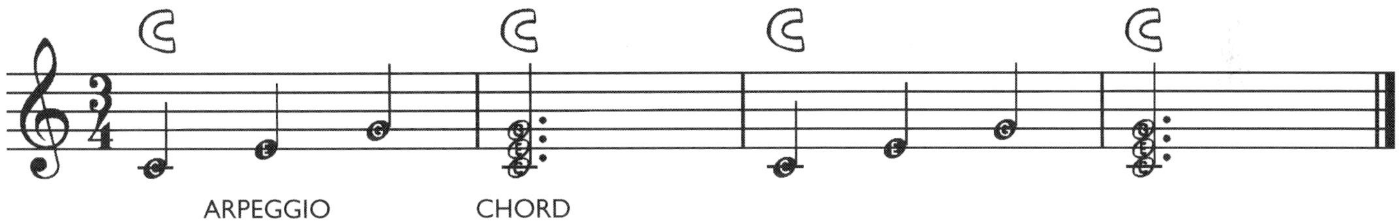

4. PRACTICE left hand arpeggios and chords until they are smooth.

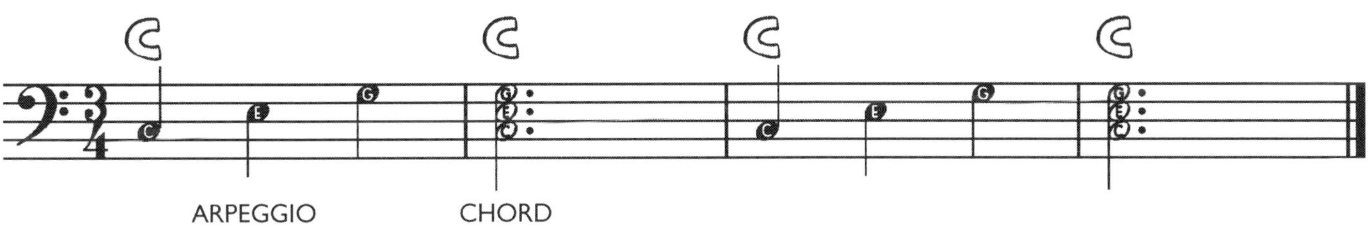

#4. CHORD SCALE CLIMB

Climb up the scale using arpeggios and chords. Say/think: "arpeggio, arpeggio, chord, chord."

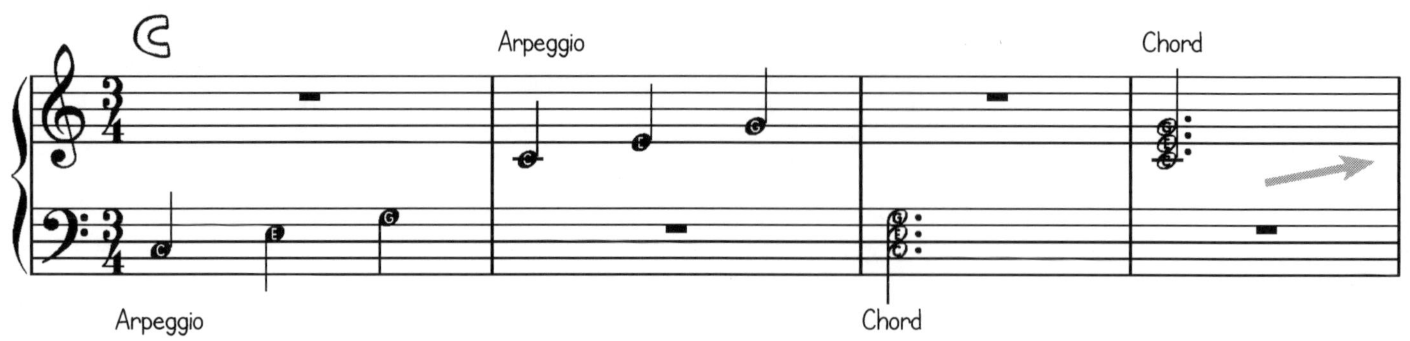

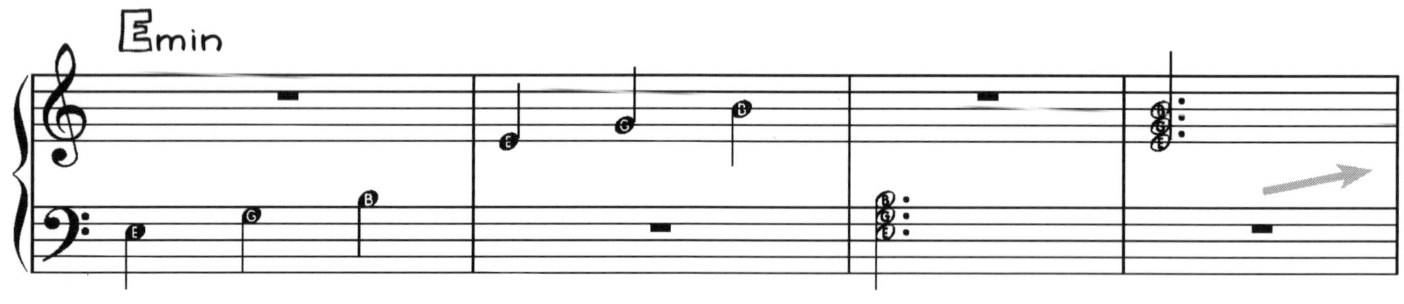

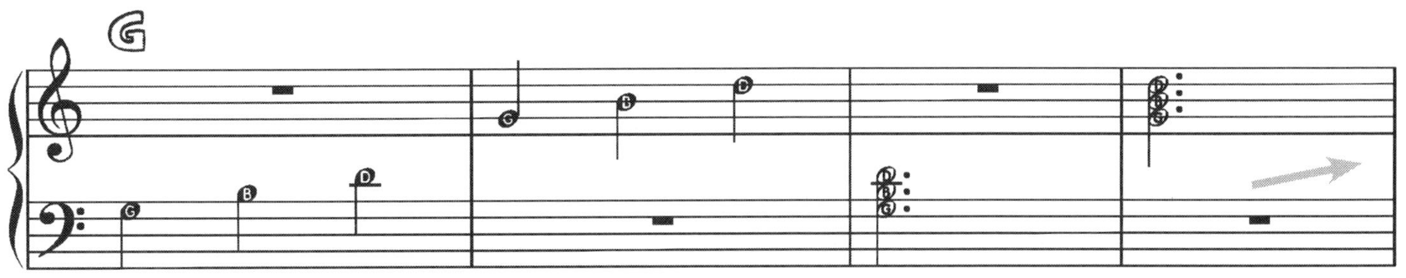
G

Amin

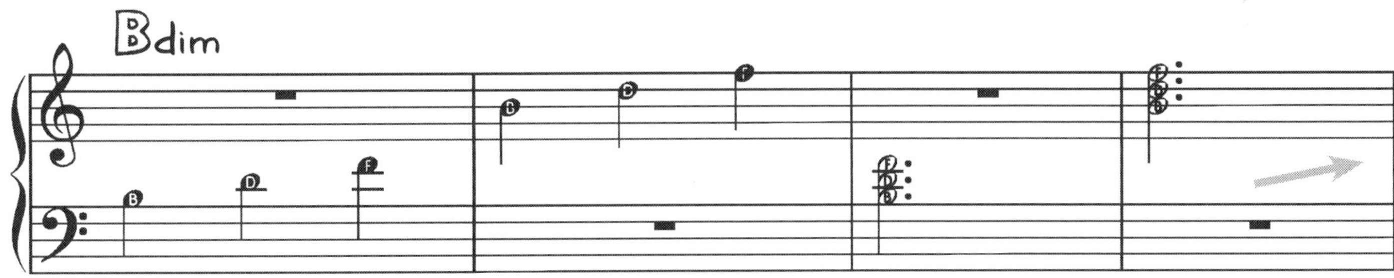
Bdim

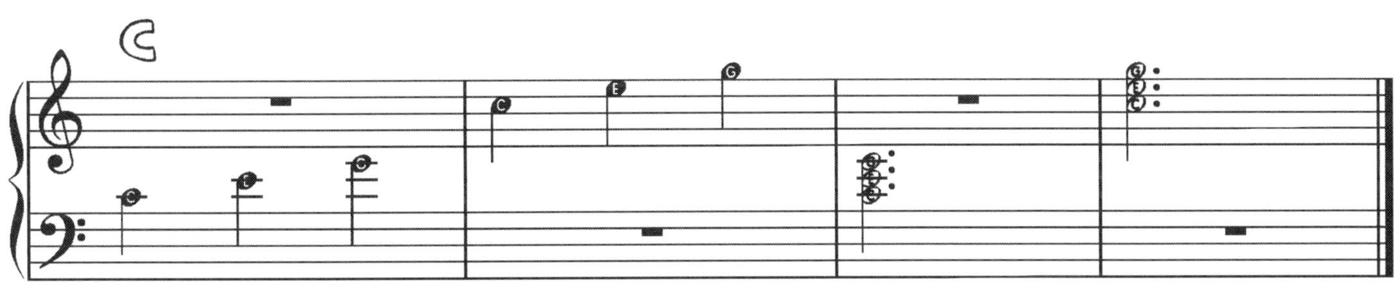
C

Congratulations! You just completed a chord scale!
Great! Er... What's a chord scale?
TURN THE PAGE TO FIND OUT!

CHORD SCALE CRASH COURSE

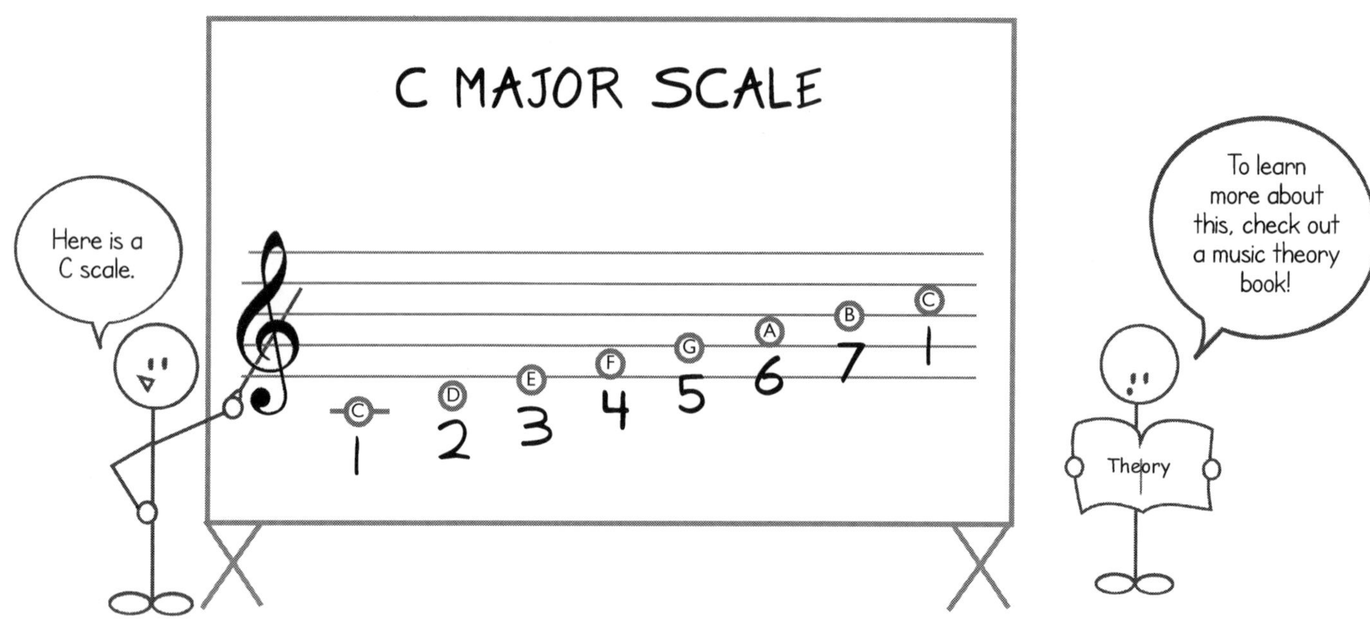

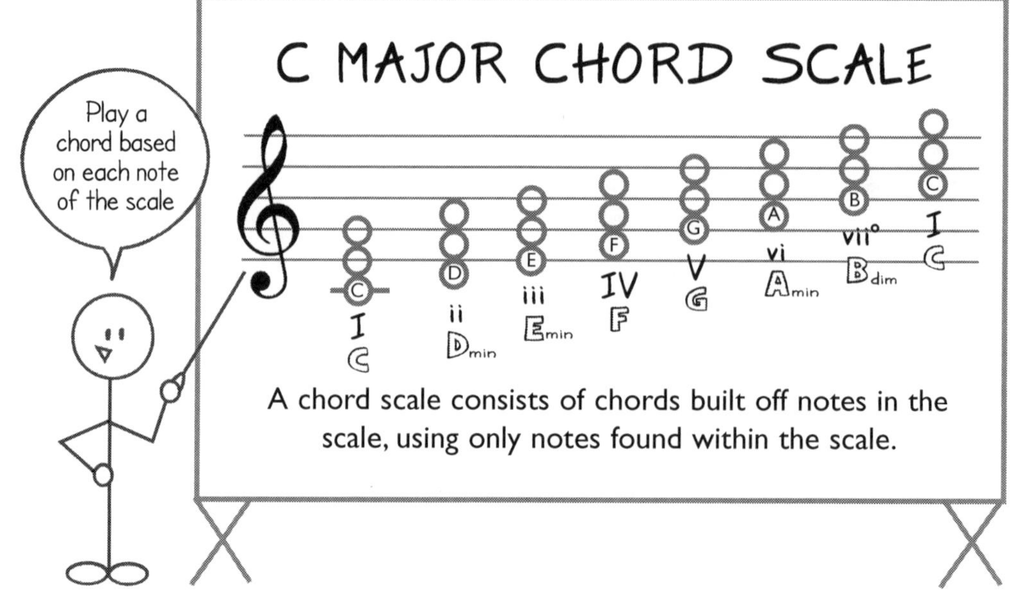

For a downloadable full color PDF of these charts, visit mwfunstuff.com/CCC!

CHORD SCALE CRASH COURSE

THE CHORD SCALE MAP

Roman numerals say which step of the scale you are on.

Major chords are capitalized and minor chords are lower case.*

Diminished chords sound strange because the fifth is lowered.

I	C	MAJOR
ii	D	MINOR
iii	E	MINOR
IV	F	MAJOR
V	G	MAJOR
vi	A	MINOR
vii°	B	DIMINISHED
I	C	MAJOR

Turn the page to see how this works when playing songs.

TOOL

For a downloadable full color PDF of these charts, visit mwfunstuff.com/CCC!

*Major and minor chords have their own chapter later in this book.

#5. CHORD SCALE SUMMIT

Play your way up the chord scale. Say it and play it!

CHAPTER 2

CHORD PROGRESSIONS

Just like a band, you're ready to play interesting songs that sound great.

In fact, you can actually make an infinite number of songs just by putting chords into different orders.

When you put chords in a song in a specific order, it's called a "chord progression."

Now that you have learned how to play chords and arpeggios, you are well on your way to playing countless songs and creating your own. The next step is to learn about chord progressions. What's a chord progression? A progression is when you take several chords and put them in a set order.

In this chapter, you will learn how to play arpeggios and chords in different orders to create all kinds of progressions, from rock songs to gypsy songs. And you won't just learn some famous progressions – you'll learn how to make your own.

#6. MALAGUENA

Start with your hands in A position. Play a left hand arpeggio, followed by a right hand arpeggio. Then move to the next chord/position and repeat.

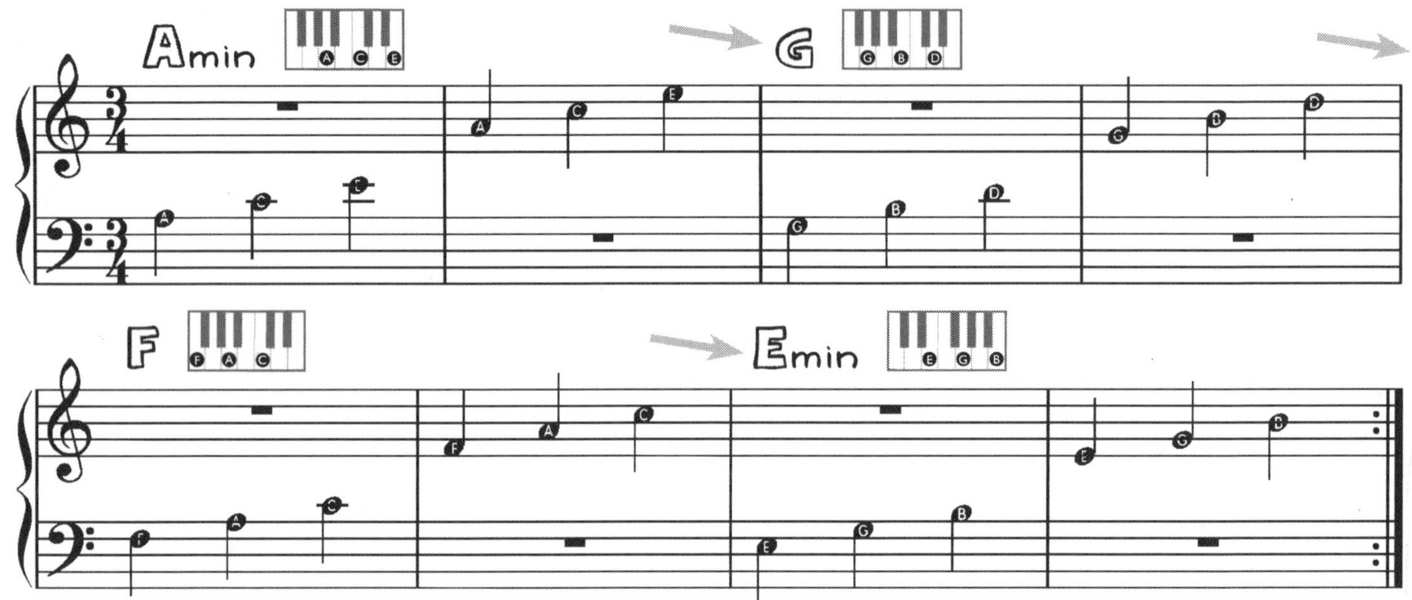

#7. MALAGUENA CHORD COMBINATION 1

Now play the Malaguena progression by using a left hand chord and right hand arpeggio pattern.

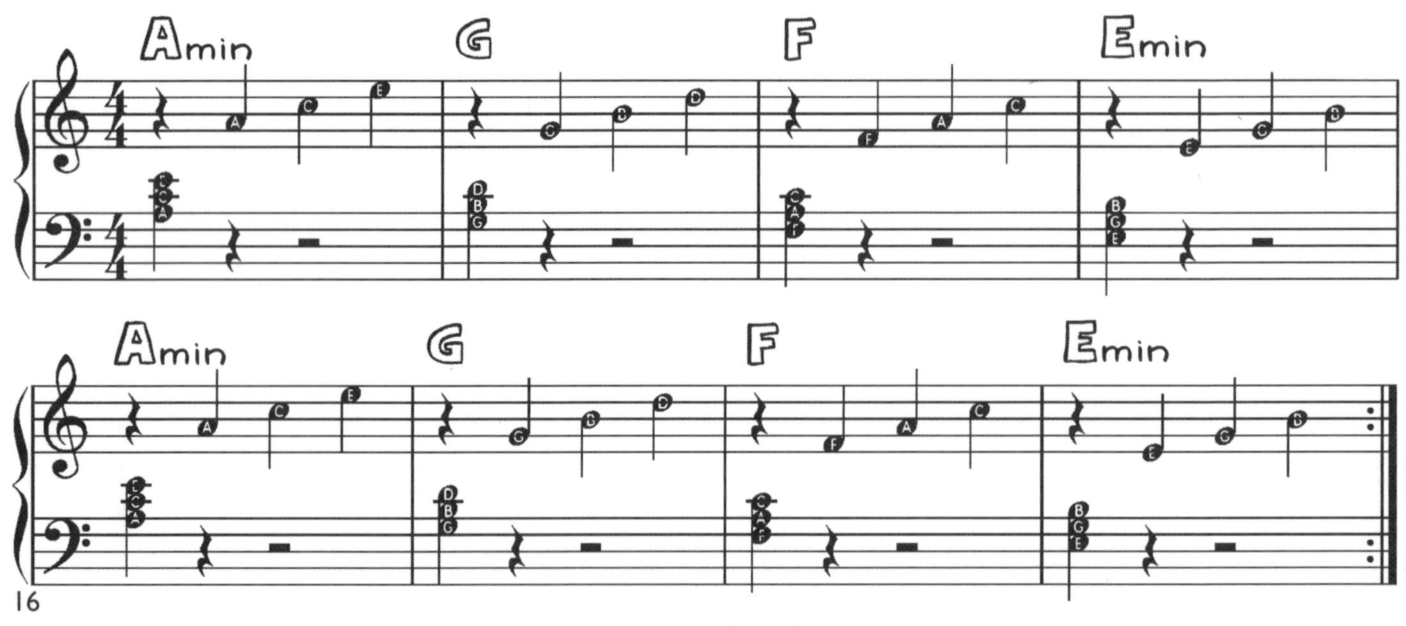

#8. MALAGUENA CHORD COMBINATION 2

Hands alternate! Say/think: "left, right, left, right."

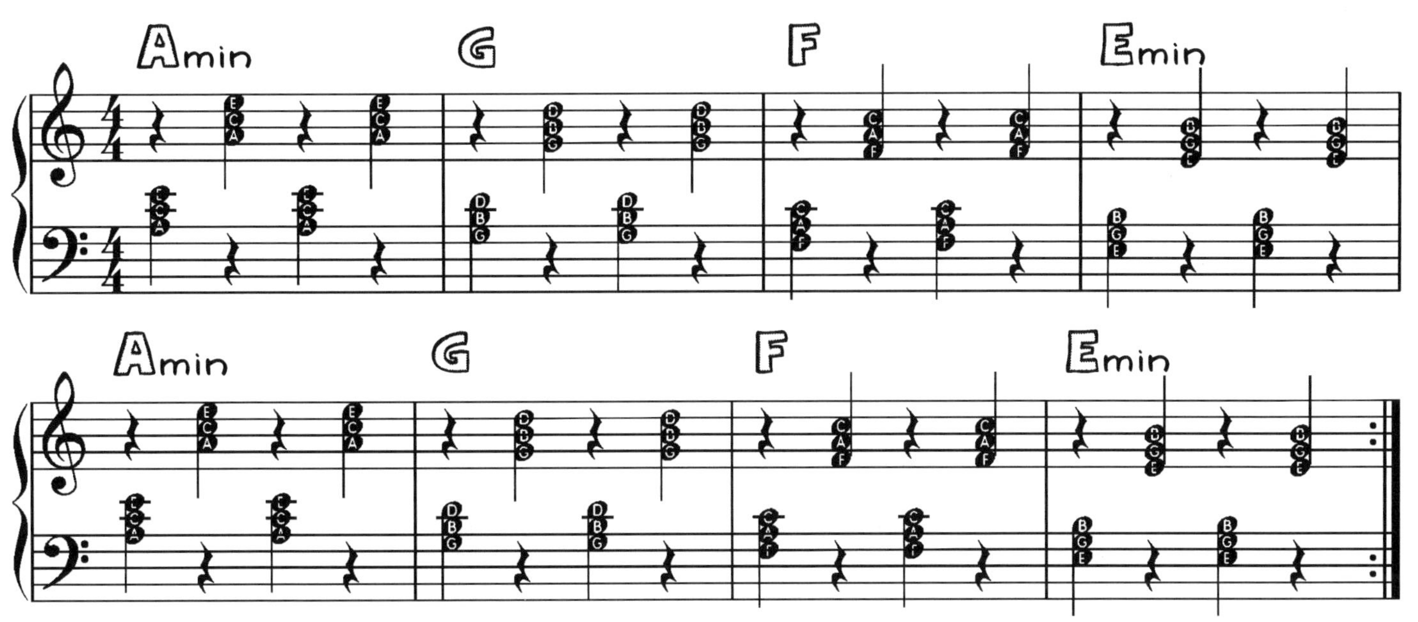

EXPERIMENT

Add interest and emotion to these exercises and others by using the boxes below.

PLAY LOUD

PLAY SLOW

PLAY WITH PEDAL

PLAY SOFT

PLAY HIGH

ADD EXTRA NOTES

PLAY FAST

PLAY LOW

CREATE AN ENDING

POWER PROGRESSIONS

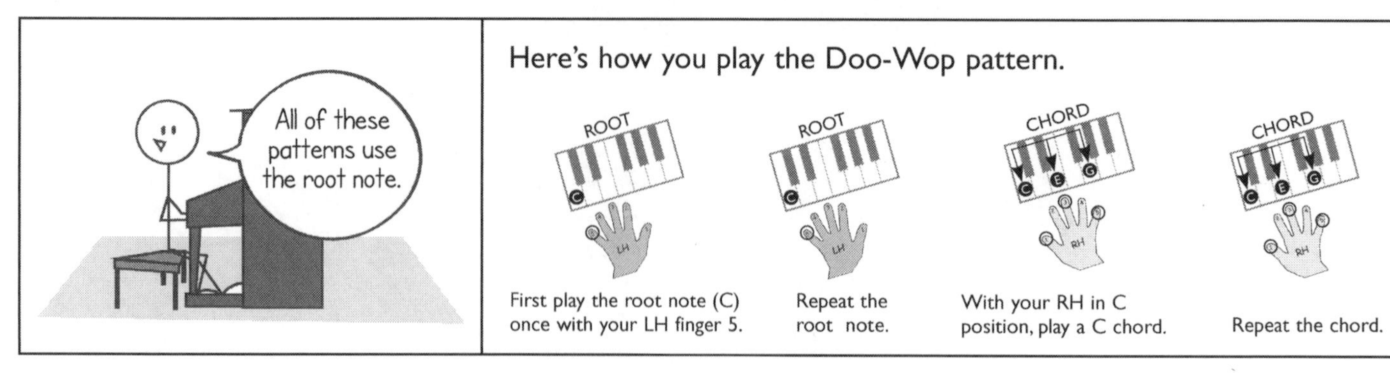

#9. DOO-WOP

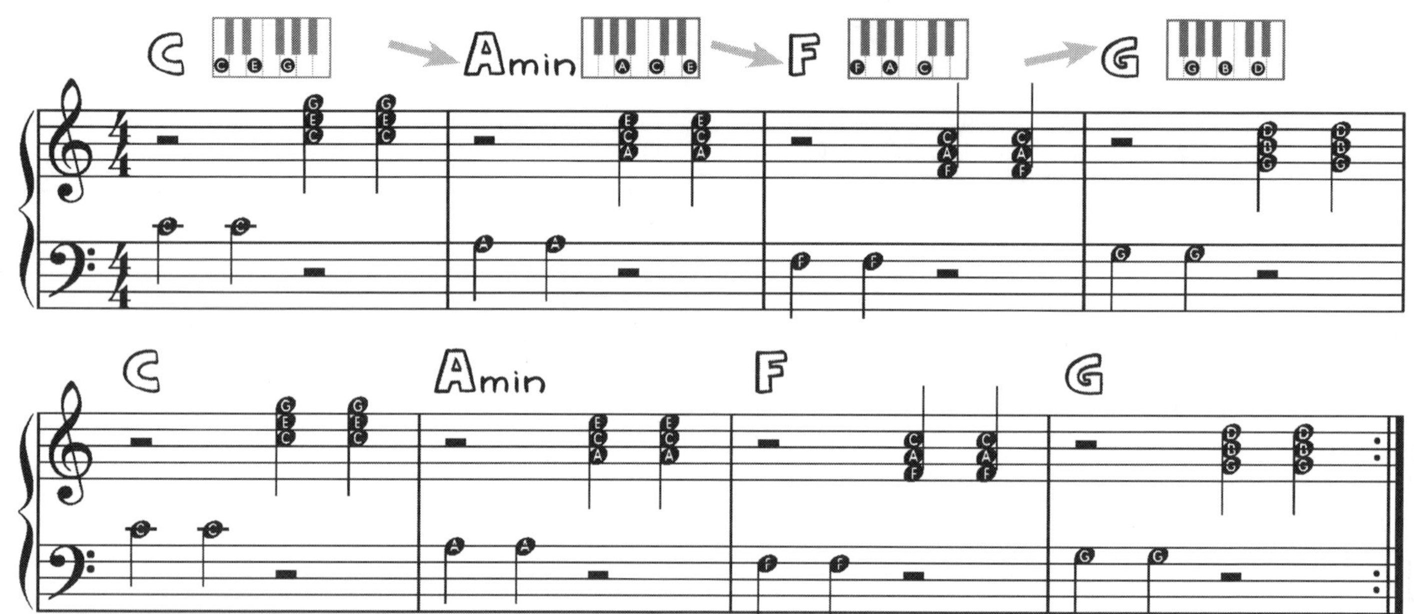

#10. BALLAD

This progression uses a left hand root note, right hand arpeggio pattern.

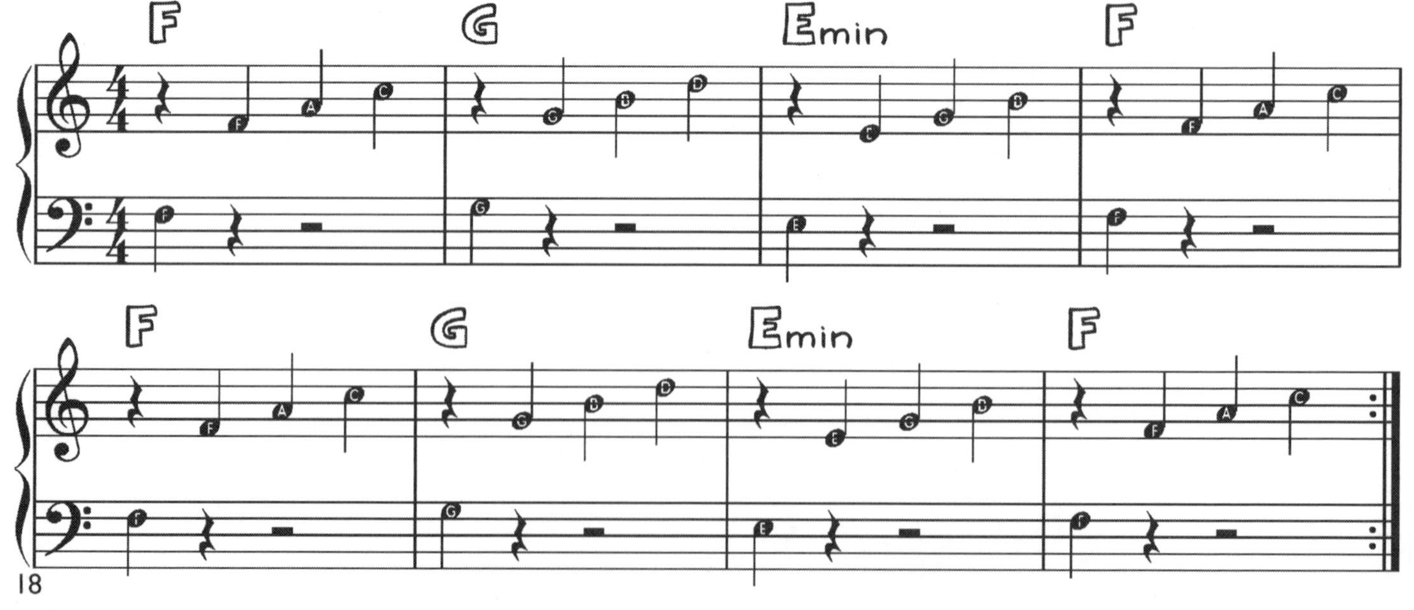

#11. ROCK PROGRESSION

This progression uses a root-root chord pattern.

CHORD FACTS

In bands, the bass player often plays the root note. The root note is the bottom note of the chord and also matches the chord symbol.

Bands use the chord symbols more than reading music. Just read the chord symbol above the staff and play!

Because they often just use the chord symbols to play, bands use "chord charts" to notate their songs. These charts normally just contain the chord symbols, measures or barlines to show how long to play the chords, and lyrics.

Just like there are countless chord progressions, there are actually tons of different types of chords. In this book, we're learning the basic type of chord, known as a triad. There are also seventh chords, "sus" chords, tensions (sounds tense!) and many more!

PACHELBEL'S CANON

Composed over 300 years ago, Pachelbel's Canon has never gone out of style, making this one of the most popular chord progressions of all time.

THE PROGRESSION:

C G Amin Emin F C F G

#12. PATTERN 1: ARPEGGIO, ARPEGGIO

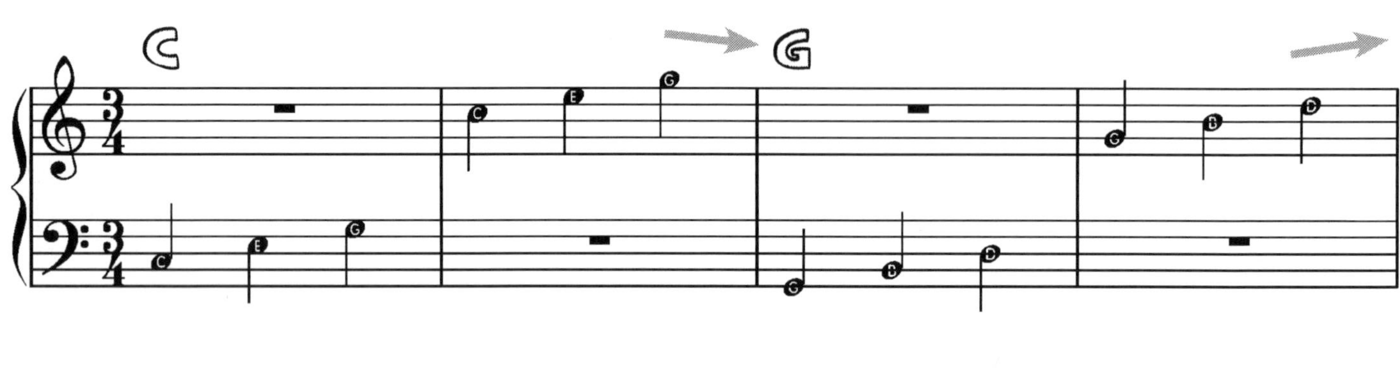

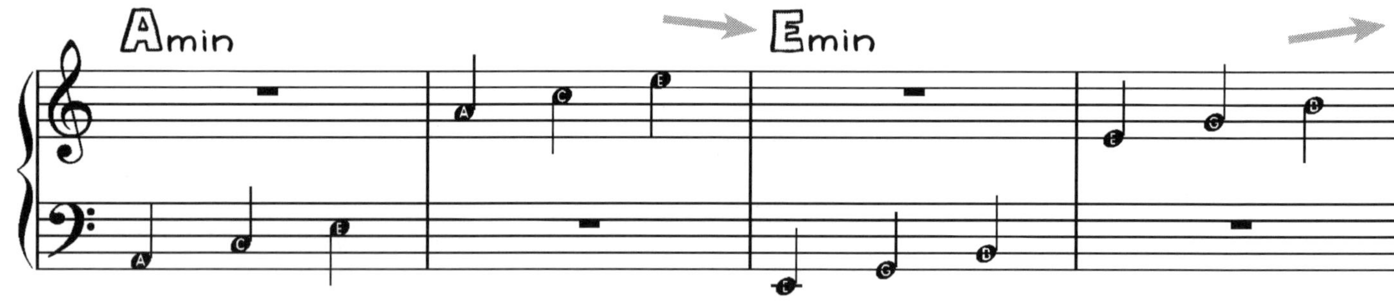

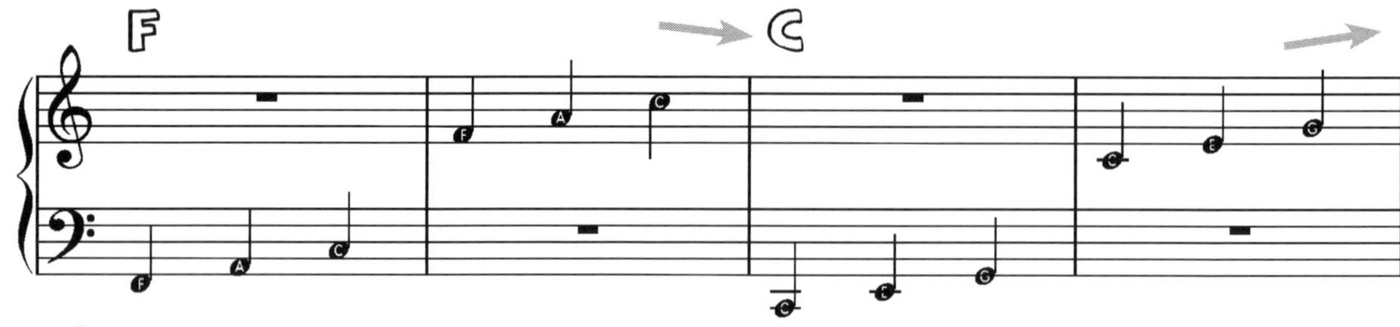

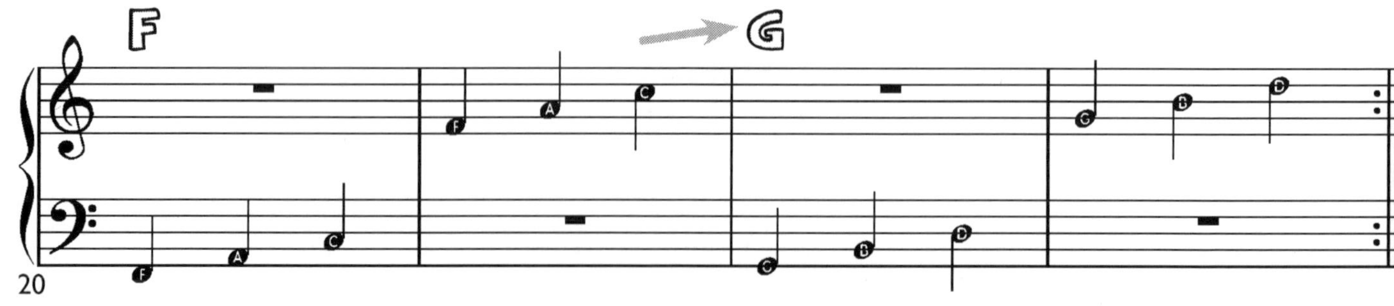

#13. PATTERN 2: ROOT, ARPEGGIO

Say/think: "left, right, right, right."

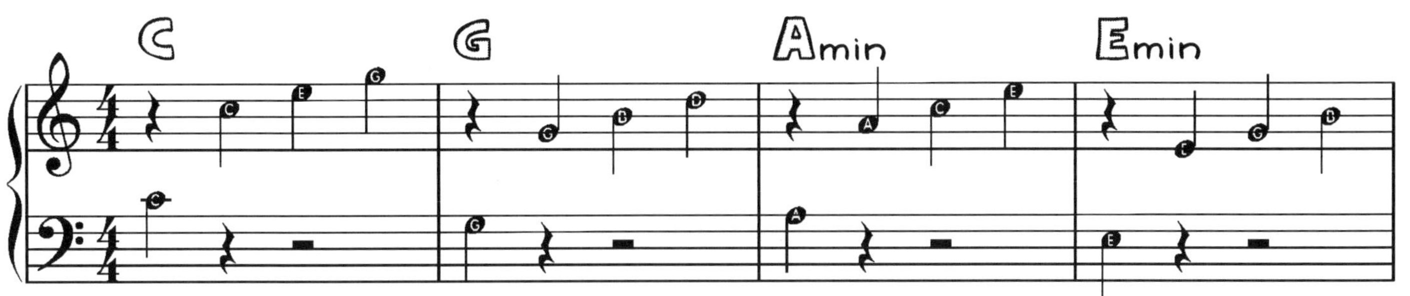

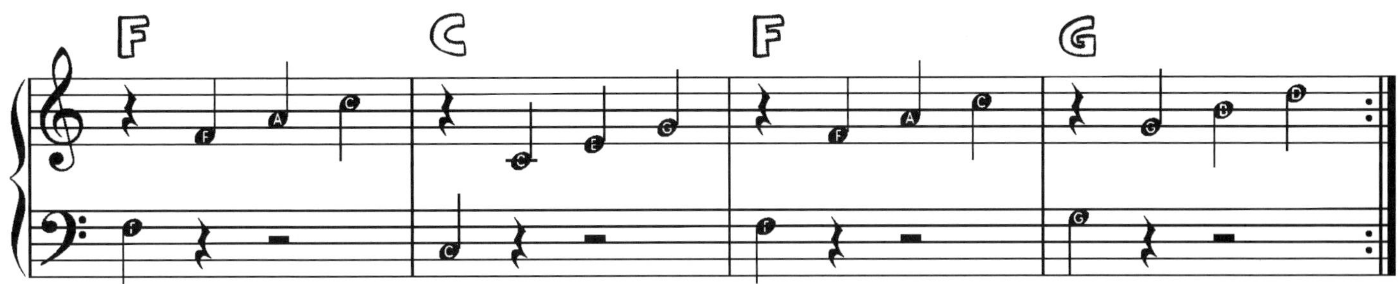

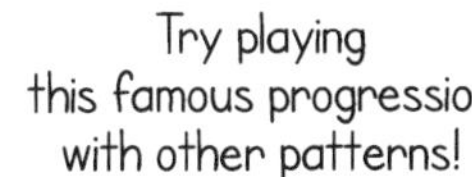

#14. PATTERN 3: ARPEGGIO, CHORD

Say/think: "left, left, left, right."

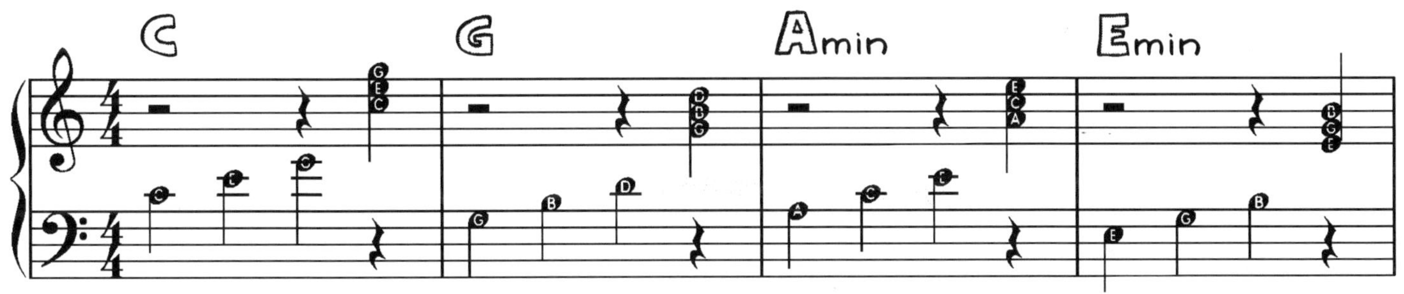

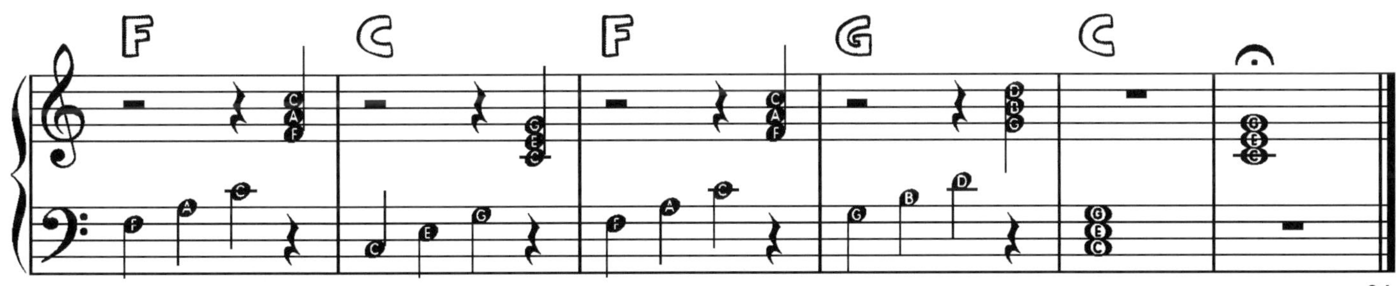

CHORD COMPOSER

In this activity, you will get to use the concepts you have learned so far to make your own chord progressions.

Just choose your chords and play - it's as simple as building with blocks.

A
C G F E

STEP 1: CHOOSE FROM THESE CHORDS OR JUST IMPROVISE

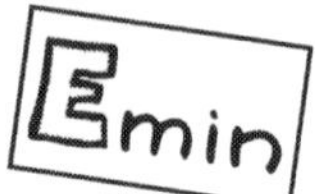

STEP 2: WRITE A FEW CHORD PROGRESSIONS OF YOUR OWN

Create your own progression by writing a chord symbol in each box. Then try playing them with different rhythmic patterns. (Feel free to choose patterns from the book, or create your own!)

PROGRESSION 1:

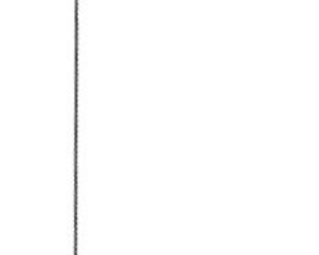

For a printable PDF of this activity, visit mwfunstuff.com/CCC

PROGRESSION 2:

PROGRESSION 3:

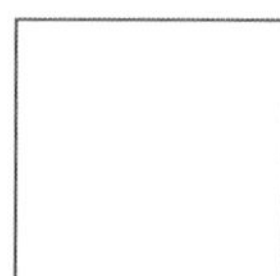
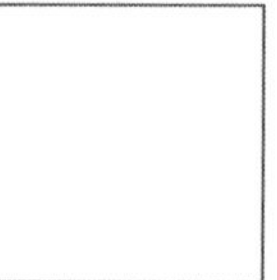

CHAPTER 3
INTERVALS

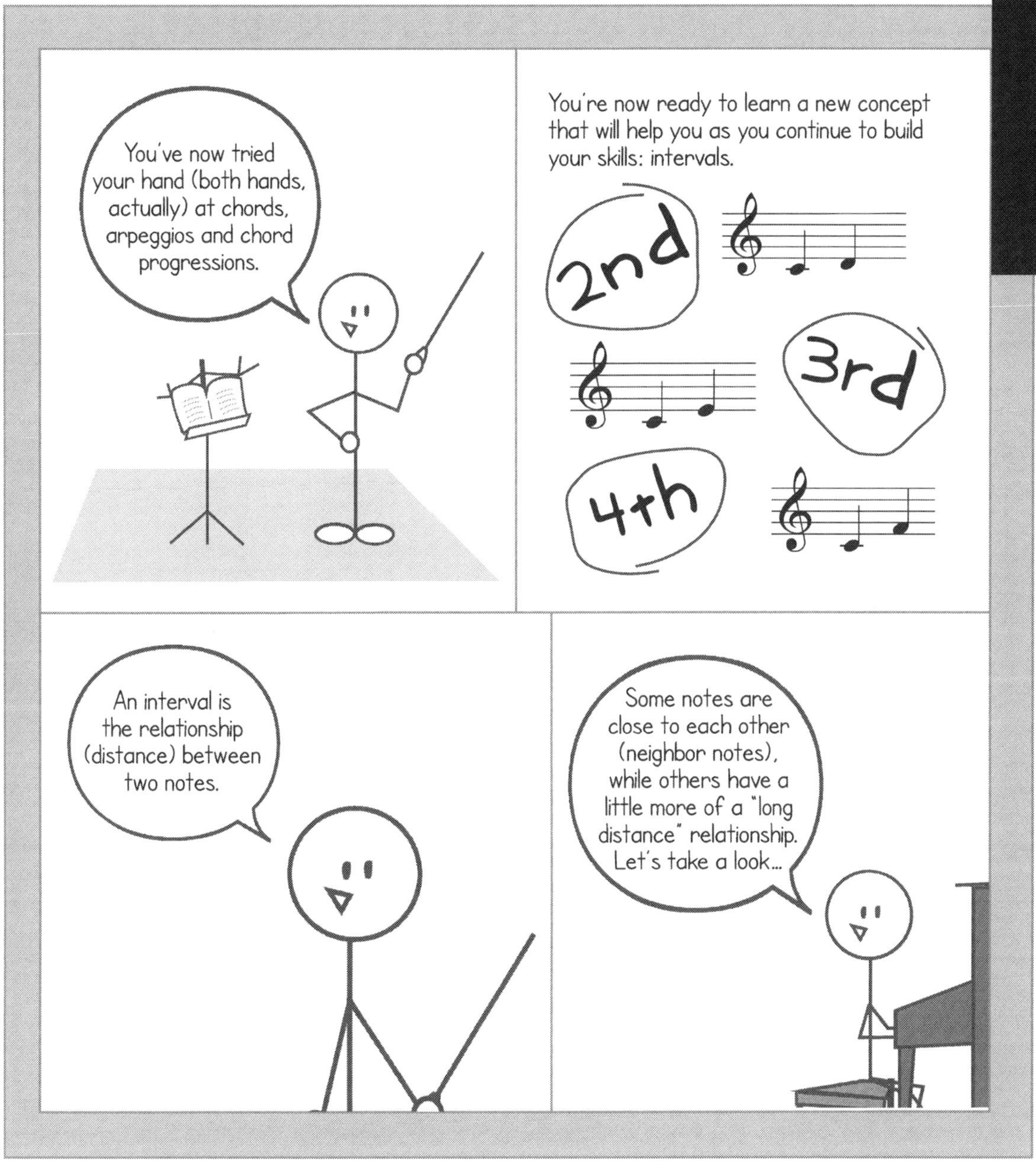

You've now tried your hand (both hands, actually) at chords, arpeggios and chord progressions.

You're now ready to learn a new concept that will help you as you continue to build your skills: intervals.

2nd

3rd

4th

An interval is the relationship (distance) between two notes.

Some notes are close to each other (neighbor notes), while others have a little more of a "long distance" relationship. Let's take a look...

This next chapter takes a look at a new concept: intervals. An interval is the relationship (or distance) between two notes or pitches. Think of them as stepping stones that allow us to make music. Each type of interval has its own distinct personality and sound. Get ready to see how they work together to make incredible music.

Psst! You'll learn about even more intervals in Chord Crash Course Book 2

SECONDS

PRACTICE PLAYING SECONDS

They can be played one at a time (a melodic 2nd) or at the same time (a harmonic 2nd).

Melodic Second Harmonic Second

EXTRA KNOWLEDGE!

There are actually two different types of seconds: major and minor. (Don't worry – you don't need to know the difference to play these exercises!) A major second is also called a whole step, and a minor second is called a half step. Look it up, or ask your teacher to show you the difference between the two!

#15. TOCCATA IN SECONDS

Your left hand will move around, while your right hand stays in one place playing melodic seconds. Try using pedal!

#16. WHIMSICAL WALTZ

In this exercise, your RH will stay put, playing a harmonic second of F and G.

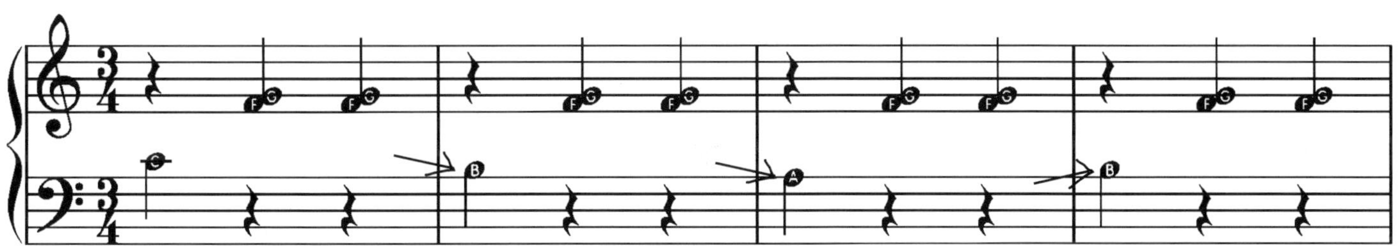

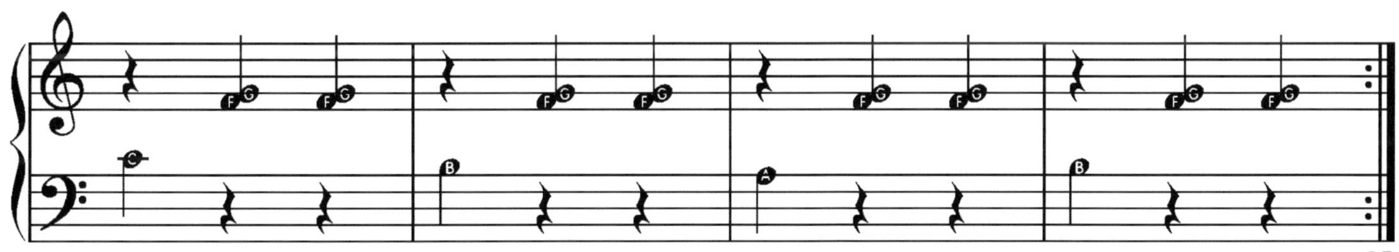

MELODIC THIRDS

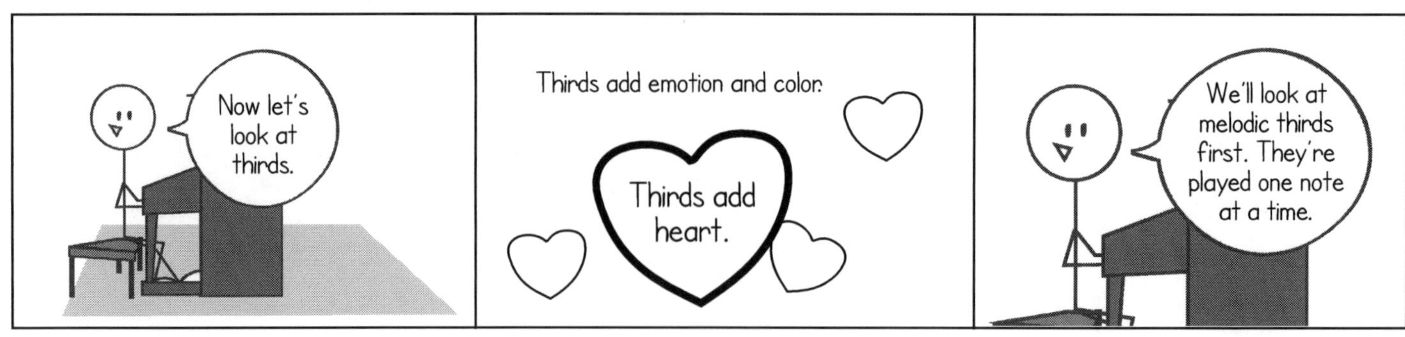

PRACTICE PLAYING A MELODIC THIRD

First with your left hand...

Here's what it looks like on the staff:

Then with your right hand...

Here's what it looks like on the staff:

EXTRA KNOWLEDGE!

Like seconds, there are two types of thirds: major and minor. You'll get to learn more about them in Chapter 5!

#17. LONG AGO

Your left hand will play a chord, followed by a melodic third in your right hand.

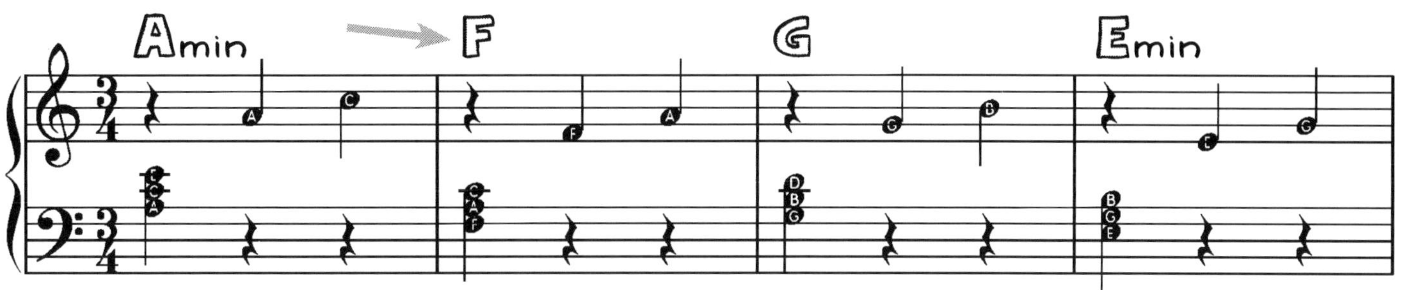

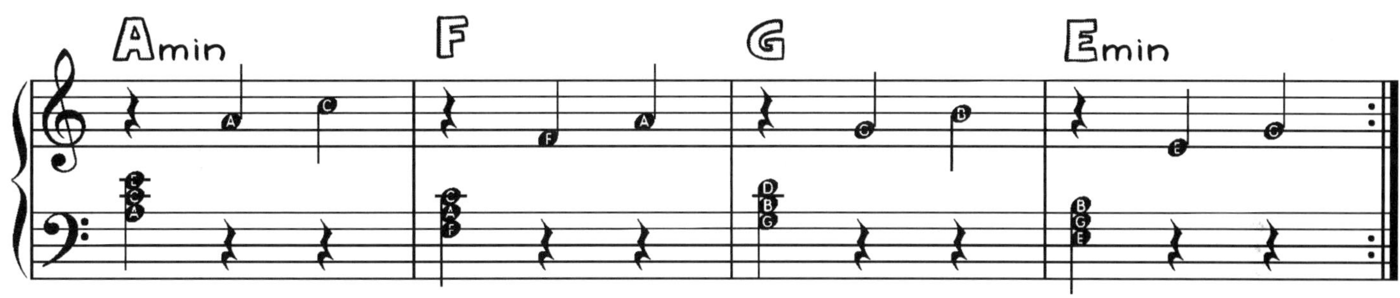

#18. EVER AFTER

Now you'll play the same pattern, but with a different progression.

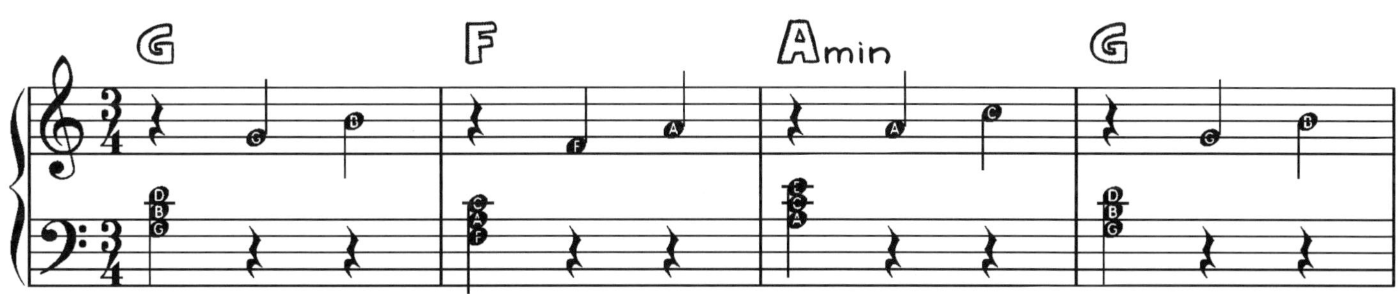

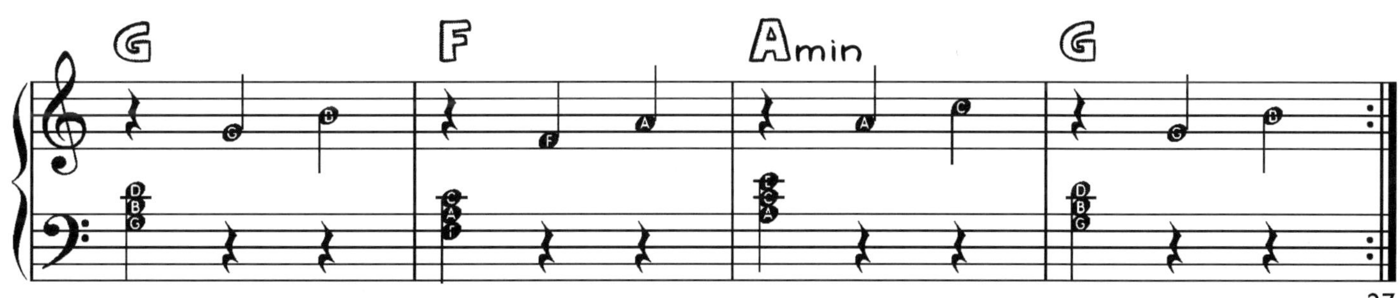

HARMONIC THIRDS

PREPARE HANDS

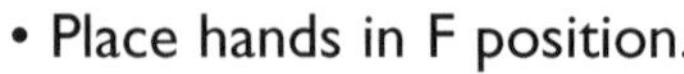

- Place hands in F position.
- LH plays an arpeggio.
- RH follows by playing a harmonic third (fingers 1 and 3 at the same time).
- Move hands up to G position and repeat.
- Continue the pattern all the way through the progression.

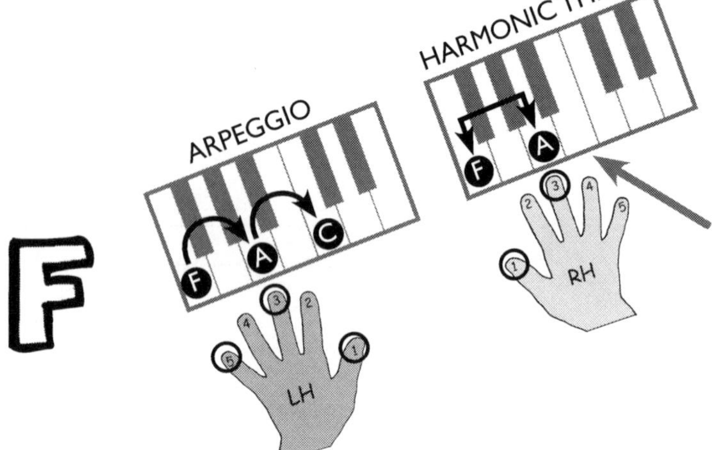

Play both notes at the same time.

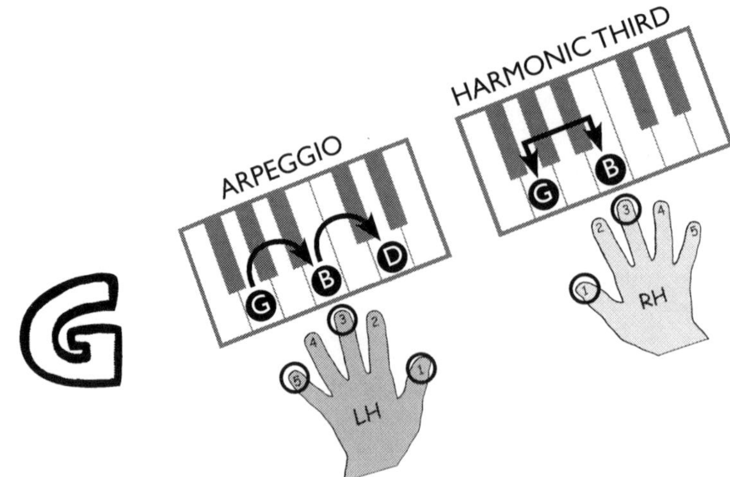

#19. DREAMING CLOUDS

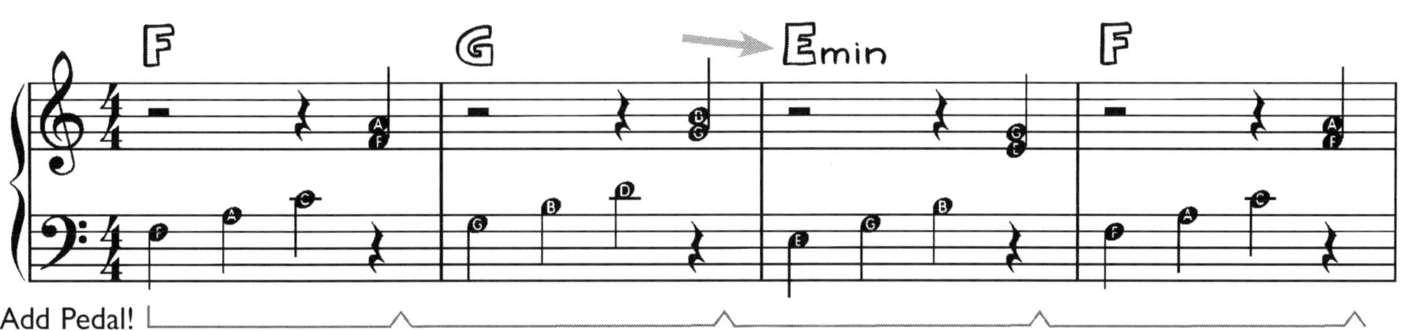

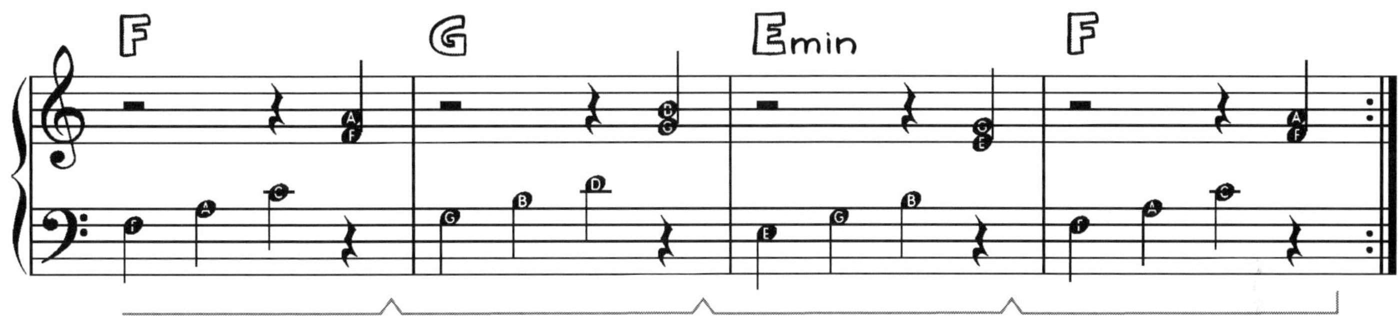

#20. IMPROV

Get into the flow.

Play an F arpeggio with your left hand while moving around your right hand to improvise with thirds. Try adding pedal for an extra dreamy effect.

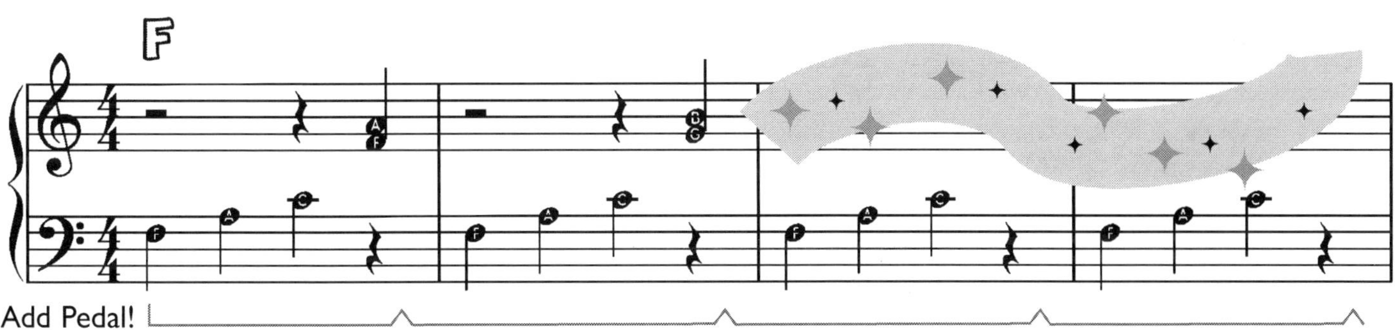

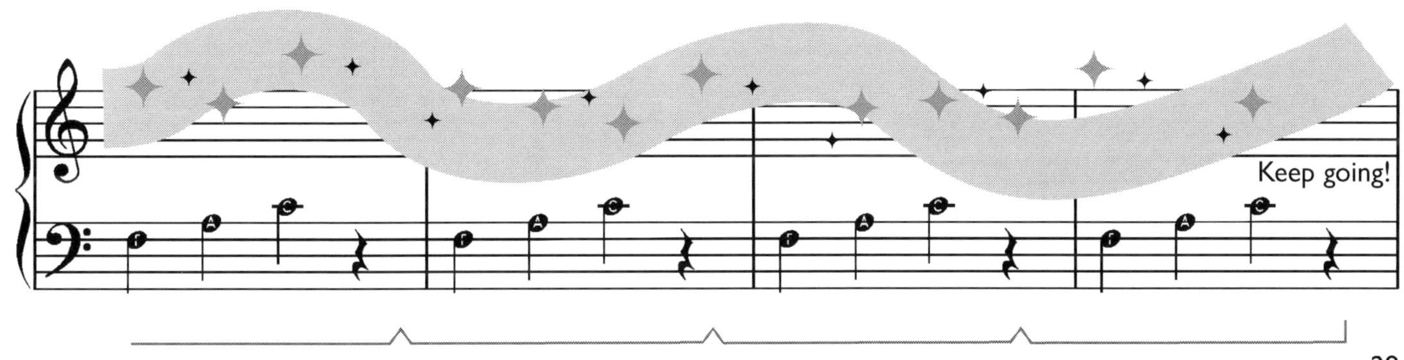

FOURTHS

PRACTICE PLAYING A HARMONIC FOURTH

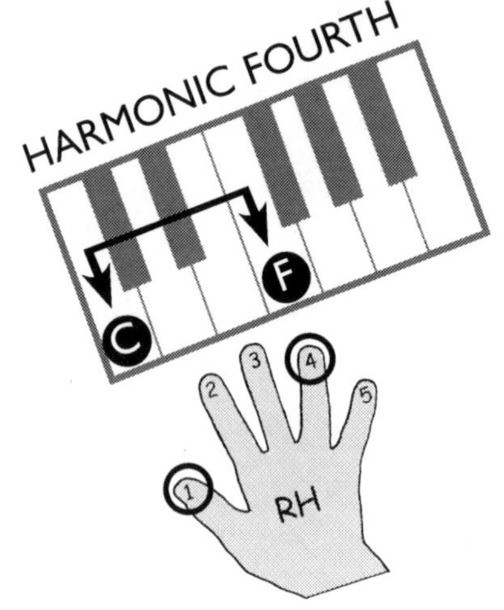

HERE IS WHAT IT LOOKS LIKE ON THE STAFF:

EXTRA KNOWLEDGE!

When we say "fourth" here, we are referring to what is technically known as a "perfect fourth." There is also a less common type of fourth known as the "tritone." The distance between the two notes in the tritone is an additional half step, and it was practically banned from classical music! If you're curious, ask your teacher to play you a tritone. How does it sound compared to a perfect fourth?

#21. INTERVAL INTERPLAY

This exercise will combine fourths with the other intervals you've learned. It'll even include a fifth (which you'll learn all about in the next chapter).

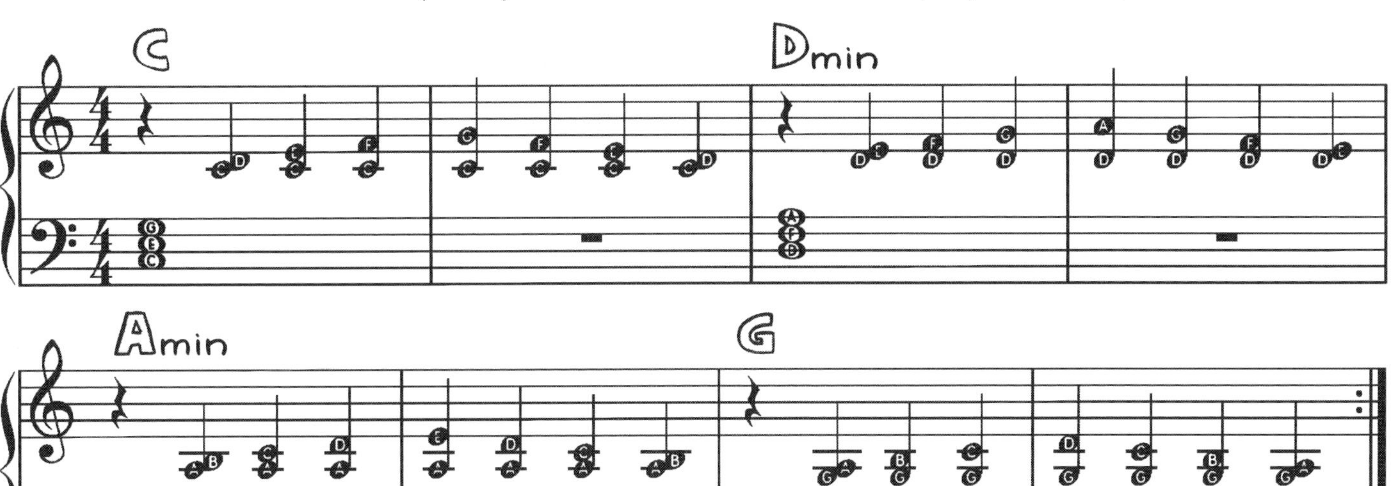

INTERVAL INSIGHTS

SECONDS

Seconds are "wanderers." They like to move toward and away from stable places.

Minor Seconds are dissonant, tense, and want to return to the root. Example: The *Jaws* Theme

Major Seconds are also known as whole steps or neighbor notes. They create a step-like motion and like to resolve to the 1 or the 3. Example: *Happy Birthday*

THIRDS

Thirds add emotion and color, and are what define a chord as "major" or "minor." (You'll learn about that in a few chapters.)

Minor Thirds are often described as sounding sad, mysterious or scary. Example: *Lullaby*

Major Thirds can be described as sounding harmonious, happy or joyous. Example: *Oh When the Saints*

FOURTHS

Fourths are unique intervals in that they sometimes sound powerful, and other times sound tense.

Perfect Fourths are powerful intervals that often want to resolve to the fifth. They're also used in a type of chord known as a "sus" chord. Example: *Here Comes the Bride*

The Tritone is also known as an augmented fourth. This very tense interval was called "the devil's interval" during the Middle Ages, and was banned from churches and most classical music. The tritone wants to resolve to the fifth. Example: the theme from *The Simpsons*.

FIFTHS

Fifths are full of power and strength, and are a very stable interval. Fifths are also known as "perfect," and give chords their power. (They even get their own chapter in this book.) Example: *Twinkle, Twinkle Little Star*

SIXTHS, SEVENTHS, OCTAVES

Of course, there are more intervals beyond fifths. (We just won't be studying them in this book.) Keep an eye out for them in your next "Crash Course," or study them further by looking online or in a music theory book.

INTERVAL INSPIRATION

Ways to play:

- The teacher plays an interval, and you name which interval it is. (Bonus challenge: close your eyes and try to name it by listening!)
- Point and play! Close your eyes, point to an interval, and play it!
- Pick a starting note, then build the chosen interval on top of that note.
- Create your own way to play!

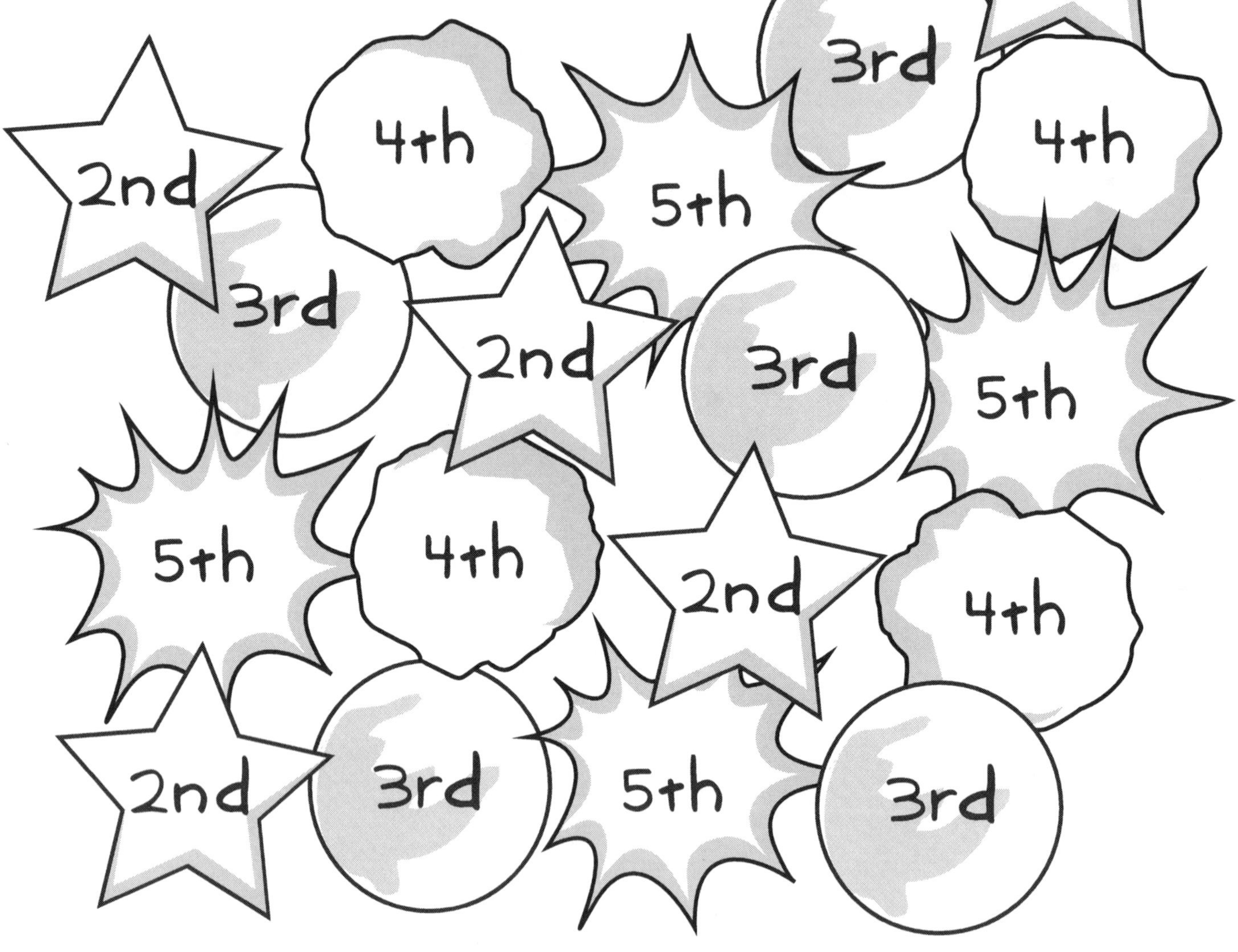

2nd

3rd

4th

2nd

4th

5th

3rd

2nd

3rd

5th

5th

4th

2nd

4th

2nd

3rd

5th

3rd

CHAPTER 4

POWER CHORDS: FIFTHS

In this chapter we'll look at fifths, including harmonic fifths, which are also known as "power chords." Think of fifths as the heavyweights of music: the distance between the notes creates a big, strong sound. This powerful sound creates a stability that is naturally pleasing to the ear. It's time to learn about fifths, and then use them to create power and strength in your own playing.

HOW TO PLAY A POWER CHORD (HARMONIC FIFTH)

HARMONIC FIFTHS (POWER CHORDS) ARE PLAYED AT THE SAME TIME, LIKE CHORDS

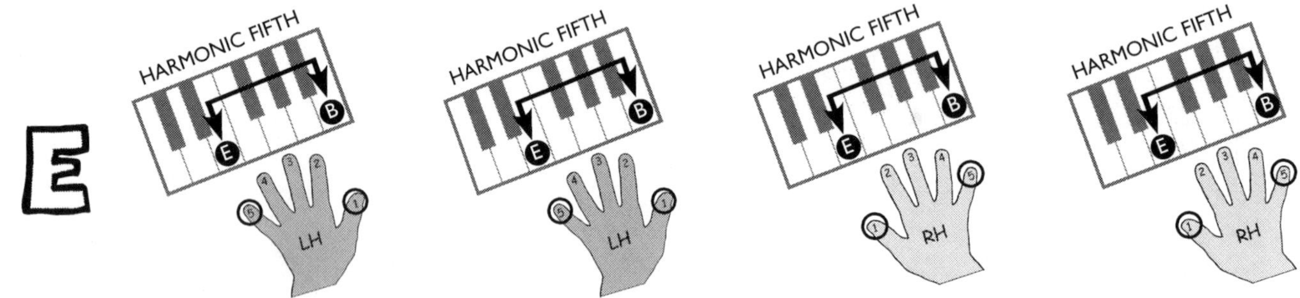

Place your hands in E position. With the LH play fingers 5 and 1 at the same time. This is a harmonic fifth.

Play it again.

With the RH, echo by playing a harmonic fifth.

Play it again.

#22. FIRE PHOENIX

Play the pattern up the Phrygian scale. Say/think: "left, left, right, right."

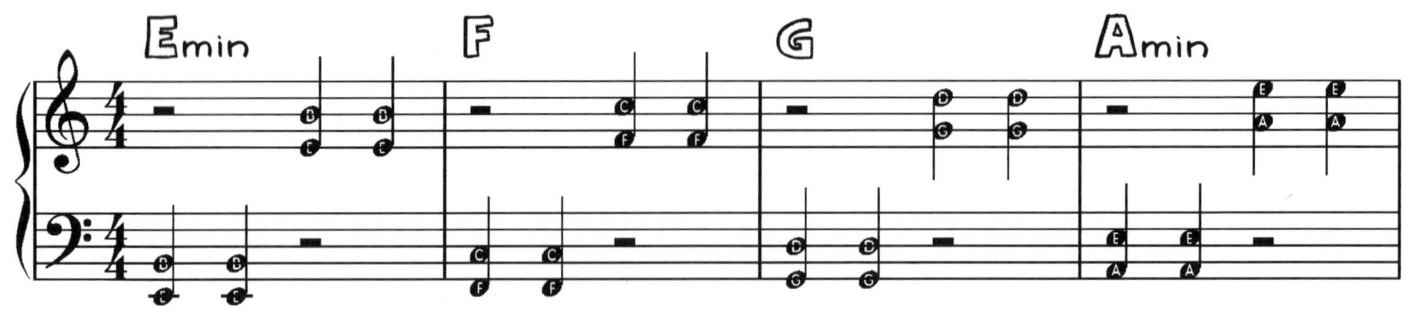

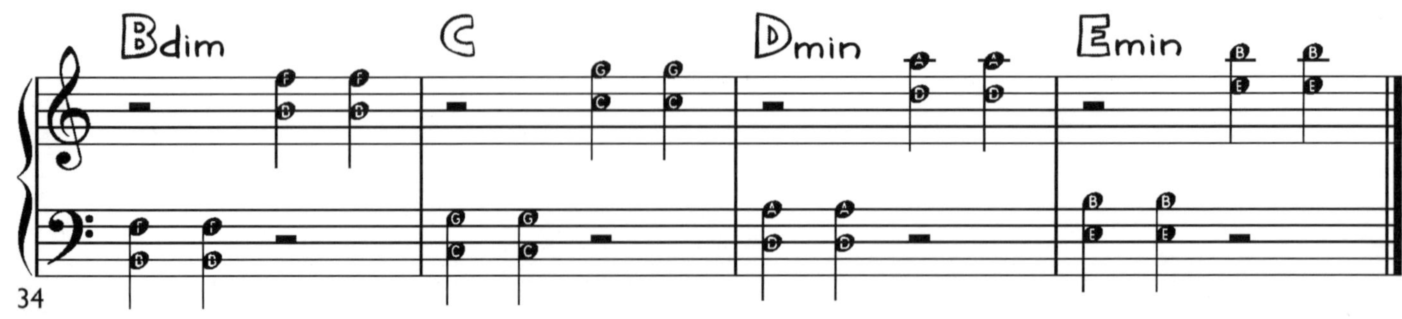

#23. HEAVY METAL THUNDER

Now play power chords with a new rhythm and chord progression. Say/think: "left, left, right."

Try this progression with different chord patterns you've learned. Make a song!

#24. HEAVY METAL LIGHTNING

"Rock" back and forth between hands. Say/think: "left, right, left, right."

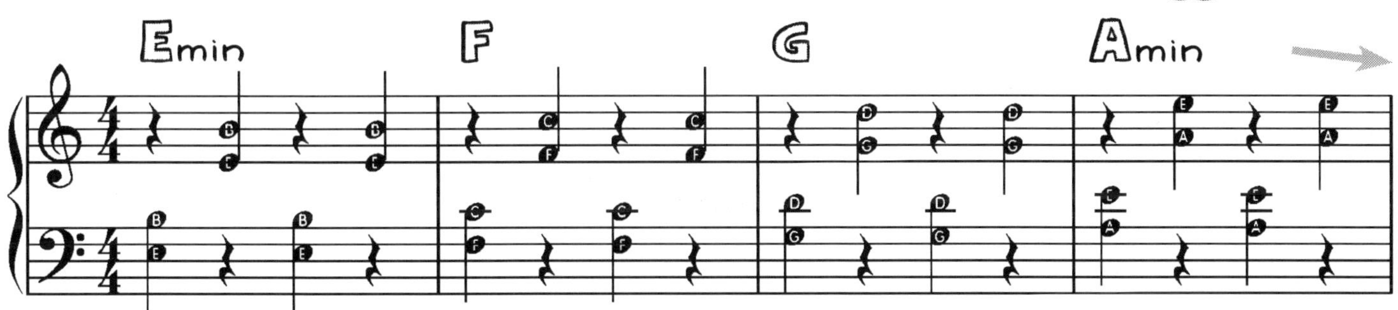

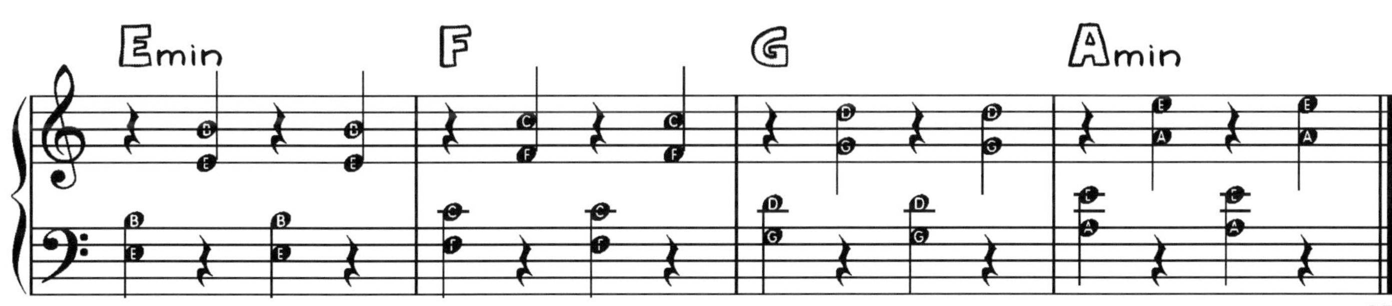

HOW TO PLAY MELODIC FIFTHS

MELODIC FIFTHS ARE PLAYED ONE NOTE AT A TIME, LIKE ARPEGGIOS.

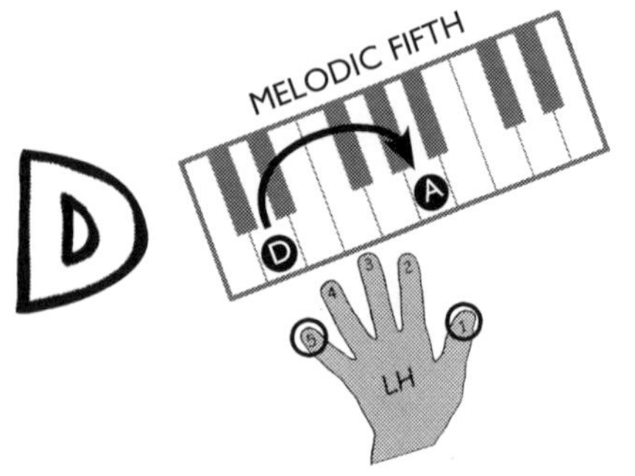

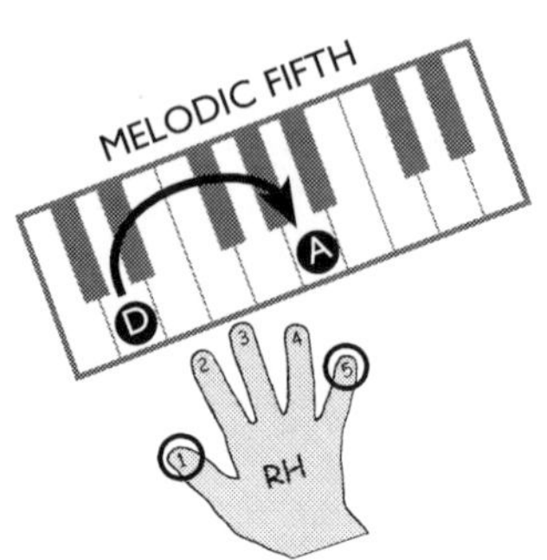

- Place your hands in D position.
- Play D with LH finger 5 (pinky).
- Play A with LH finger 1.

- Play D with RH finger 1.
- Play A with RH finger 5.

#25. DRAGON WARRIOR

For this exercise, play the melodic fifth pattern from above with this chord progression. Say/think: "left, left, right, right."

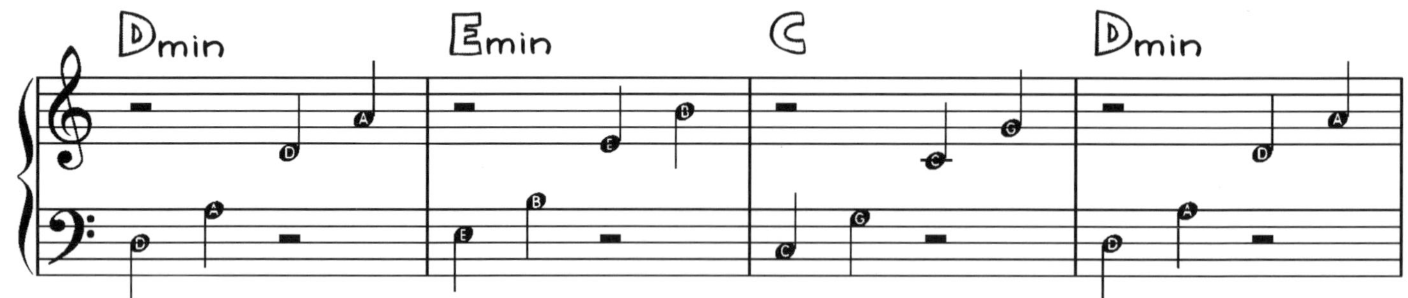

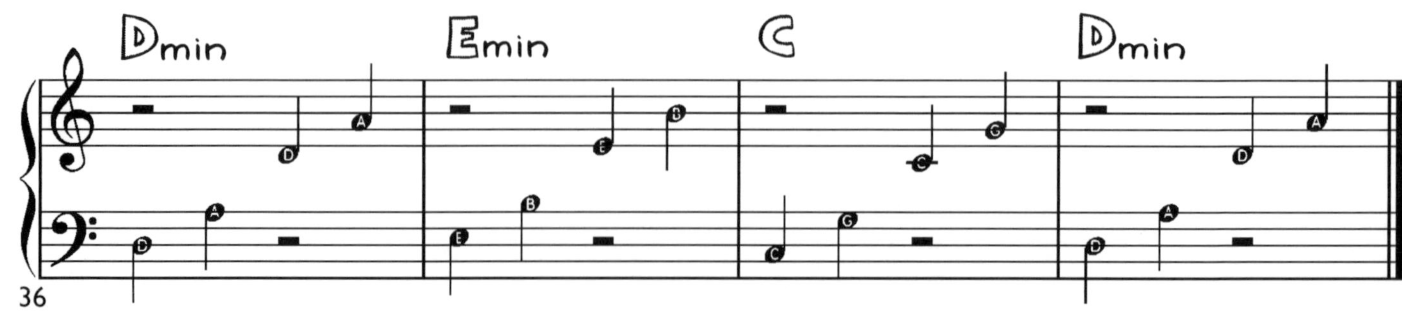

#26. POWER ROCK

Now play the melodic fifths pattern you learned with this popular pop/rock chord progression.

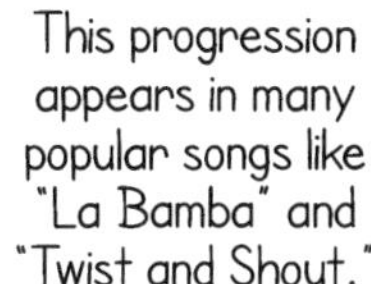

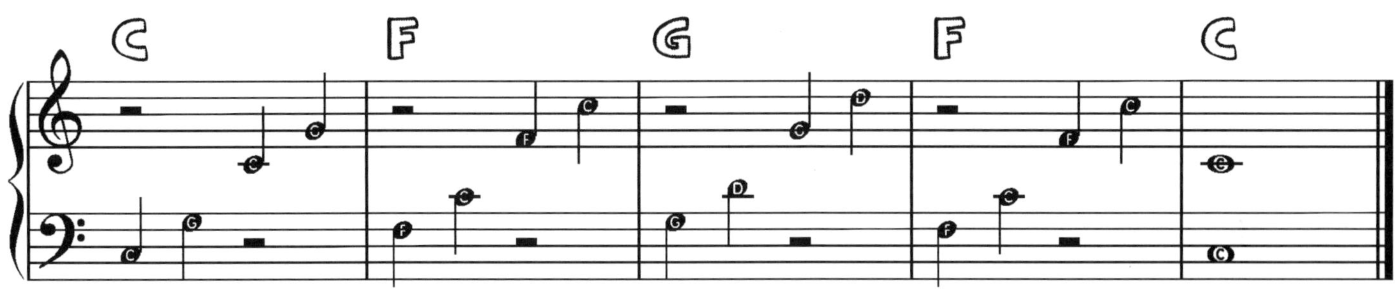

#27. IMPROVISE WITH THE PATTERN

Now play the melodic fifths pattern all over the keyboard, using any root notes/positions you choose. Get into the flow!

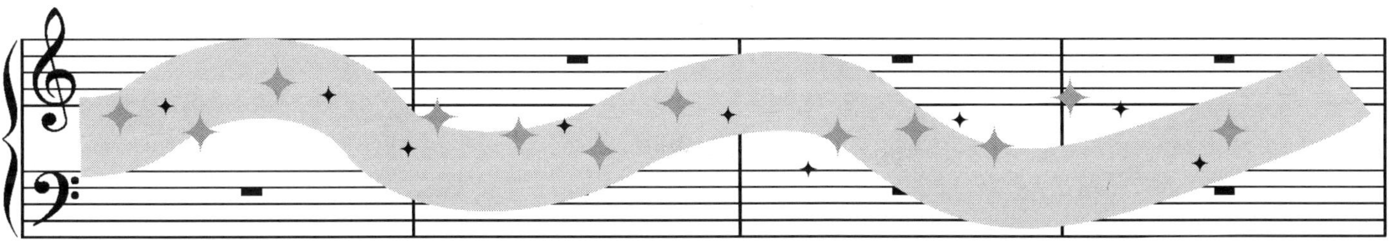

Improvise for at least 3 minutes.

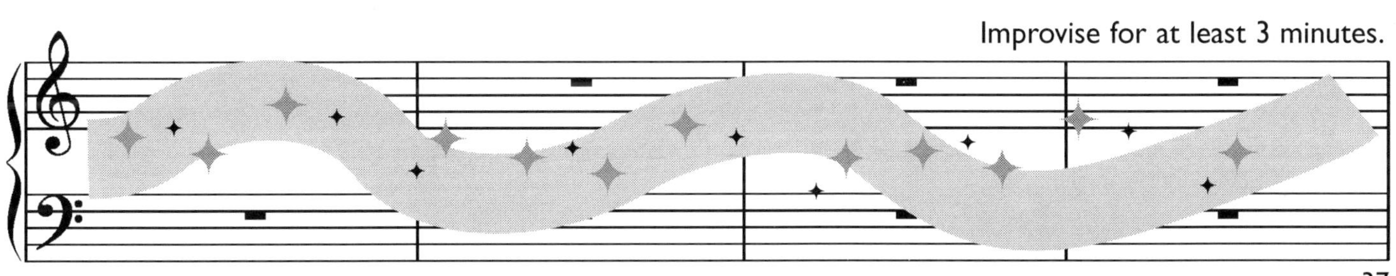

#28. MYSTERIOUS MOON

Repeat the ending and fade out.

#29. WARRIOR HEART

This song combines left hand melodic fifths
with right hand melodic thirds.

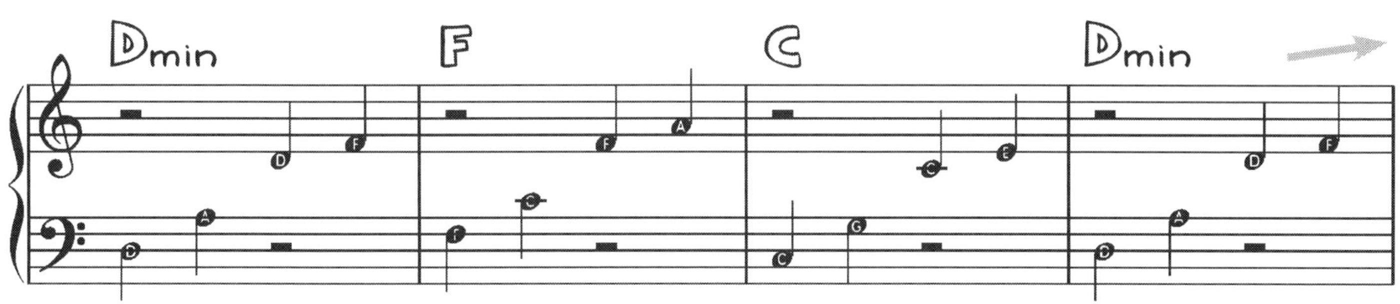

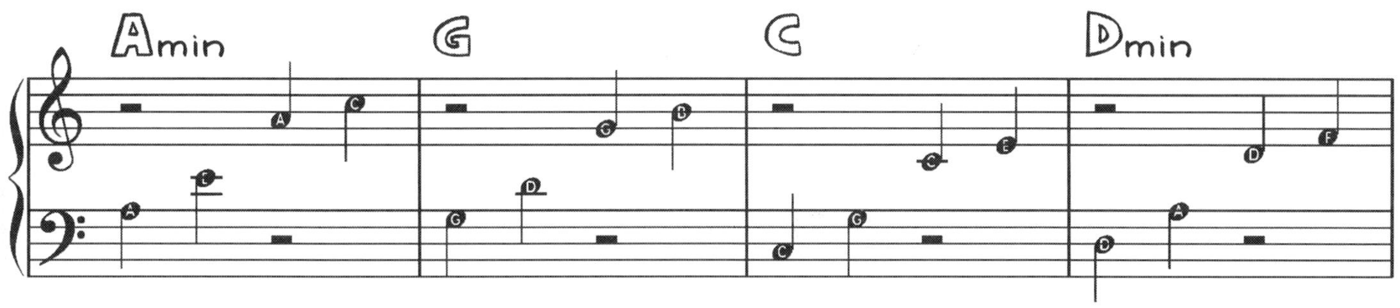

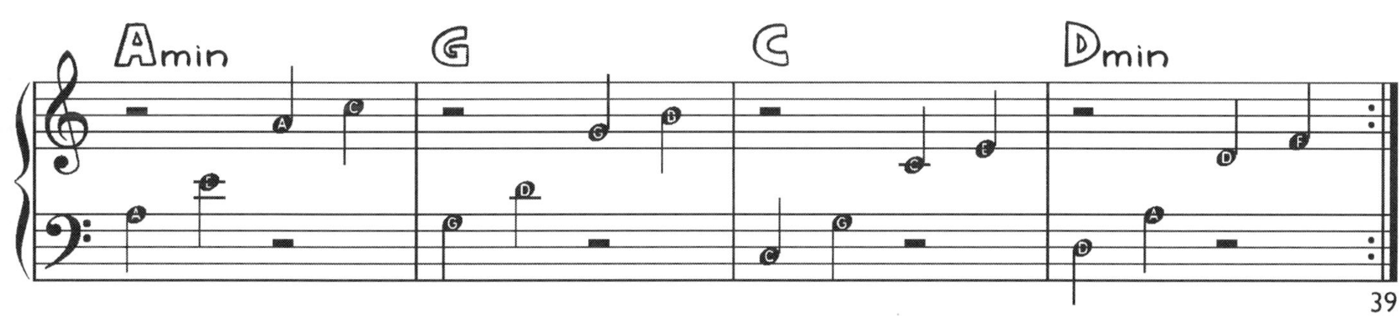

HEART OF ROCK

PATTERN 1

Play this pattern with Heart of Rock 1.

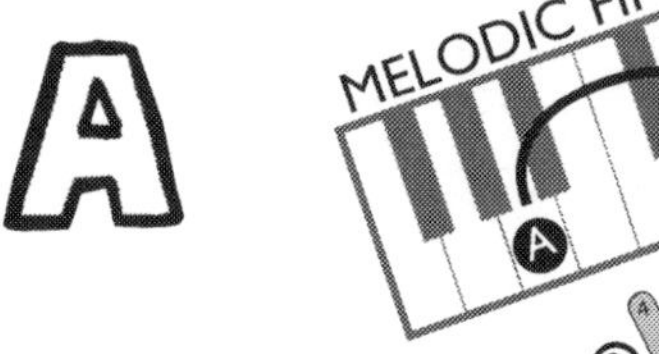

With your hands in A position, play a melodic fifth with your LH.

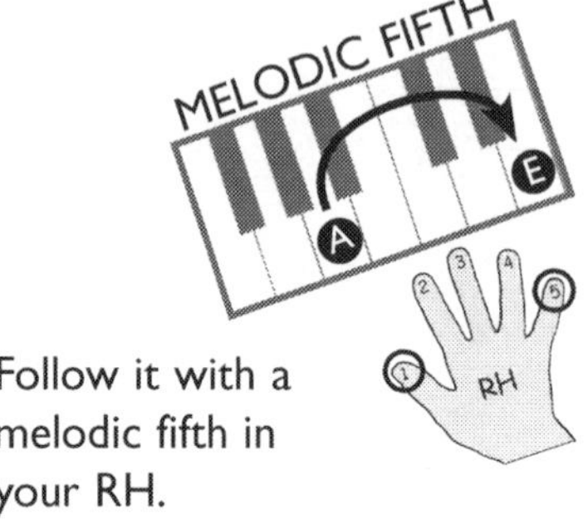

Follow it with a melodic fifth in your RH.

PATTERN 2

Play this pattern with Heart of Rock 2.

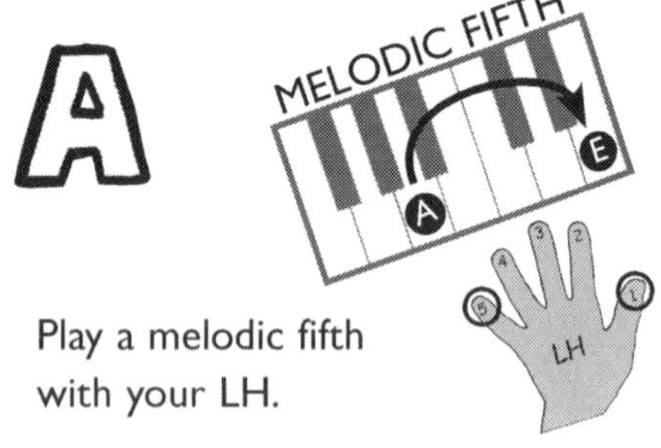

Play a melodic fifth with your LH.

Follow it with a harmonic fifth in your RH. Hold for TWO beats.

PATTERN 3

Play this pattern with Heart of Rock 3.

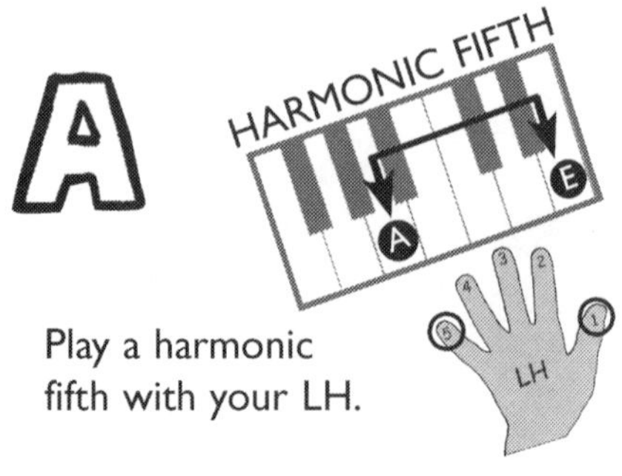

Play a harmonic fifth with your LH.

Repeat the LH harmonic fifth.

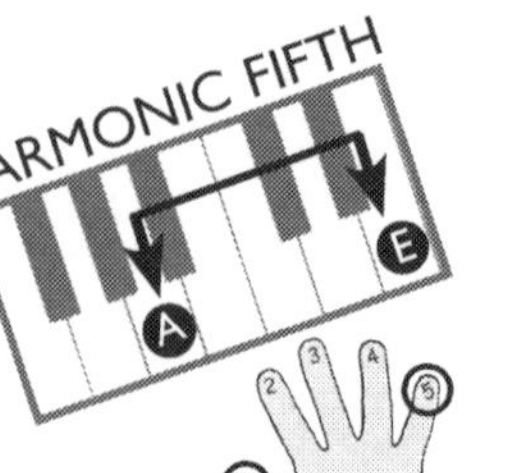

Follow it with a harmonic fifth in your RH. Hold for TWO beats.

#30. HEART OF ROCK 1

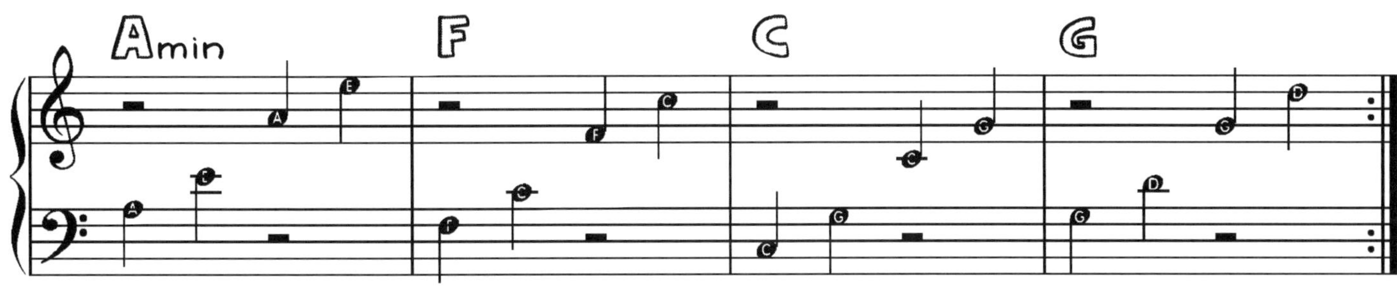

#31. HEART OF ROCK 2

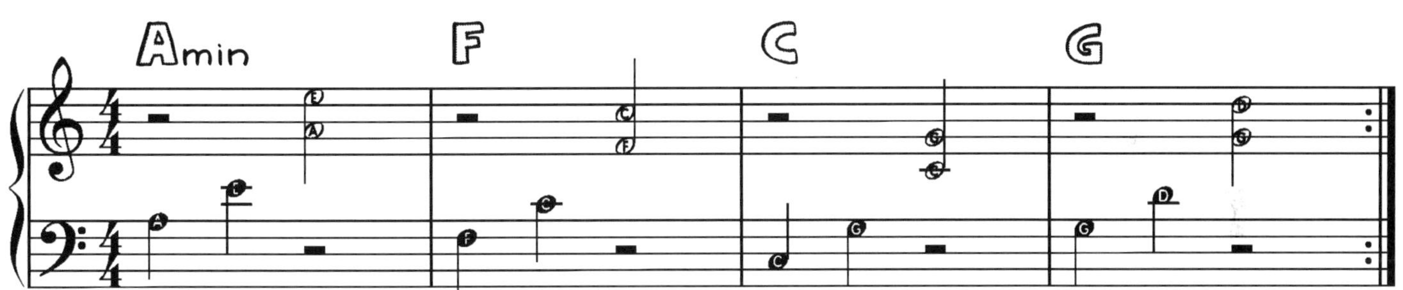

#32. HEART OF ROCK 3

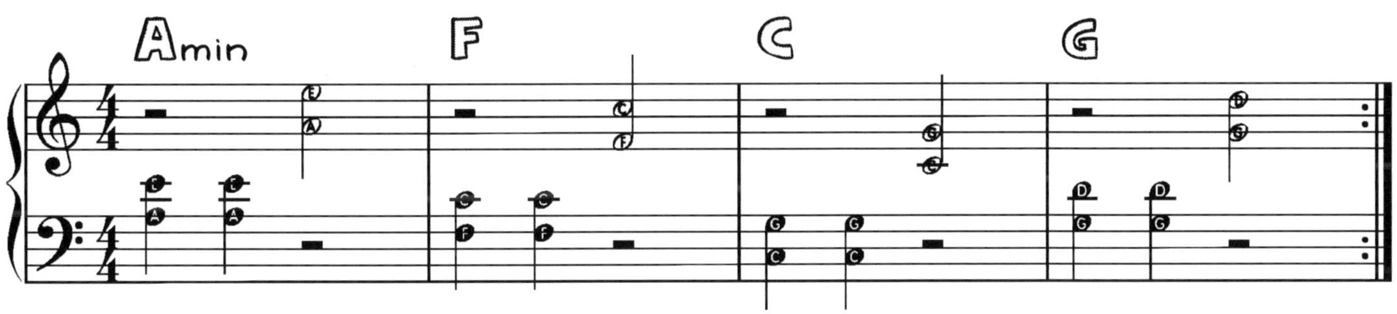

FIFTHS CHORD COMPOSER

STEP 1: CHOOSE FROM THESE CHORDS

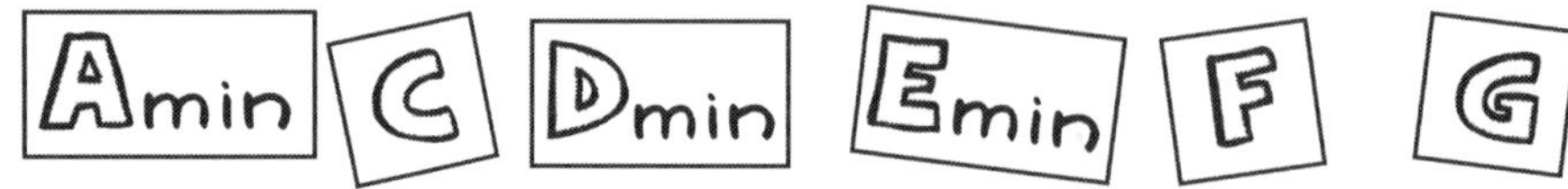

STEP 2: WRITE A FEW CHORD PROGRESSIONS OF YOUR OWN

Create your own progression by writing a chord symbol in each box. Then try playing them with different rhythmic patterns.

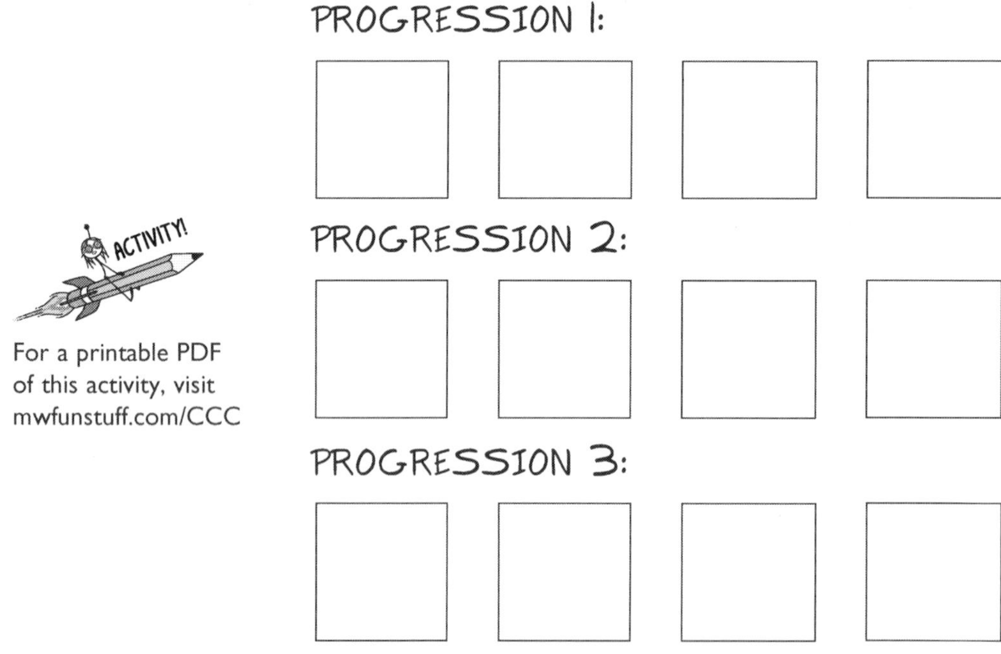

For a printable PDF of this activity, visit mwfunstuff.com/CCC

CHAPTER 5
MAJOR AND MINOR CHORDS

Music has the power to make us laugh or cry, and to make us excited or scared.

Much of that has to do with whether the chords are major or minor.

MAJOR

MINOR

...And that's decided by just one note: the third (or middle note).

Changing that one note can totally alter the mood.

In this chapter you will learn about major and minor chords. While major chords have 4 half steps between the root and third, minor chords only have 3. You'll learn that changing this one note can make a happy song sad, a cheery song spooky, or vice versa. Check it out for yourself, and learn the difference that a half step makes!

WHAT IS A MAJOR CHORD?

MAJOR CHORDS

have 4 half steps between the root and the third.

4 half steps = major

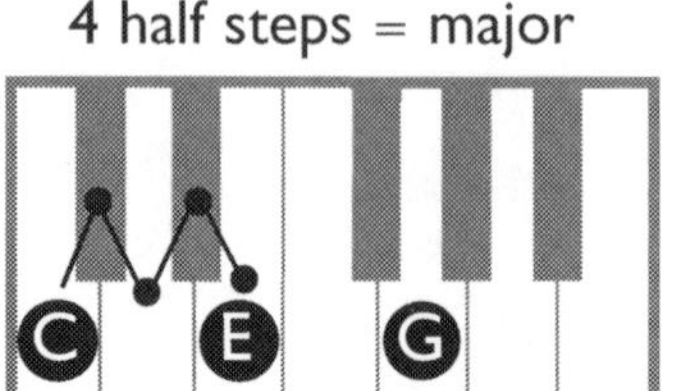

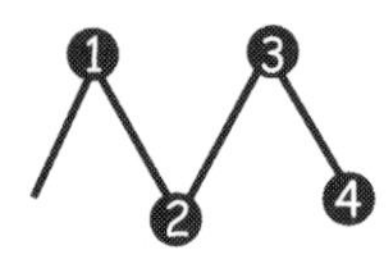

THE MAJOR CHORDS IN THE KEY OF C ARE...

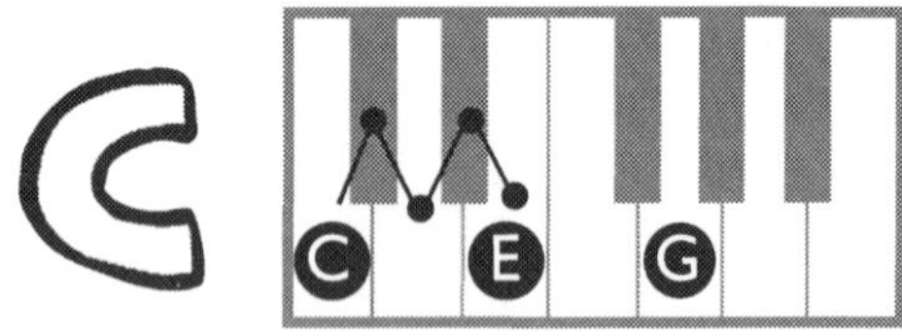

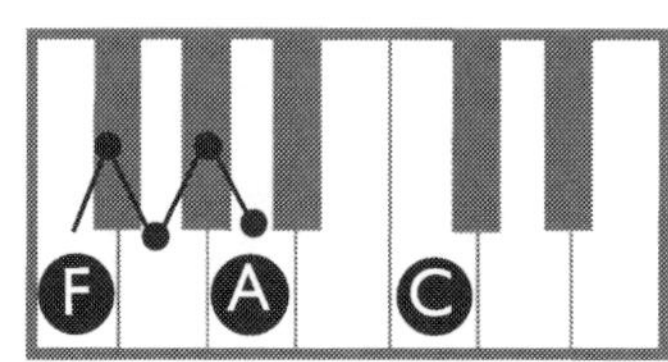

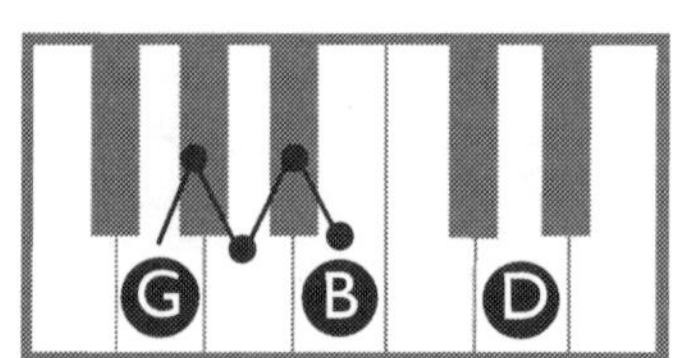

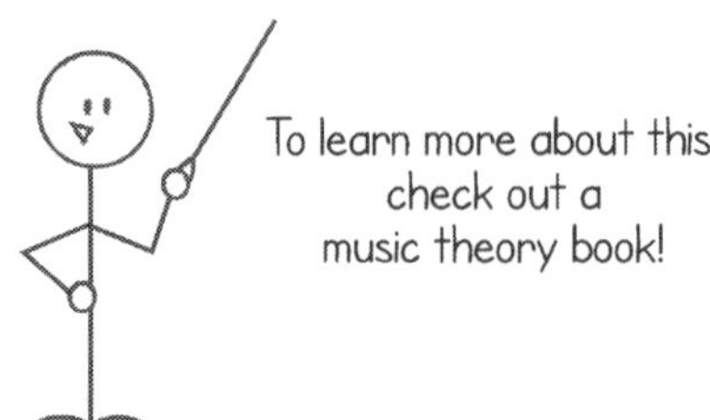

WHAT IS A MINOR CHORD?

MINOR CHORDS

have 3 half steps between the root and the third.

3 half steps = minor

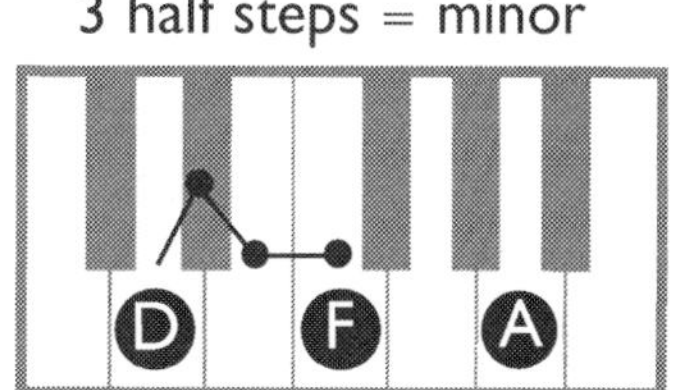

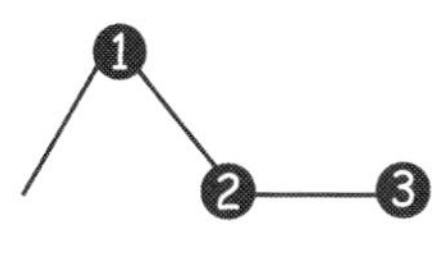

THE MINOR CHORDS IN THE KEY OF C ARE...

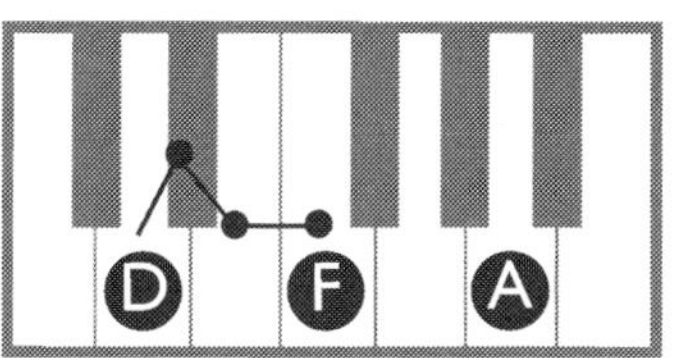

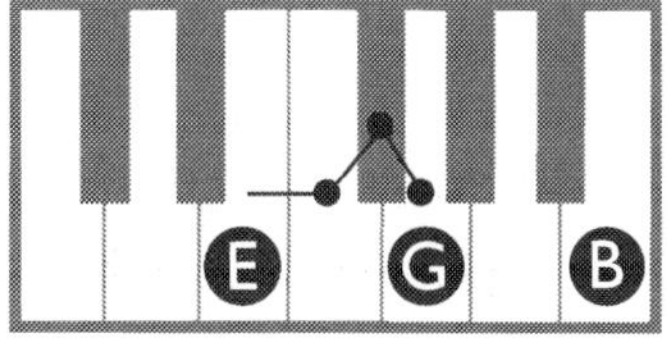

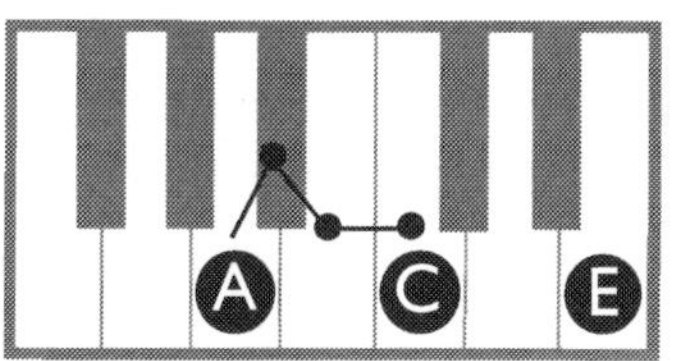

#33. MINOR CHORD MASH UP

This song uses an all-minor chord progression with an arpeggio pattern, then switches time signatures to play it with chords. Minor chords are used in sad songs or mysterious movies to build tension. Can you hear why?

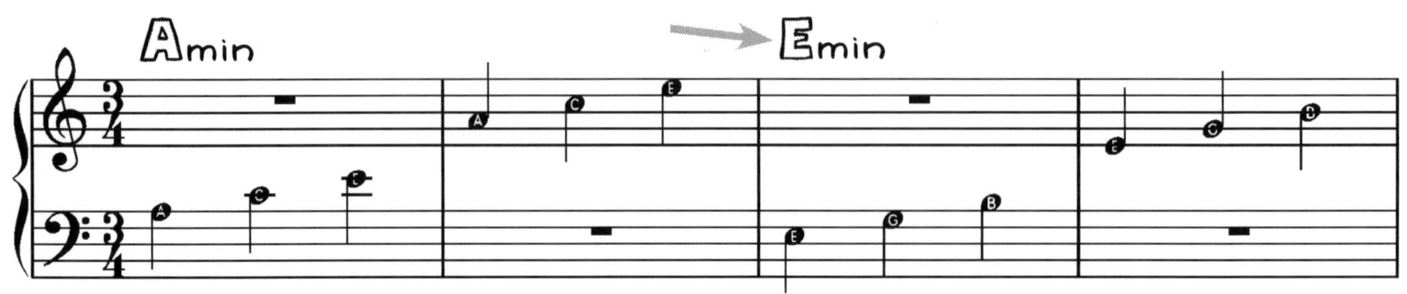

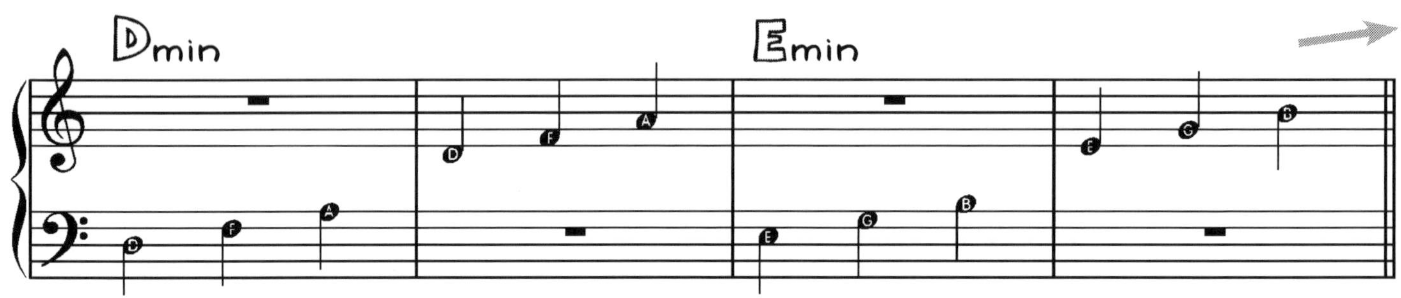

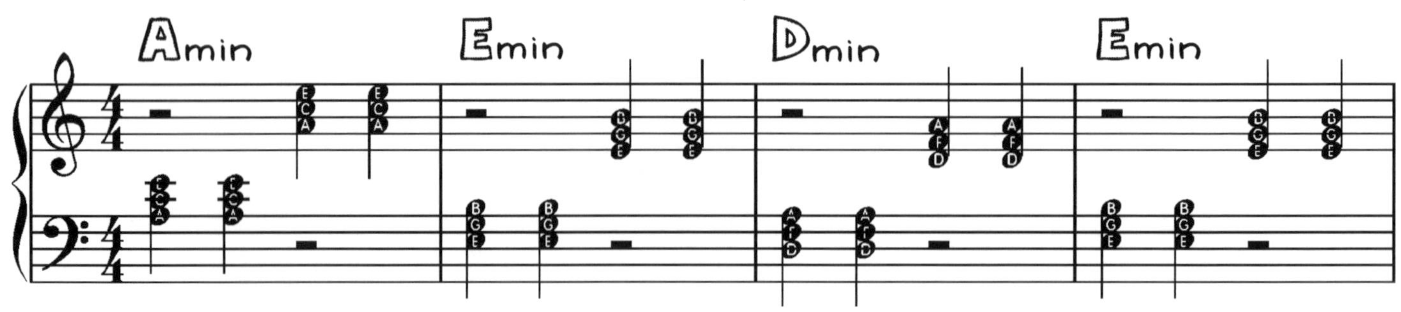

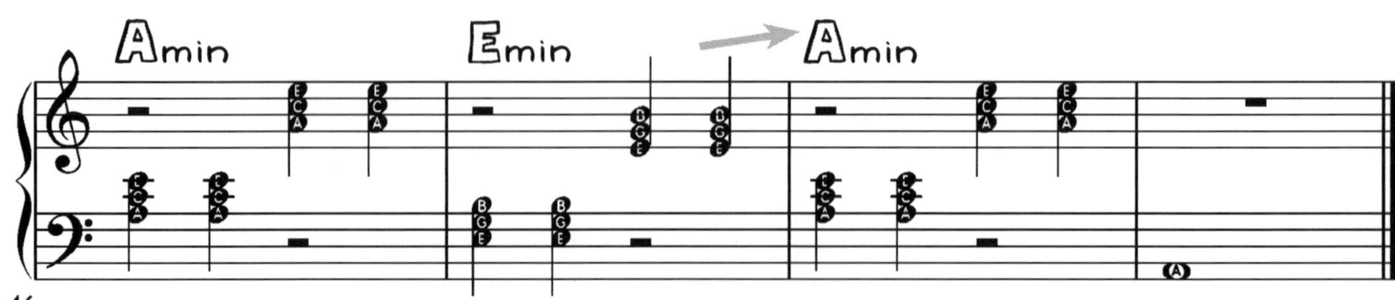

#34. MAJOR CHORD MERRIMENT

This progression uses an all-major chord progression with a variety of rhythm patterns. Can you hear and feel the difference from the last song?

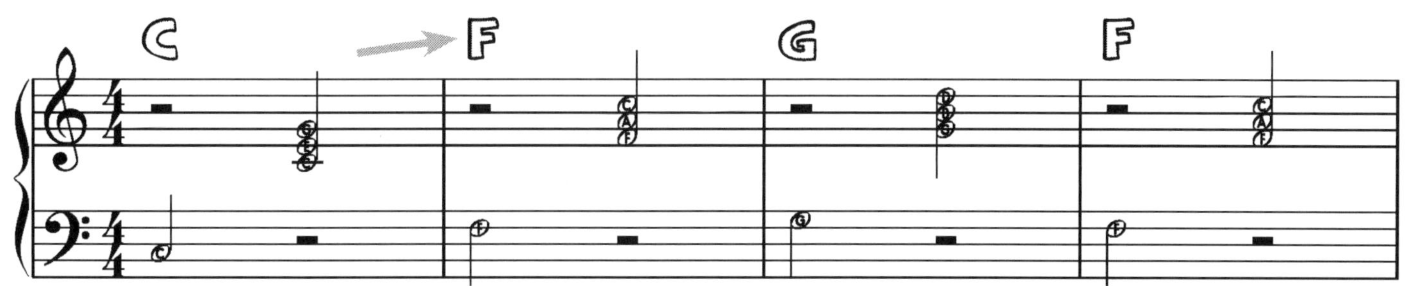

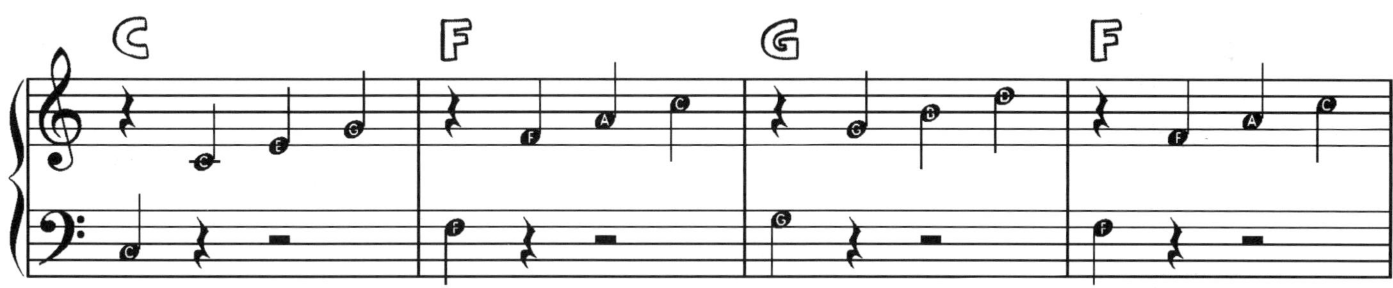

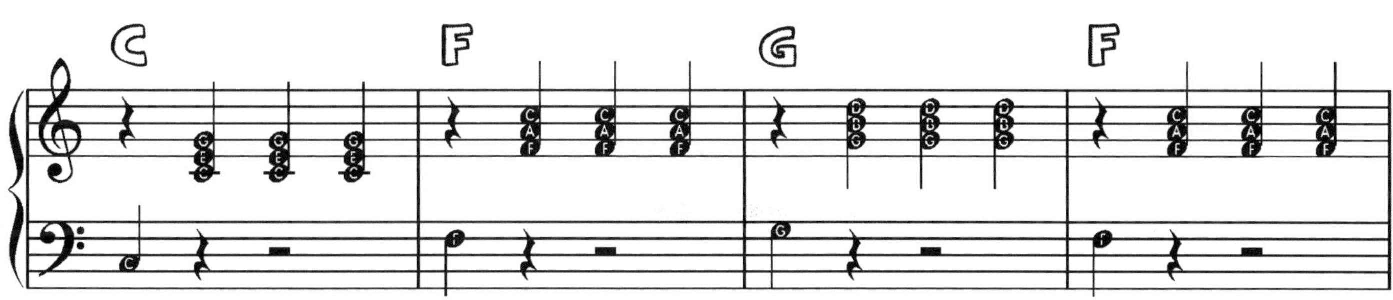

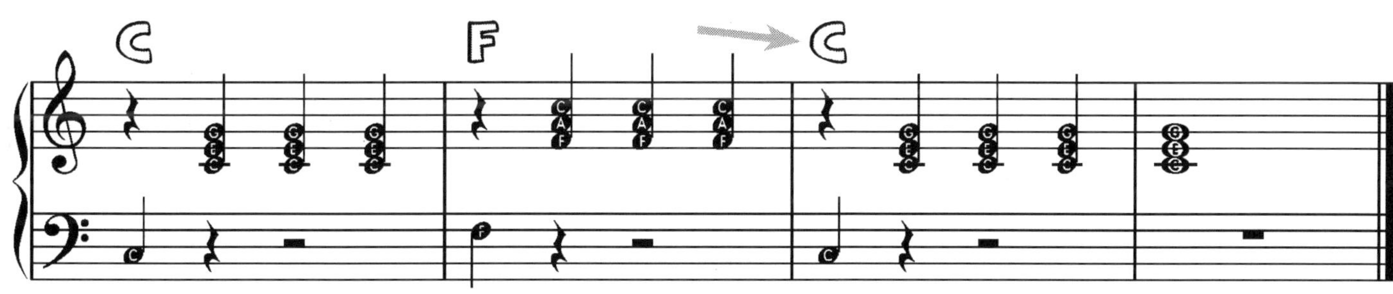

MAJOR TO MINOR (BRING IT DOWN....)

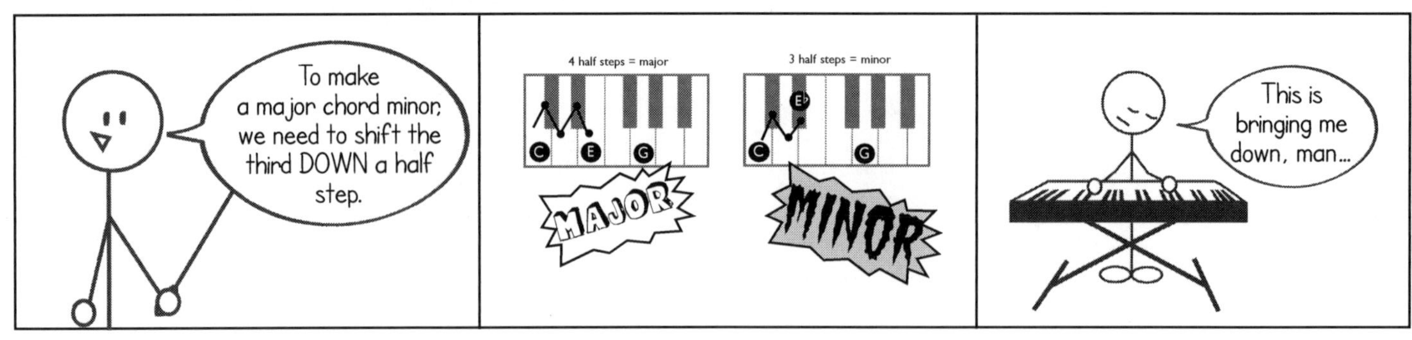

LET'S CHANGE C MAJOR INTO C MINOR...

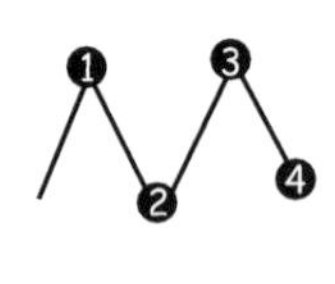

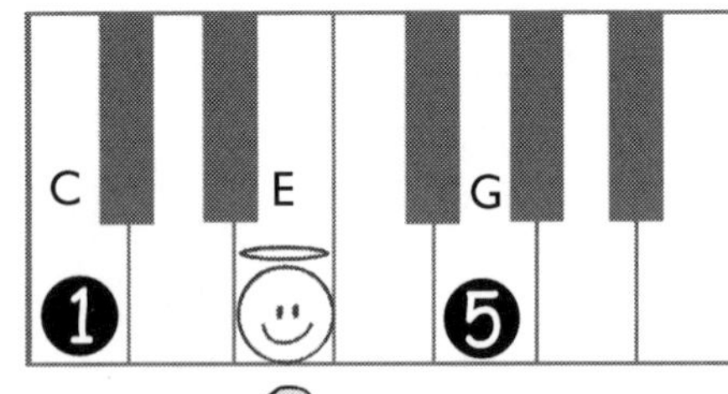

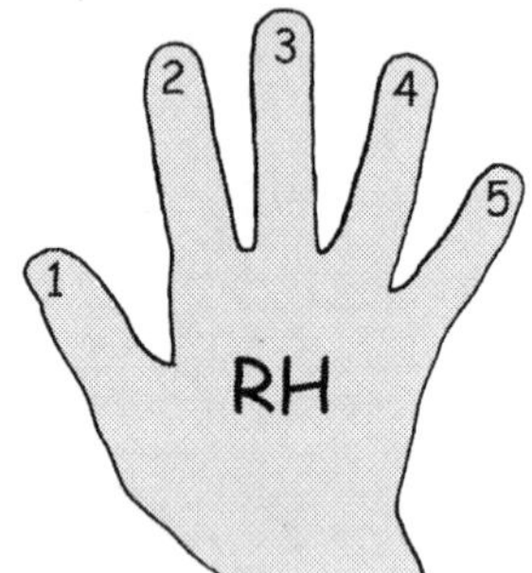

Bring the third (E) down to E♭

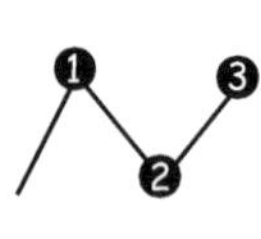

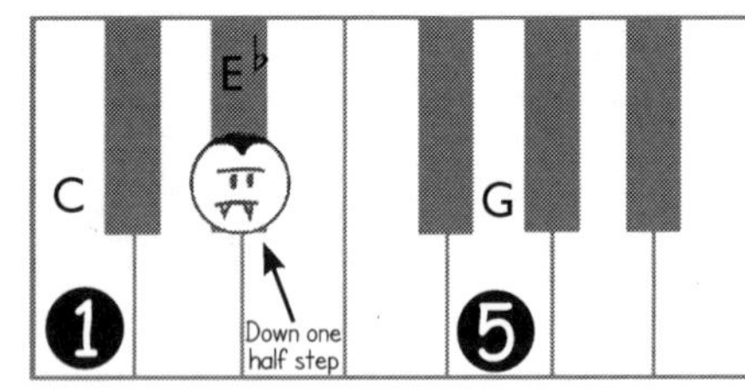

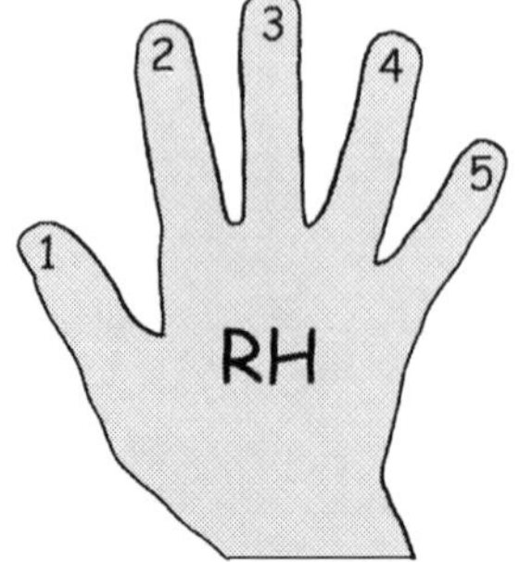

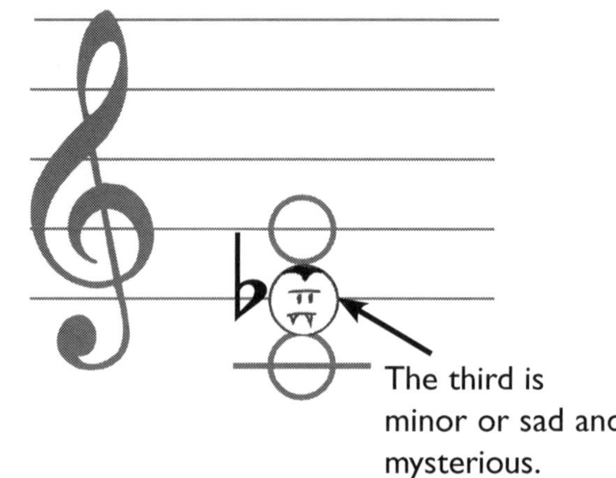

MINOR TO MAJOR (CHEER IT UP....)

To make a minor chord major, we shift the third UP a half step.
3 half steps = minor
A
C
E
MINOR
4 half steps = major
C#
A
E
MAJOR
That cheered it up.

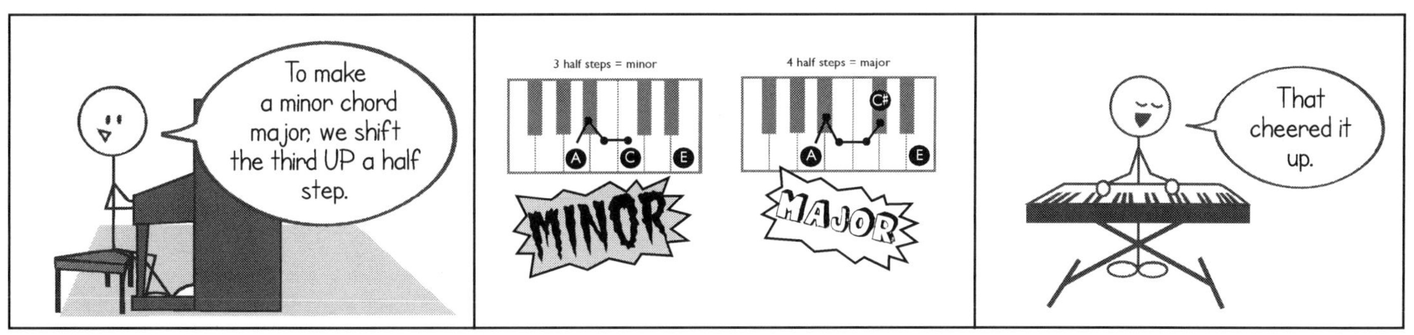

LET'S CHANGE A MINOR INTO A MAJOR...

A MINOR

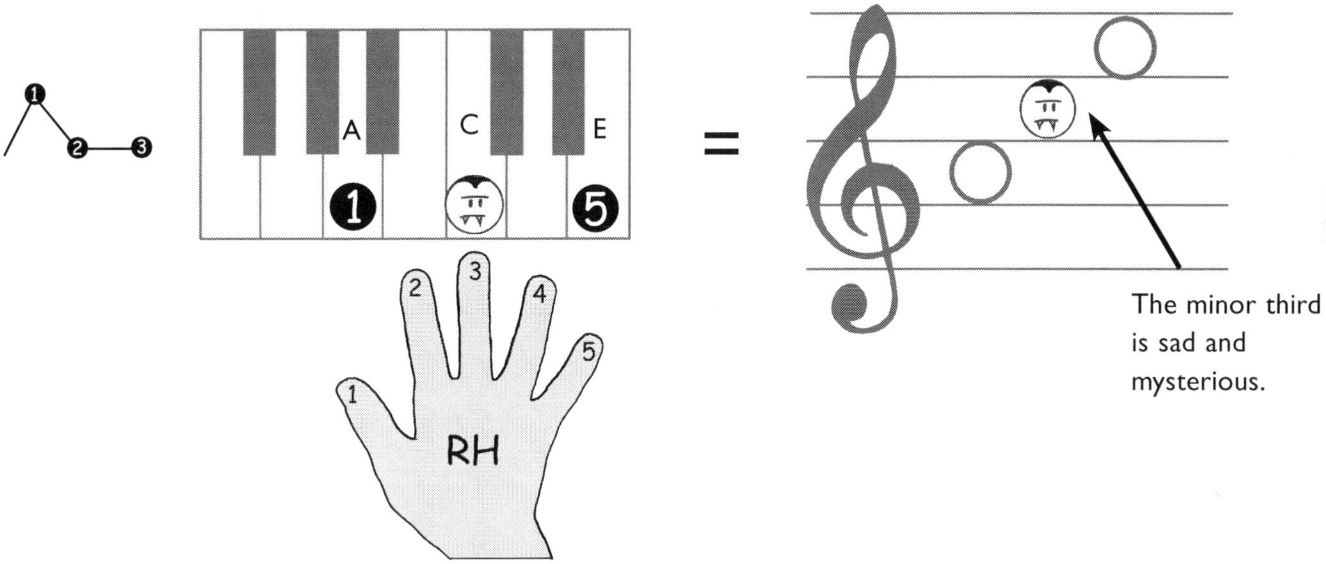

A
C
E
1
5
RH
1
2
3
4
5
=
The minor third is sad and mysterious.

A MAJOR

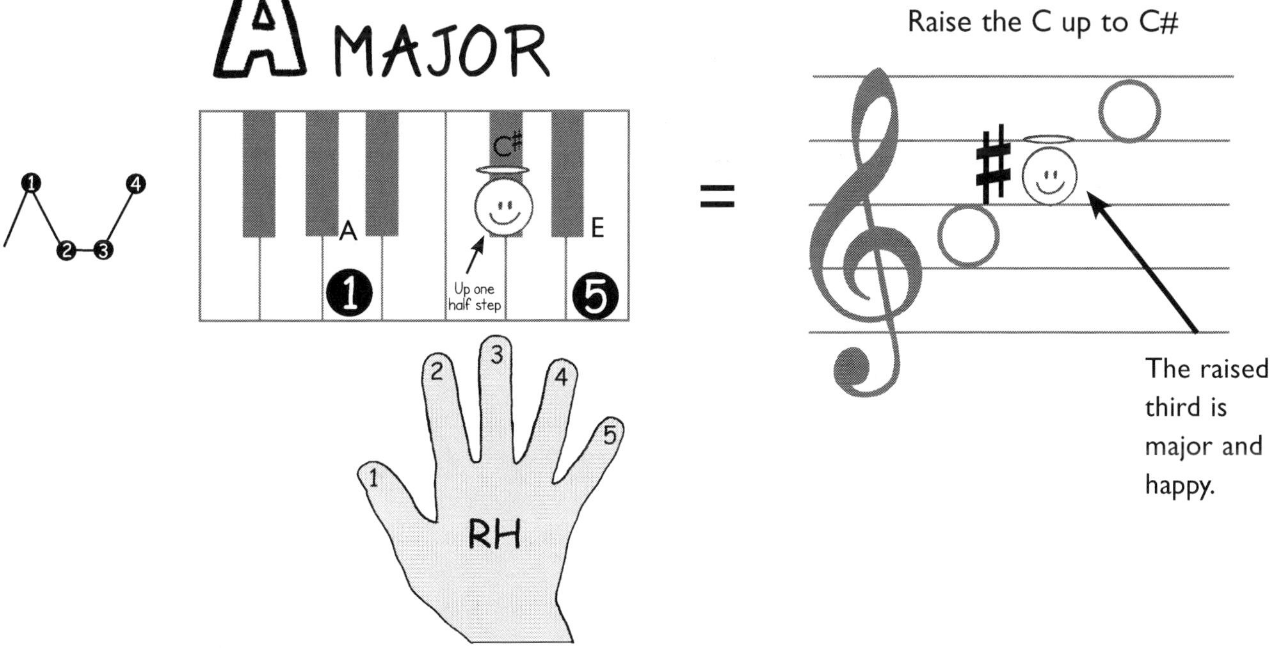

Raise the C up to C#
C#
A
E
1
5
Up one half step
RH
1
2
3
4
5
=
The raised third is major and happy.

#35. MAJOR MINOR CONCERTO

THE THIRD (MIDDLE NOTE) SETS THE MOOD

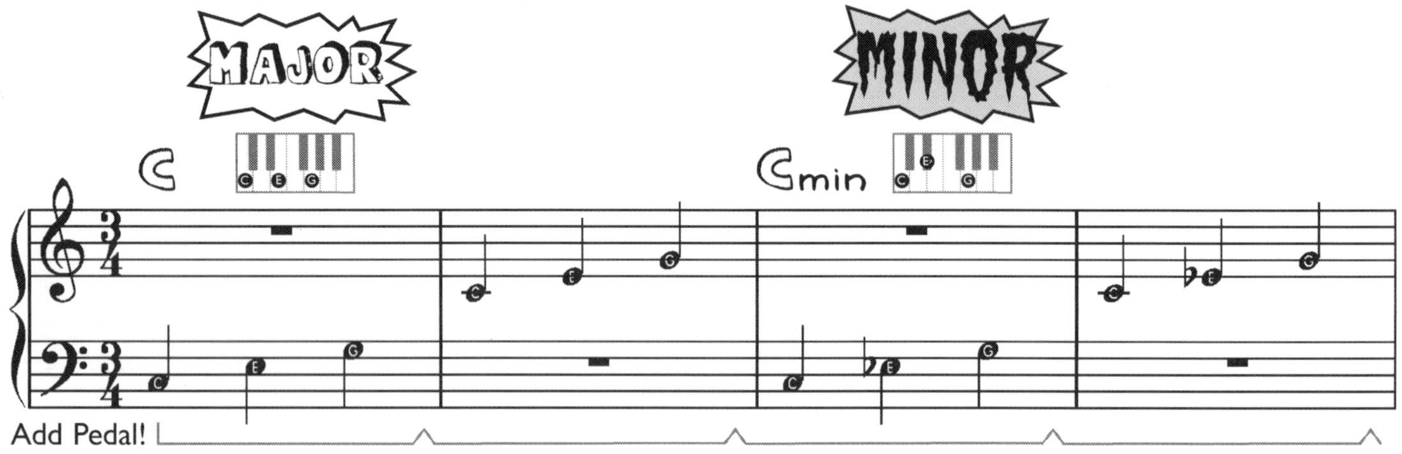

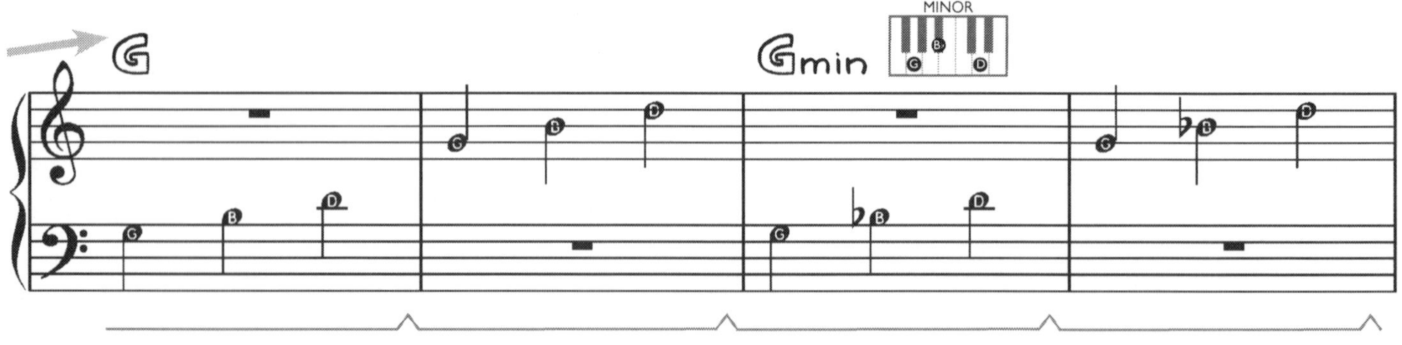

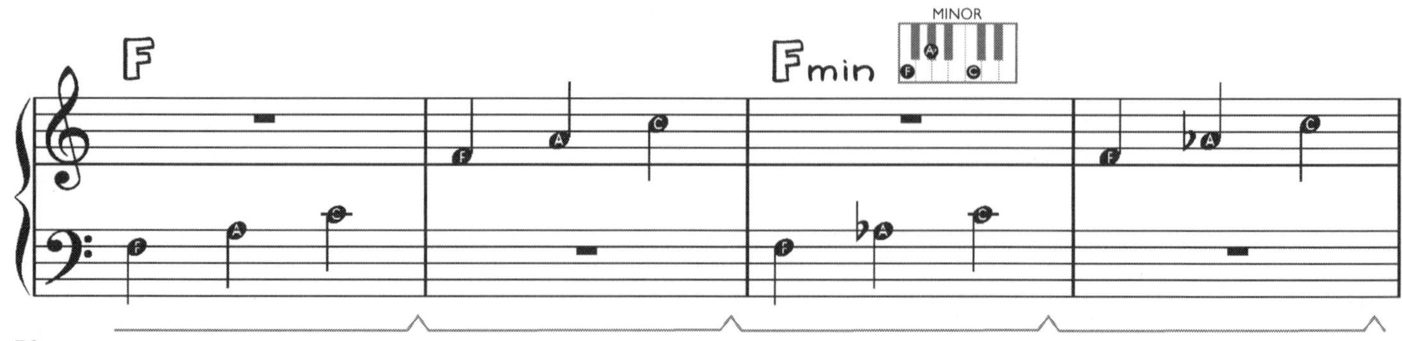

Emin
E
MAJOR
Amin
A
MAJOR
Dmin
D
MAJOR
G
Gmin
MINOR
C
Cmin
MINOR
Hold!

ACTIVITY: MAJOR MINOR QUEST

Practice building both major and minor chords on these root notes.

A C D E G C

G F E G A

A

C F D CHOOSE A ROOT NOTE!

CHAPTER 6

ARPEGGIO ACROBATICS

Now that you have mastered the basics, your journey is going to get interesting. You are going to be playing more complex patterns with both hands, up and down the scale. You will also be using these patterns with chord progressions to play whole songs. With these new arpeggio patterns, your own songs can become more interesting and adventurous. It's time for some arpeggio acrobatics!

#36. DOUBLE RAINBOW ARPEGGIO SCALE

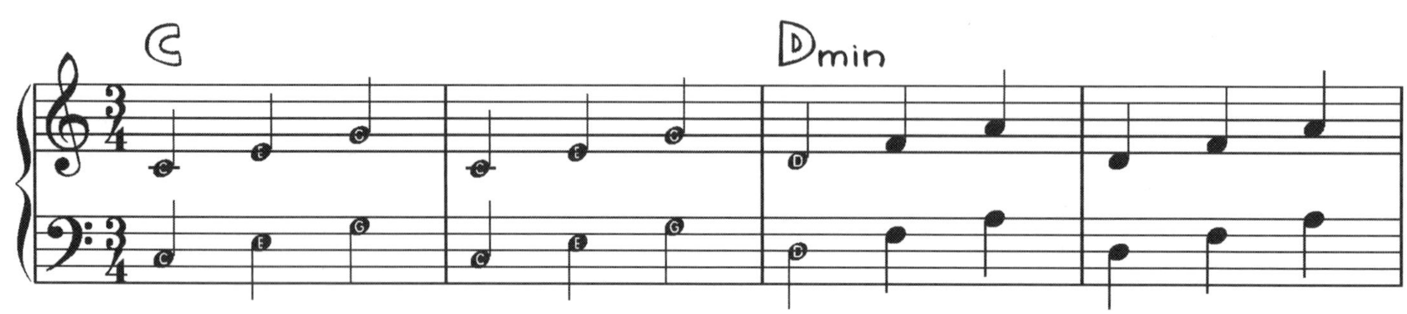

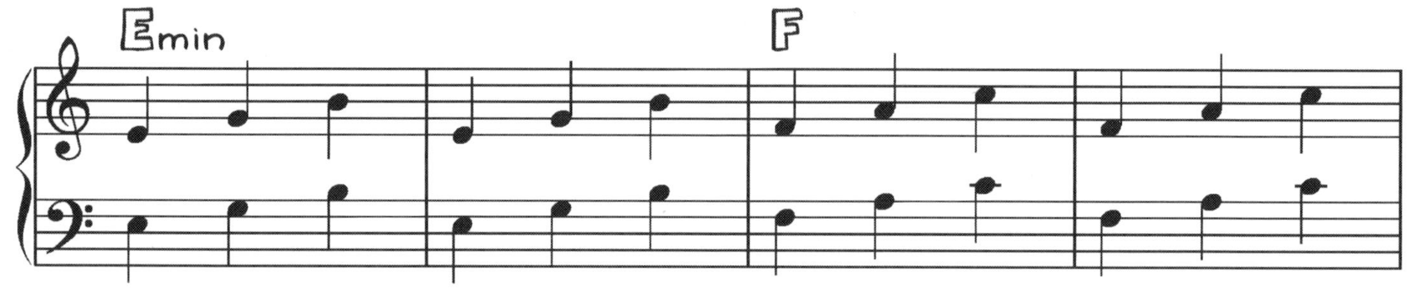

Challenge: Try playing this exercise going back down the scale.

#37. DOUBLE BUBBLE

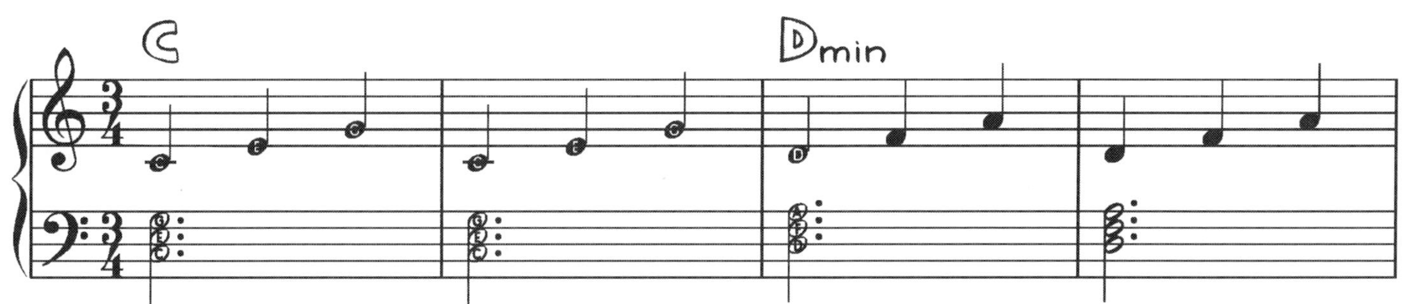

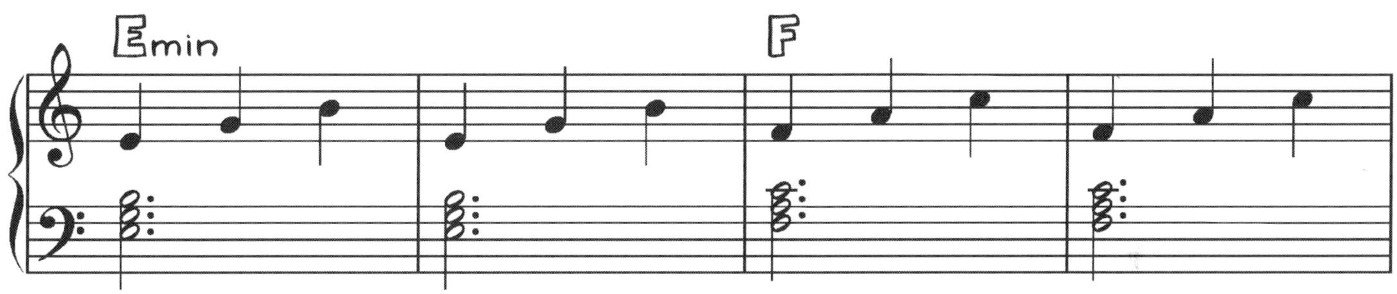

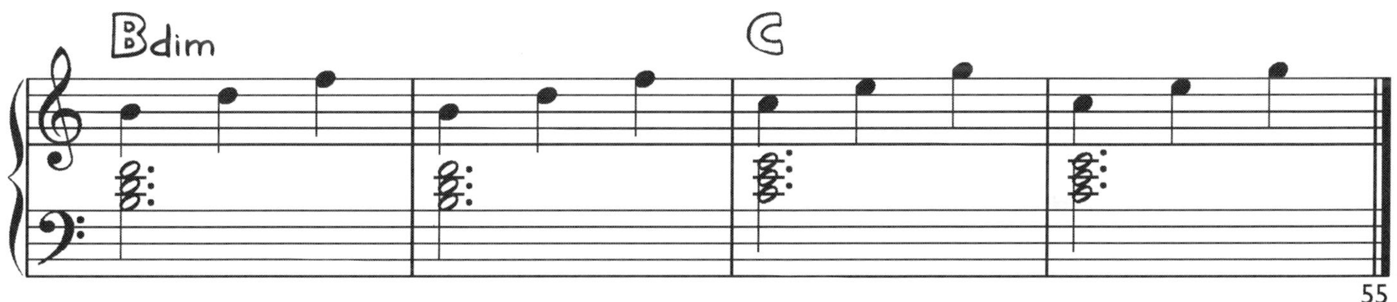

ODE TO DOUBLE RAINBOWS

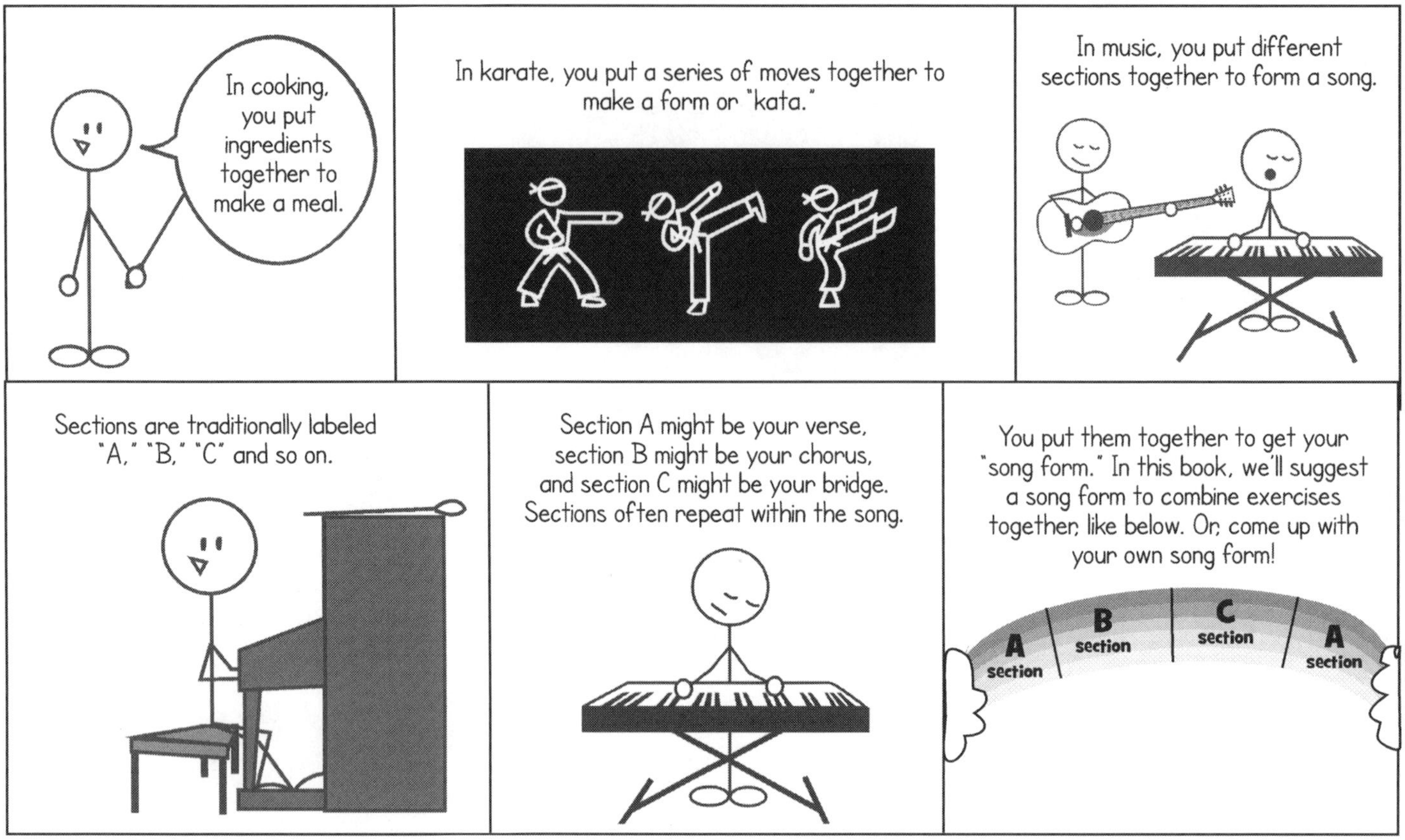

In cooking, you put ingredients together to make a meal.

In karate, you put a series of moves together to make a form or "kata."

In music, you put different sections together to form a song.

Sections are traditionally labeled "A," "B," "C" and so on.

Section A might be your verse, section B might be your chorus, and section C might be your bridge. Sections often repeat within the song.

You put them together to get your "song form." In this book, we'll suggest a song form to combine exercises together, like below. Or, come up with your own song form!

A section
B section
C section
A section

#38. A SECTION: DOUBLE ARPEGGIO

Arpeggios, hands together.

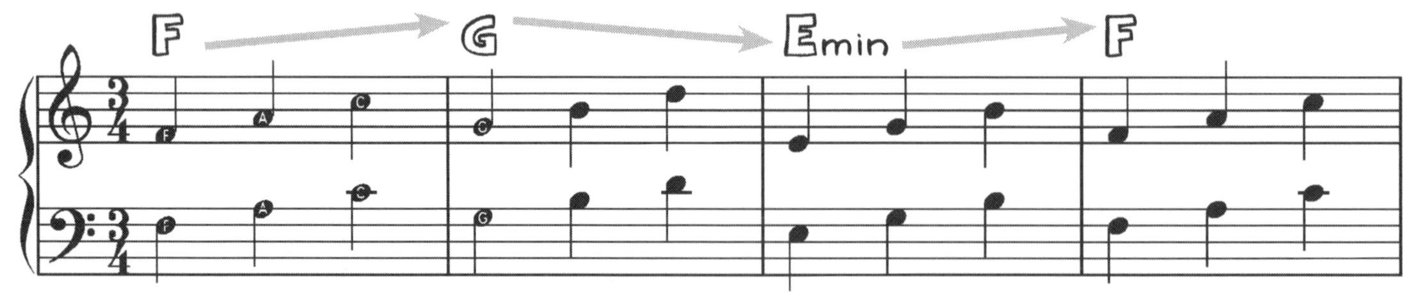

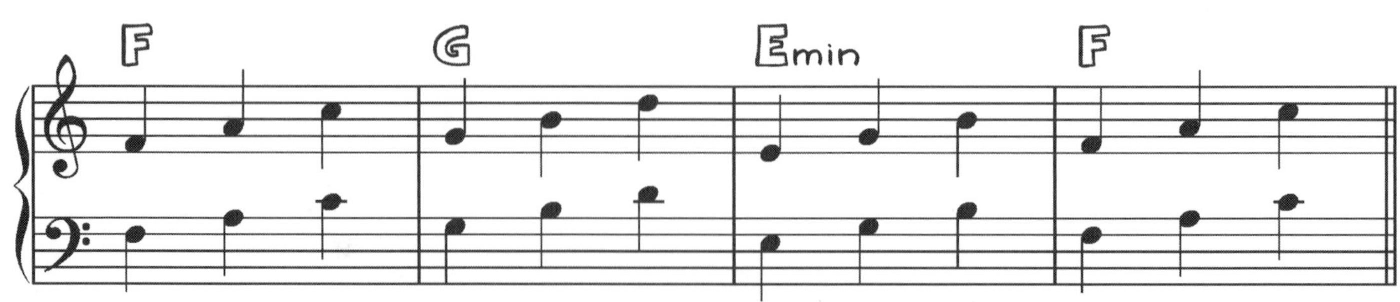

#39. B SECTION: ARPEGGIO CHORD

Left hand plays an arpeggio while your right hand plays a chord.

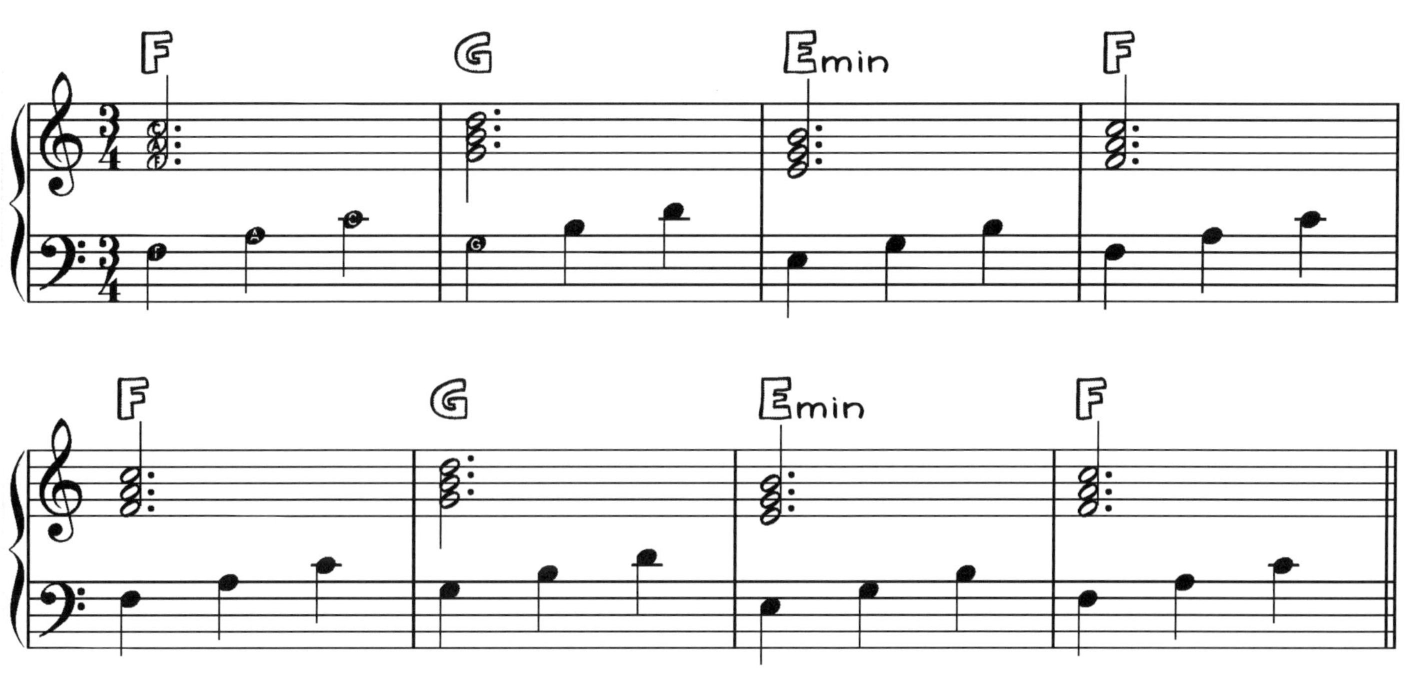

#40. C SECTION: CHORD ARPEGGIO

Left hand plays a chord while your right hand plays an arpeggio.

F G Emin F

F G Emin F

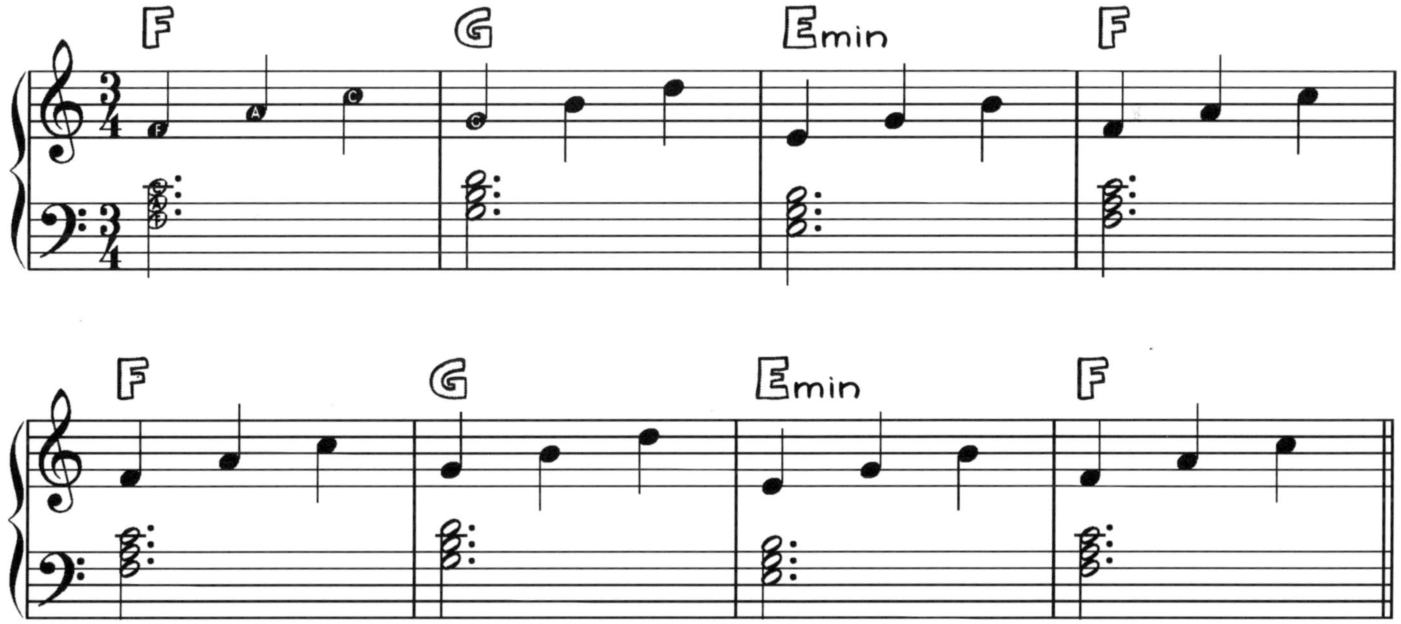

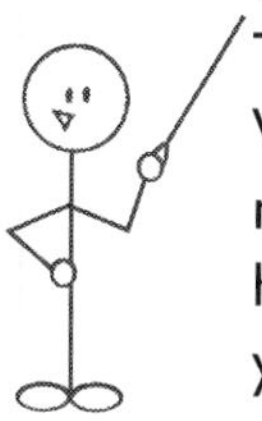

Put the sections together. The song form is A B C A. What other form can you make? Demonstrate that you have mastered this by creating your own. →

BROKEN HEART SONG

#41. A SECTION

Both hands play a root-third-fifth-third arpeggio pattern.

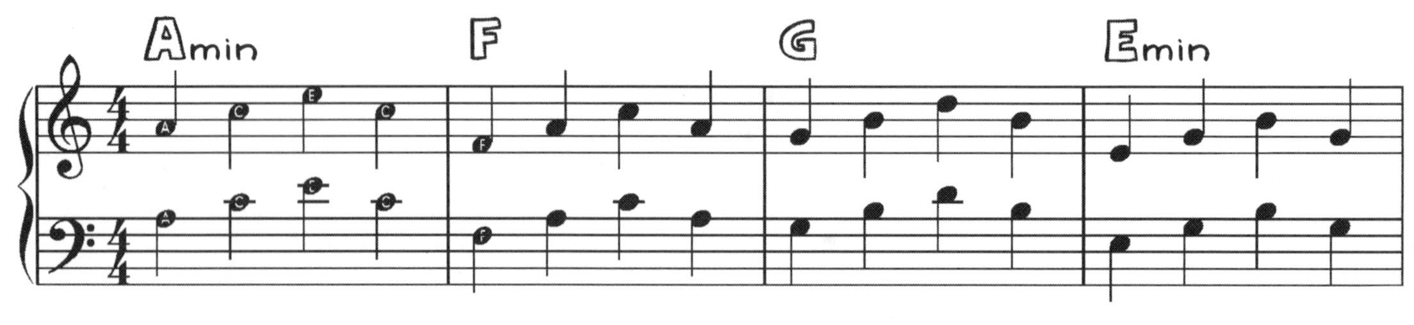

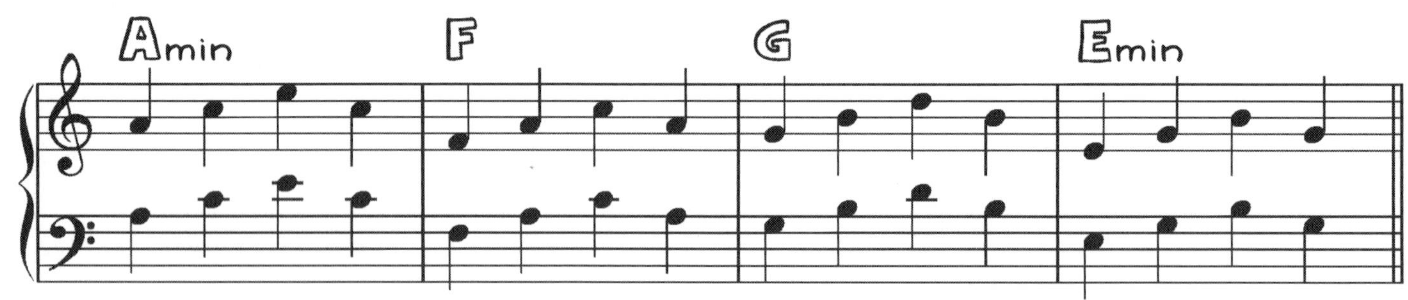

#42. B SECTION

Left hand plays a chord while the right hand plays a root-third-fifth-third arpeggio pattern.

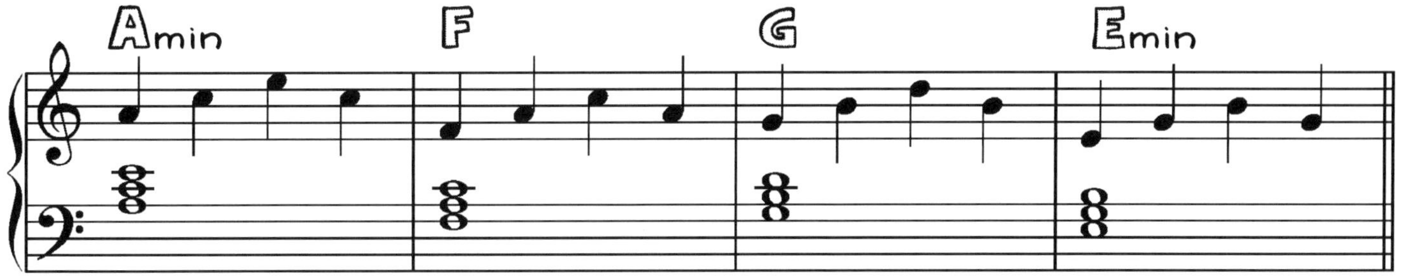

#43. C SECTION

Right hand plays a chord while the left hand plays a root-third-fifth-third arpeggio pattern.

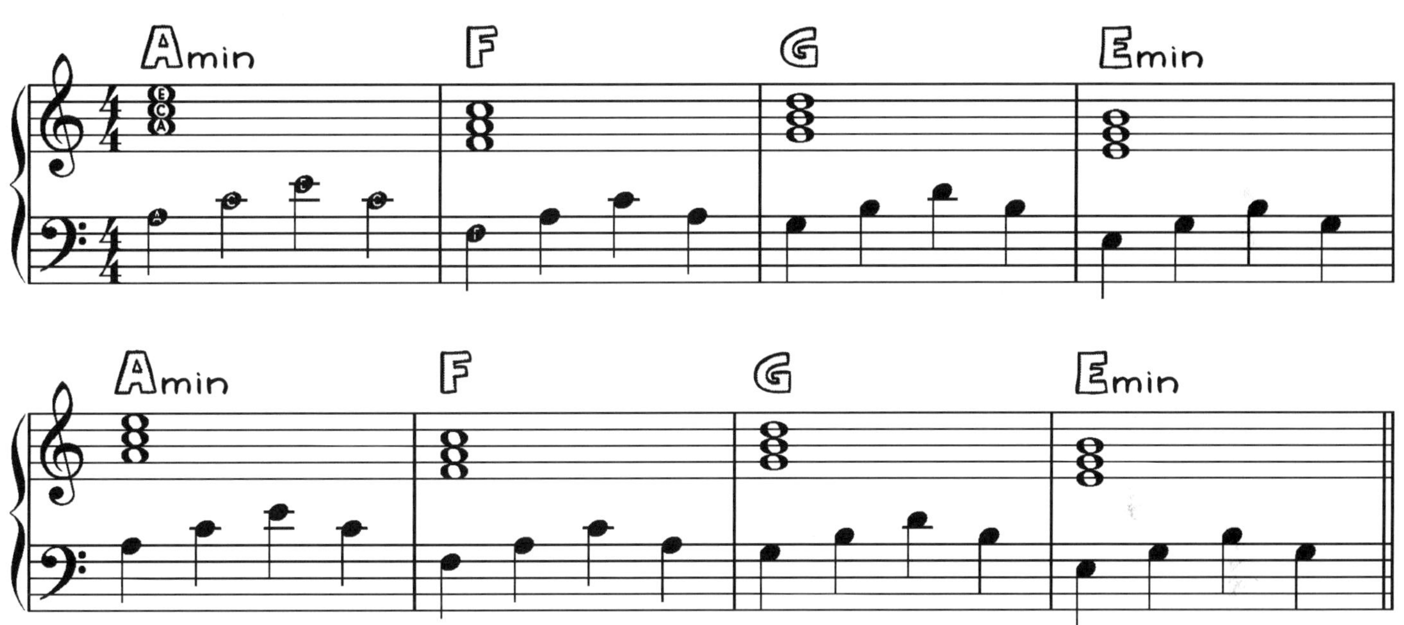

Now try making your own song form:

WHAT IS A CROSSOVER ARPEGGIO?

TO PLAY CROSSOVER ARPEGGIOS...

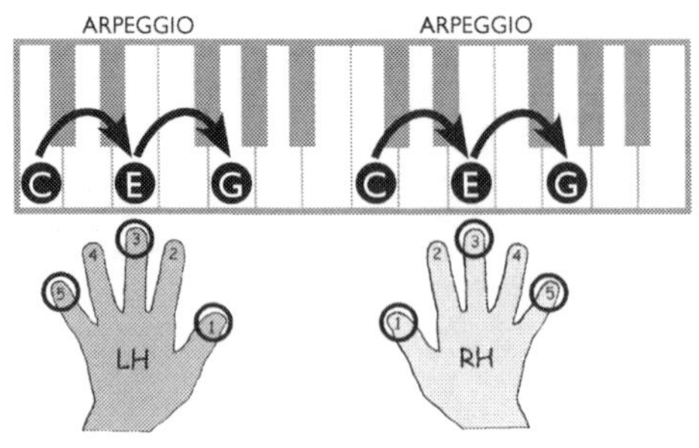

- Place your hands in low C position.
- Play a LH arpeggio and then a RH arpeggio.

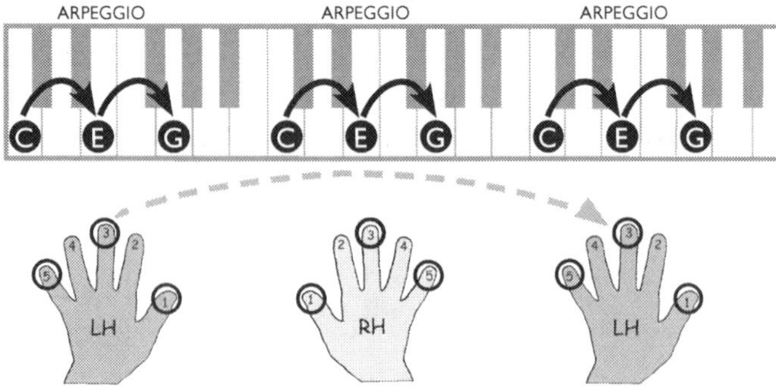

- Cross your LH over your RH, and play another C arpeggio. (Start moving your LH before your RH finishes.)

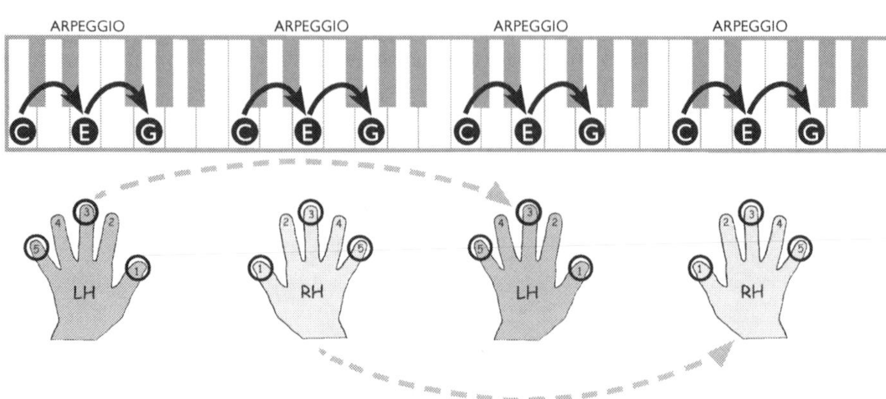

- Finish by crossing your RH under your LH to play the last C arpeggio.

#44. CROSSOVER ARPEGGIO SCALE

Keep going up the scale. End by playing high C.

#45. MALAGUENA FLOW

Play crossover arpeggios with the famous Malaguena progression.

Repeat and end on A

#46. DAYDREAMS

This progression has been used in songs like "Stand By Me," "Eternal Flame" and countless others!

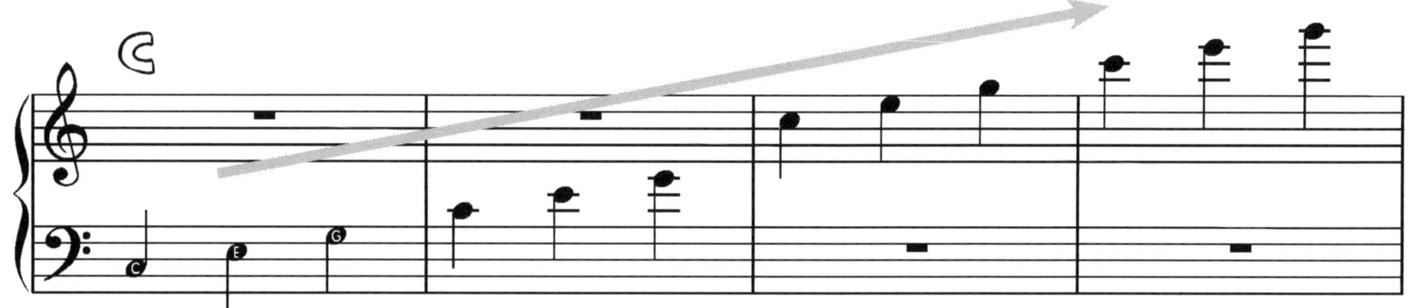

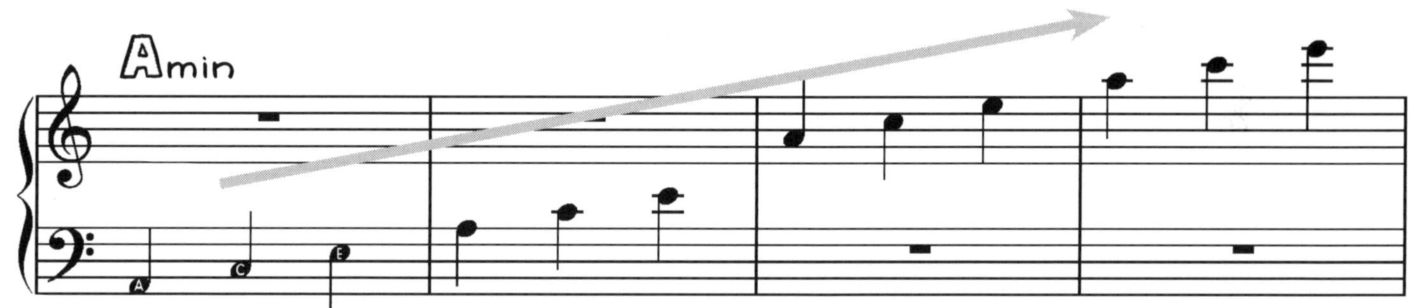

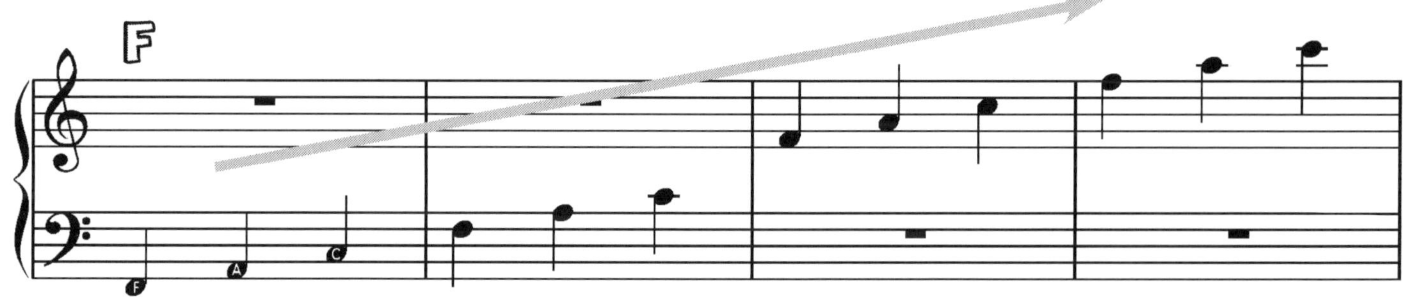

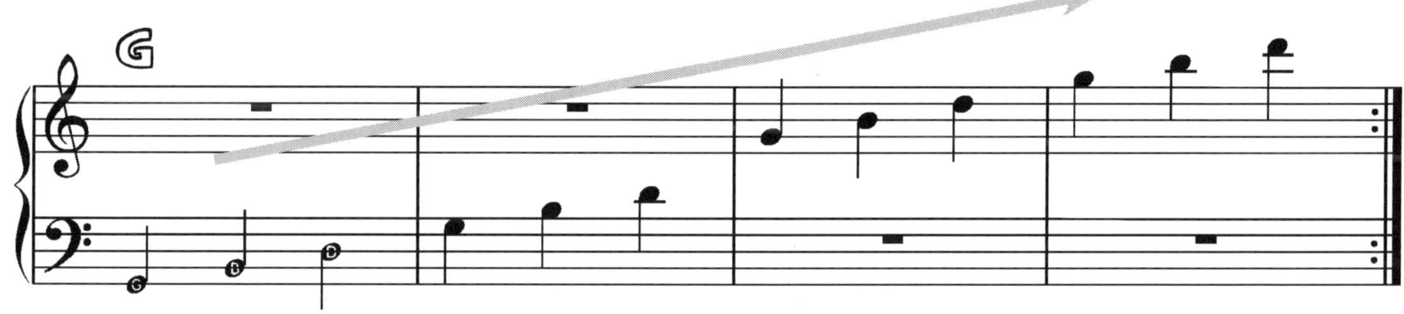

Challenge! Try playing the Major Minor Concerto on page 50 with crossover arpeggios.

CROSSOVER COMPOSER

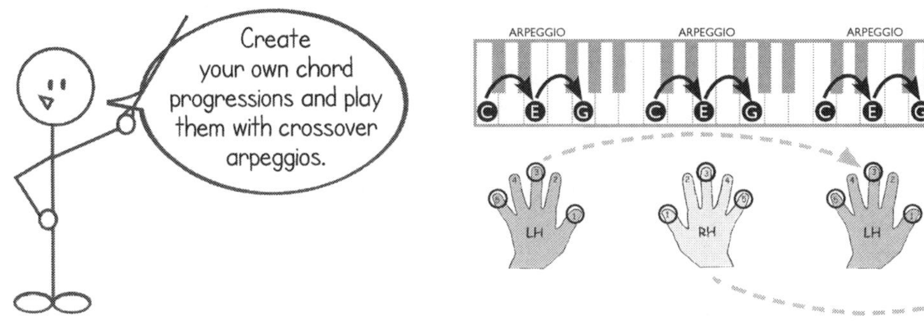

STEP 1: CHOOSE FROM THESE CHORDS

STEP 2: WRITE A FEW CHORD PROGRESSIONS OF YOUR OWN

For a printable PDF of this activity, visit mwfunstuff.com/CCC

CHAPTER 7

TRANSPOSITION

THE CHORD COMPLAINT DEPARTMENT

You may have noticed that the songs in this book (with a couple of exceptions) use exclusively white keys. We've actually done that on purpose, because with no sharps or flats, C is an easy key to learn in. There are many other keys, though! You can move chords, patterns, and melodies to any key using something called transposition, which we'll teach you in this chapter.

TOP REASONS TO TRANSPOSE

1 VOCAL RANGE

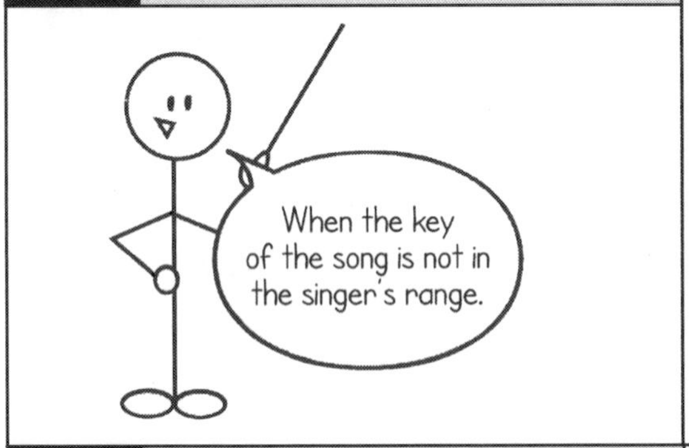

When the key of the song is not in the singer's range.

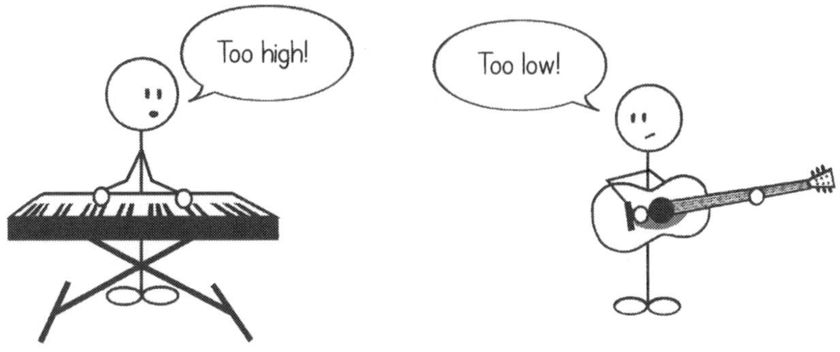

Too high!

Too low!

Your vocal range is the group of notes you are able to sing comfortably. People have different ranges, and it's common to transpose a song performed by someone else to suit your voice. Rock stars do it all the time!

2 PLAYING WITH OTHERS

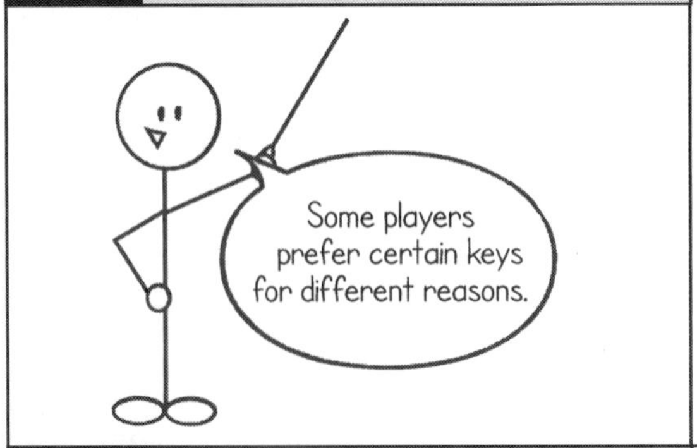

Some players prefer certain keys for different reasons.

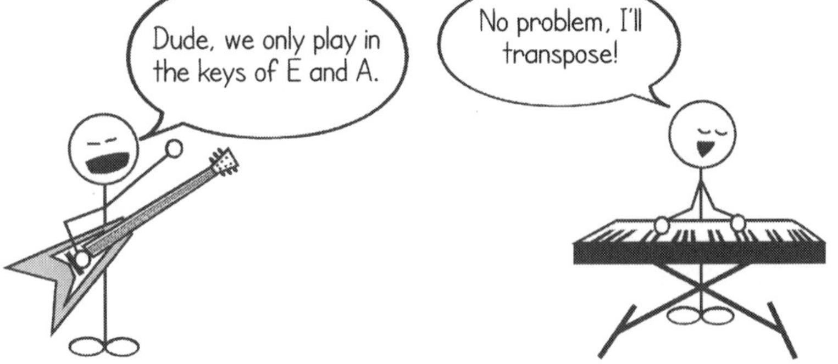

Dude, we only play in the keys of E and A.

No problem, I'll transpose!

3 DIFFICULTY OF THE SONG

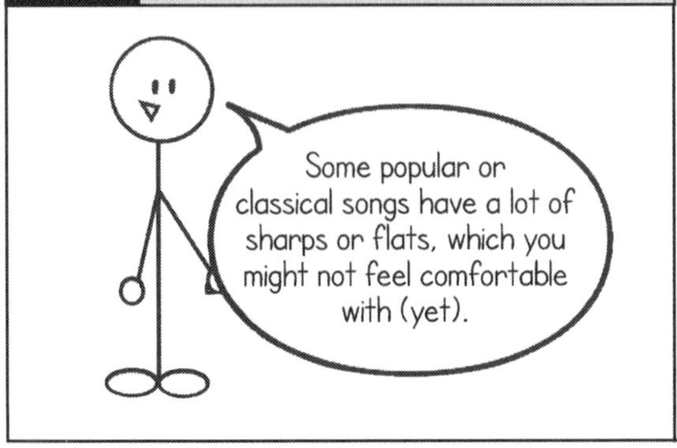

Some popular or classical songs have a lot of sharps or flats, which you might not feel comfortable with (yet).

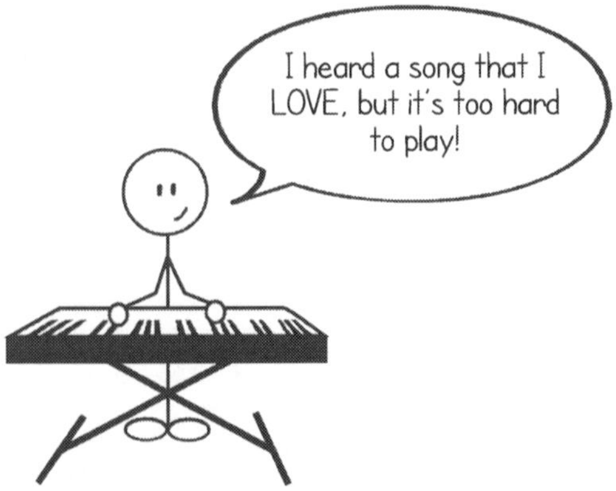

I heard a song that I LOVE, but it's too hard to play!

TRANSPOSING CHORDS IS SIMPLE

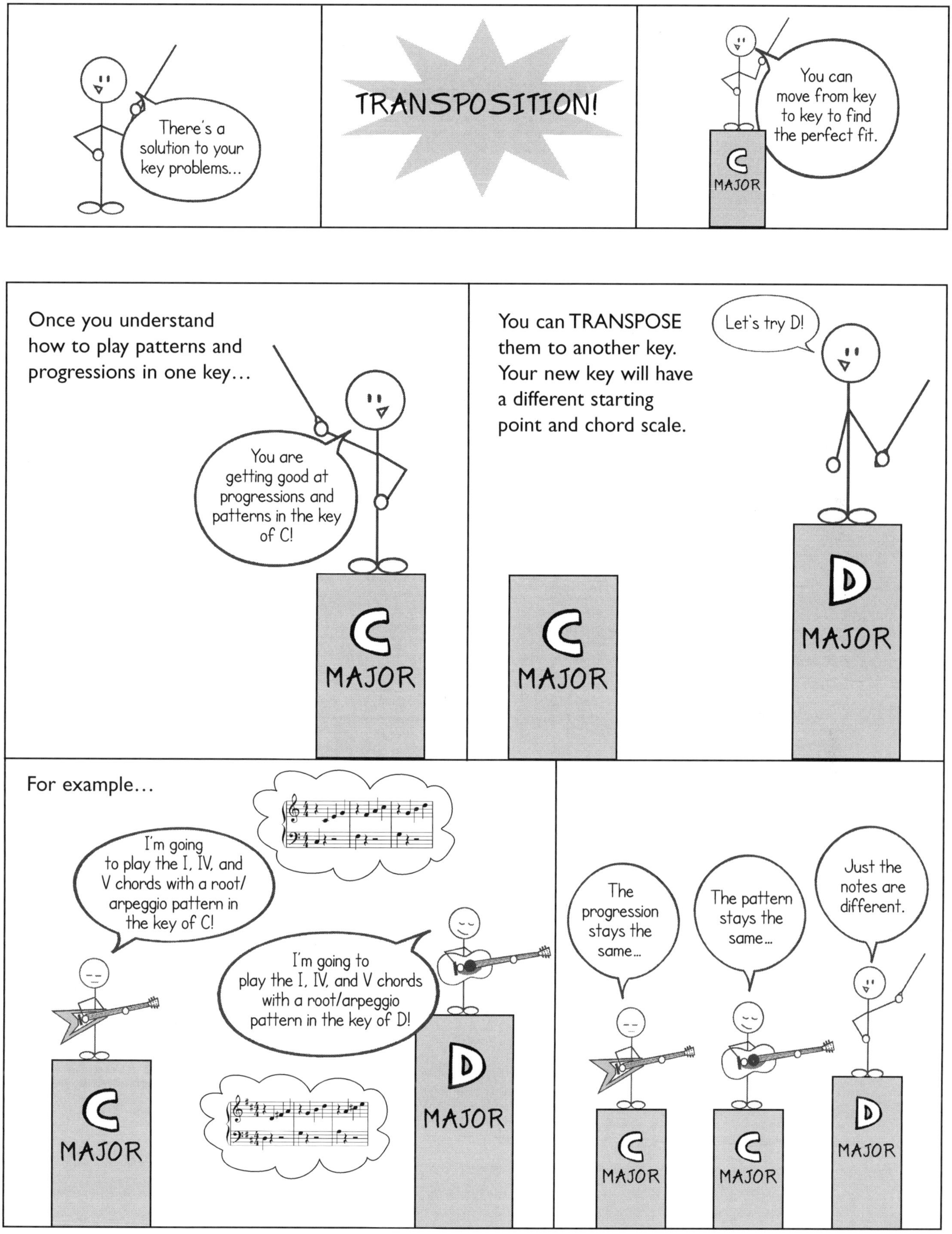

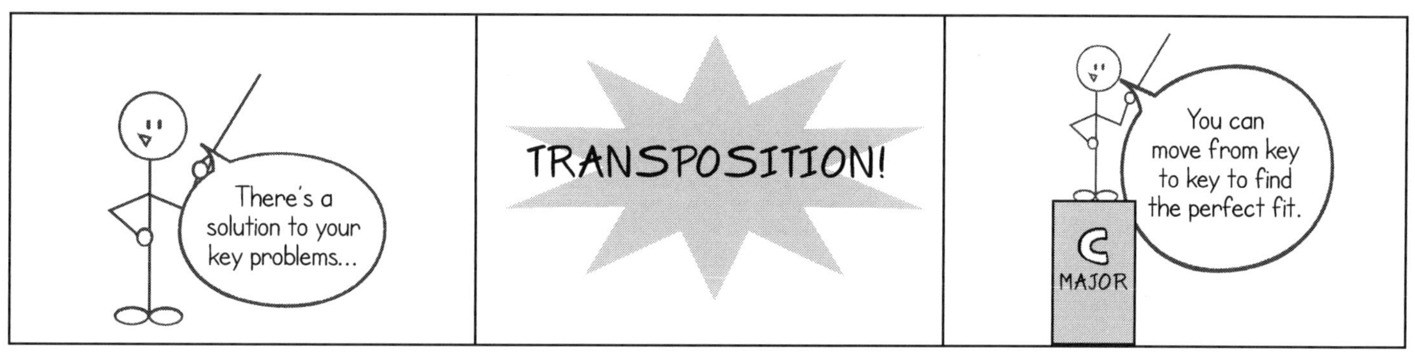

Once you understand how to play patterns and progressions in one key...

You are getting good at progressions and patterns in the key of C!

C MAJOR

You can TRANSPOSE them to another key. Your new key will have a different starting point and chord scale.

Let's try D!

C MAJOR

D MAJOR

For example...

I'm going to play the I, IV, and V chords with a root/arpeggio pattern in the key of C!

I'm going to play the I, IV, and V chords with a root/arpeggio pattern in the key of D!

C MAJOR

D MAJOR

The progression stays the same...

The pattern stays the same...

Just the notes are different.

C MAJOR

C MAJOR

D MAJOR

TACKLING TRANSPOSITION

So far we've been playing in the key of C, but you can transpose to any key, each with their own scale... and their own chord scale.

HOW TRANSPOSITION WORKS

Each major key maintains the same relationships between notes and chords, even though it starts in a different place. Some keys have sharps and flats, which are needed to maintain those relationships. Because of them, we can move from key to key without changing the character of the song. It will just sound higher or lower.

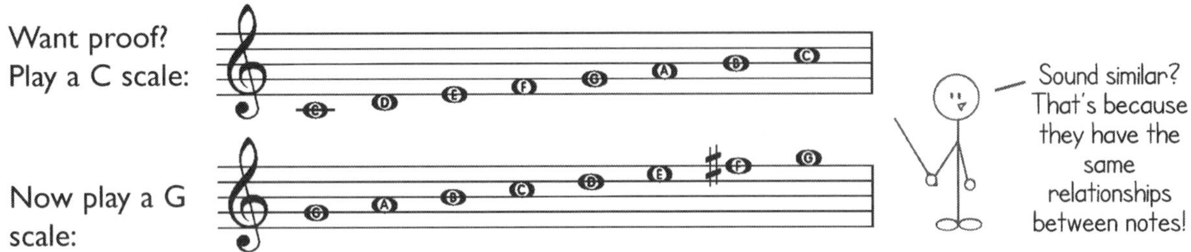

LETS LOOK AT CHORD SCALES

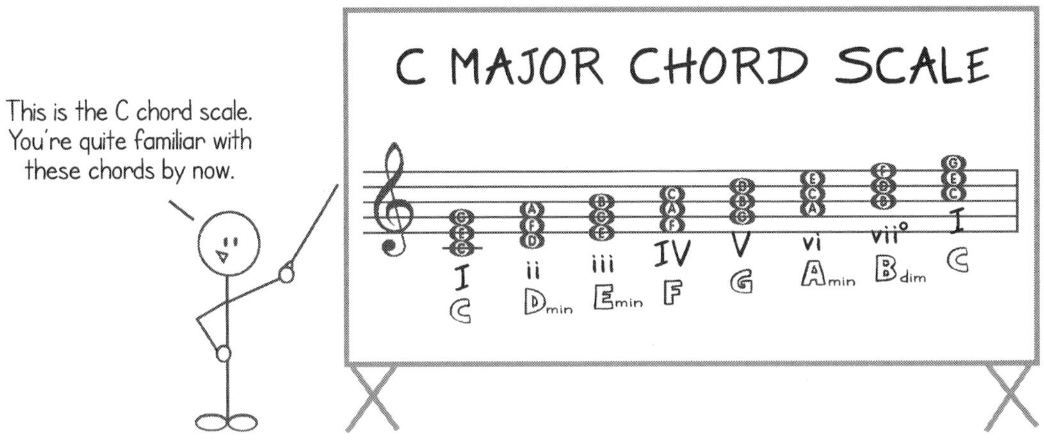

This is the G chord scale. Notice that the chord numbers stay the same. That's because the relationships are the same.

Play both chord scales. See how they sound similar?

You can use scales and chord scales to help you transpose many songs. We've got a handy chart with them on page 116. On the next page, we'll show you the steps to take to transpose your favorite Chord Crash Course songs!

TRANSPOSING IN 4 STEPS

Let's transpose this short song:

C Dmin F G C

First, look at the key signature. (If there are sharps and flats at the beginning before the time signature, you can use them to figure out the key. Having NO sharps or flats at the beginning generally means you're in the key of C major or A minor. Look at the chord scale glossary on page 116 to see the key signatures for different keys.) Still not sure? Is there a chord that feels like "home base"? If so, the name of that chord is also probably the name of the key. Songs often end on that "home base" chord, like the song above. It ends on C and has no sharps or flats. We're in the key of C major.

RH: Chord

LH: Root Note

Compare the chord progression above to the C chord scale. If we do that, we'll see that the progression is:

I ii IV V I

By referring to the chord progression using the chord numbers, we can easily change keys.

Use the chord numbers to figure out what the chord progression is in the new key. Let's transpose to the key of G.

In the key of G:

I ii IV V I = G Am C D G

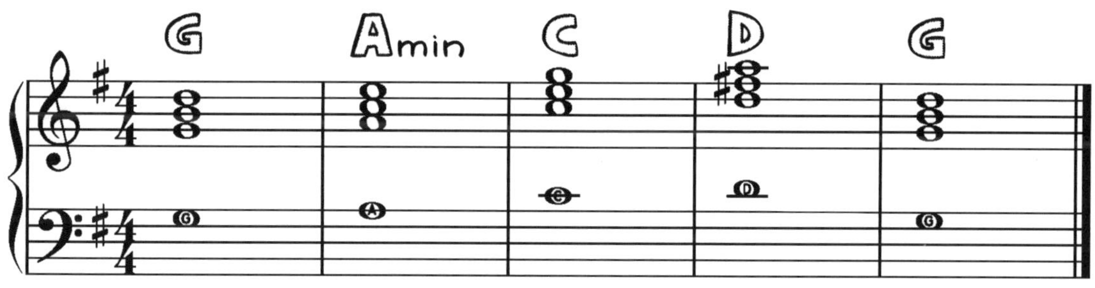

PRACTICE TRANSPOSING

Now, practice your new skill by transposing the song below to the key of D! Follow the steps and fill them in as you go! Turn to the Chord Scale Glossary on page 116 to view the chord scale for the key of D.

The song above is in the key of:

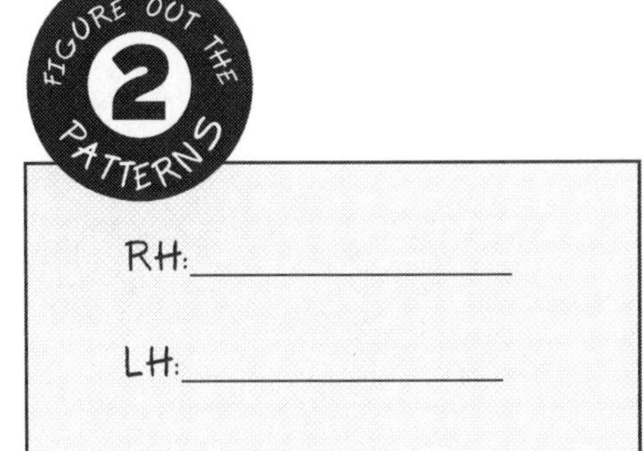

RH: ______________

LH: ______________

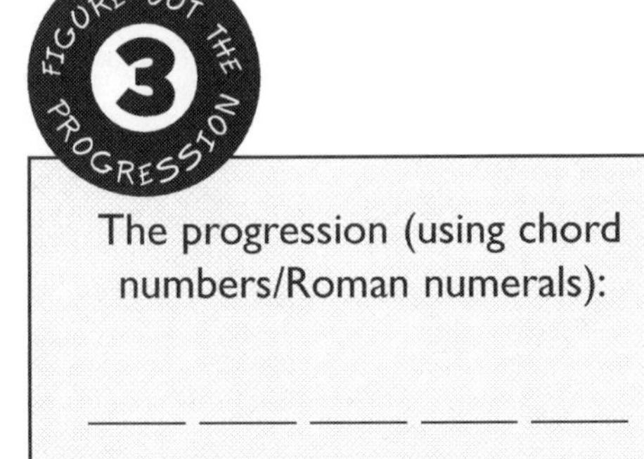

The progression (using chord numbers/Roman numerals):

____ ____ ____ ____ ____

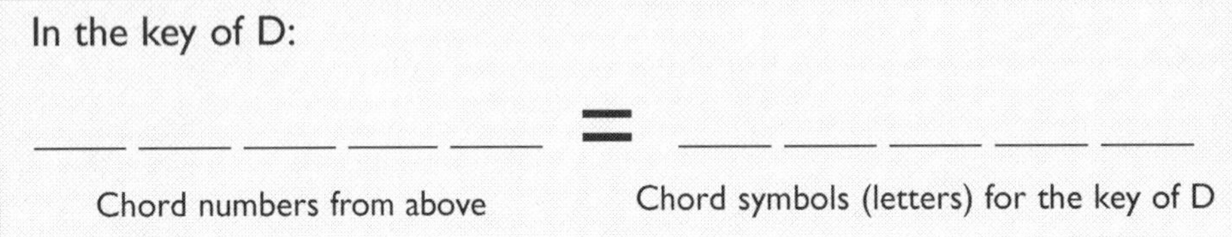

In the key of D:

____ ____ ____ ____ ____ = ____ ____ ____ ____ ____

Chord numbers from above — Chord symbols (letters) for the key of D

(For a printable PDF of this activity, visit mwfunstuff.com/CCC)

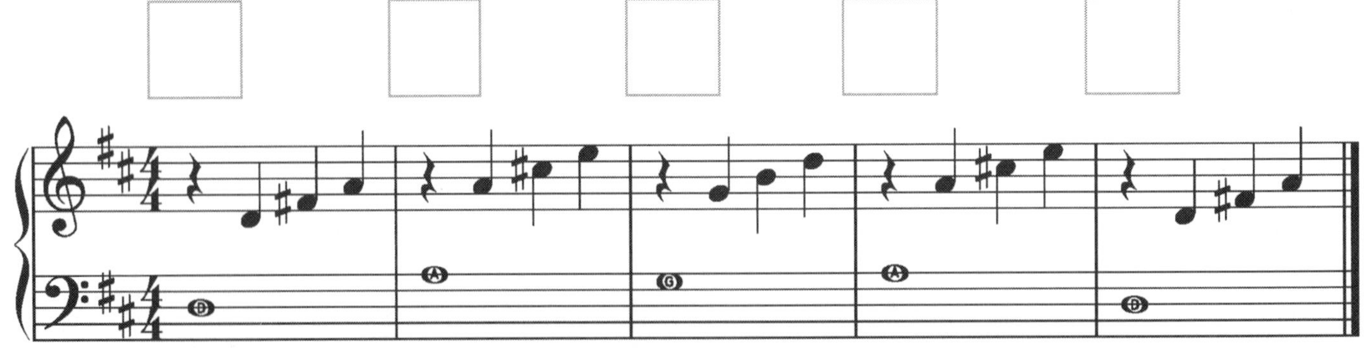

CHAPTER 8

TIMELESS STYLES

In this chapter, you'll learn some timeless accompaniment patterns that have been used in classical music, movies and more for countless years.

Oom-pah music conjures images of polka bands, circuses or, of course, the Oompa Loompas from Willy Wonka's Chocolate Factory. But the Oom-pah pattern is full of even more surprises. It is a true power pattern used in a wide variety of styles and has a rich history. European classical composers like Strauss, Brahms, and Chopin all used Oom-pah patterns in their waltzes. A popular style of Klezmer music (a traditional Jewish style) came out of this same part of the world, and also shows an Oom-pah influence. Even famous composer Danny Elfman (who has written the soundtracks for TONS of movies and TV shows... including the Simpsons' theme song) uses Oom-pah.

Alberti bass is one of the most powerful and universal arpeggio patterns in the world. The great masters of Vienna, Austria (Haydn, Mozart and Beethoven) immortalized Alberti bass by using the pattern in everything from keyboard and violin sonatas to compositions for their symphonies.

Now you get to learn these timeless styles, and use them in your own way.

OOM-PAH-PAH WALTZES

Umm...
What is an OOM?

The "oom" is the low note (the root note) on the down beat, kind of like the boom of a drum.

What is a PAH?

The "pahs" are the higher notes of the chord.

LEFT HAND

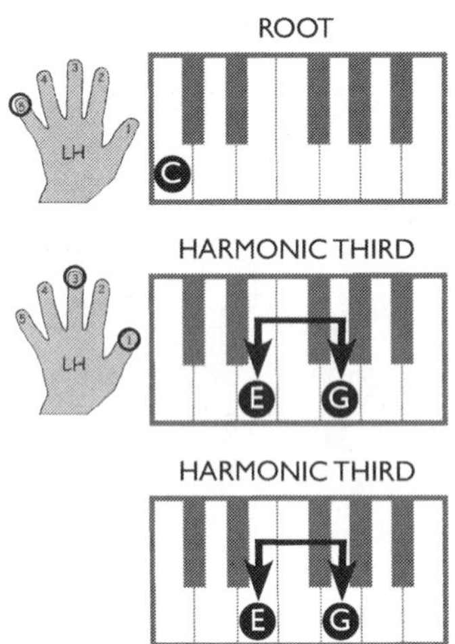

RIGHT HAND

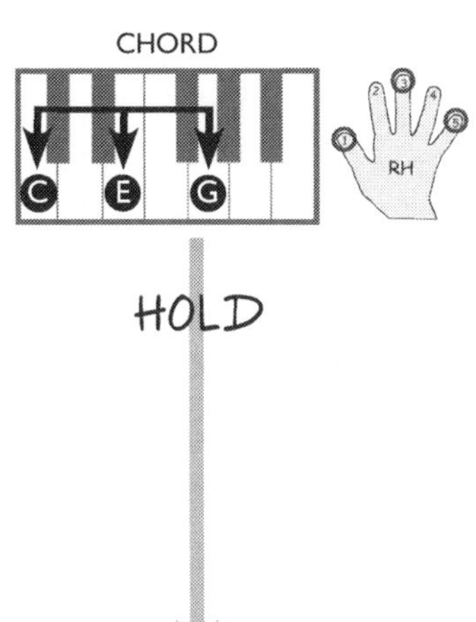

- Left hand plays the root, followed by a harmonic third (with the 1 and 3 fingers), and another harmonic third.
- Practice that until smooth, and then try adding your right hand, playing a chord while the left hand plays the root note.

#47. A SECTION: CIRCUS WALTZ

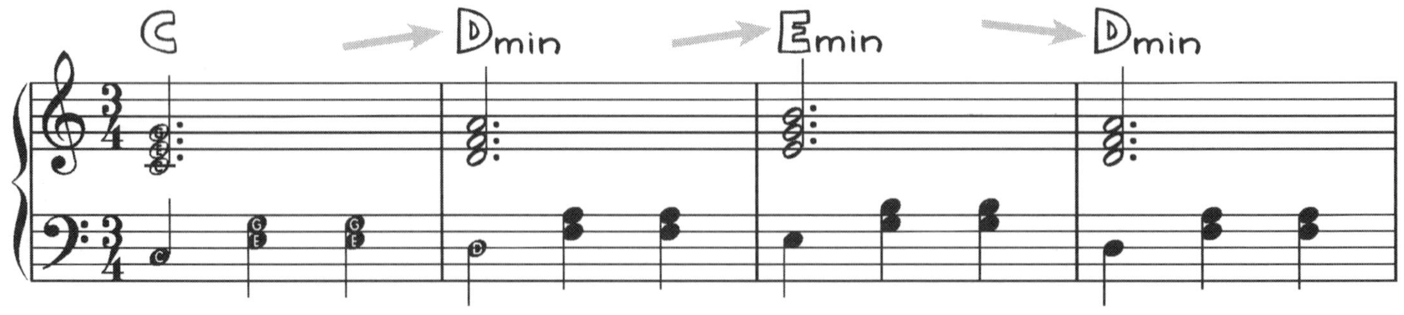

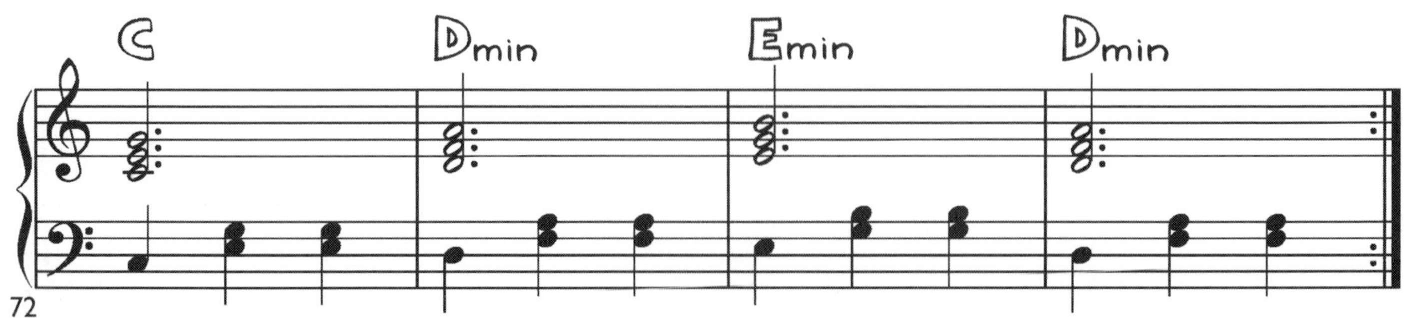

#48. B SECTION: WALTZ OF THE CLOWNS

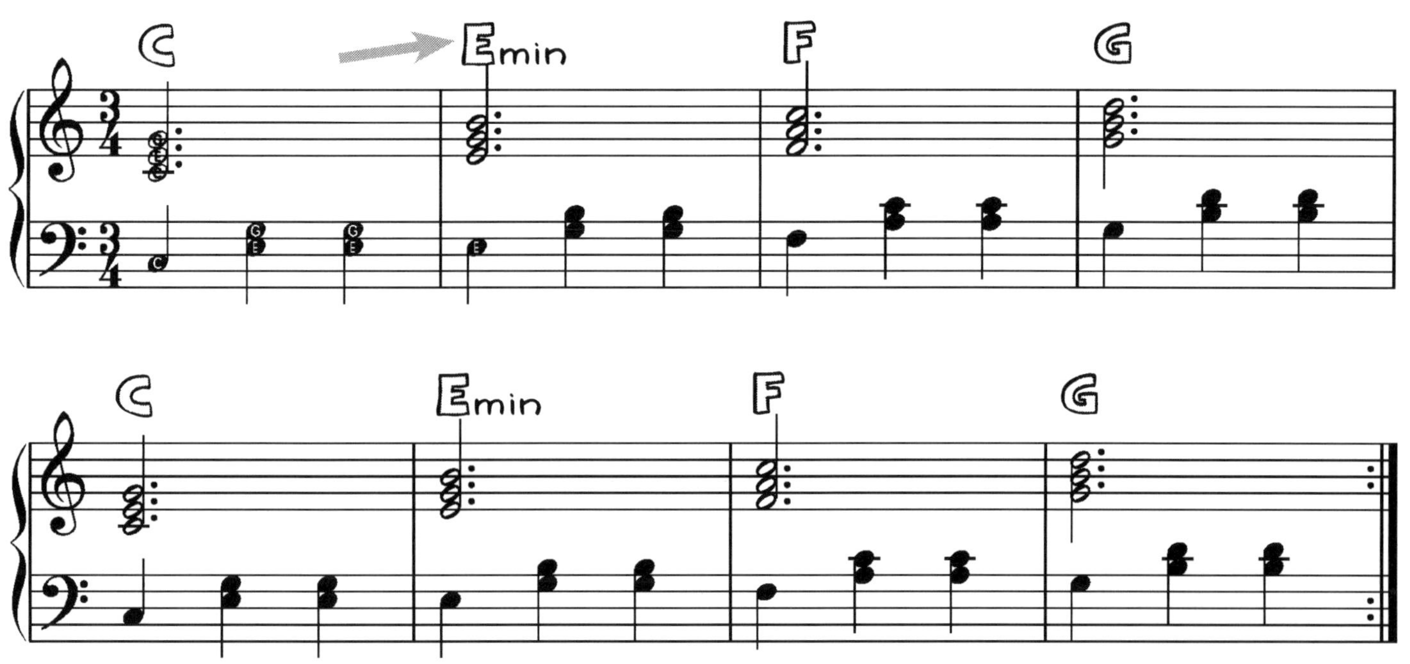

#49. C SECTION: FLYING TRAPEZE

Now that you've mastered the pattern, let's fly on over to a new key. In this exercise, we'll be transposing exercise #47, "Circus Waltz," to the key of G. Write the new chord symbols above each measure, and then play.

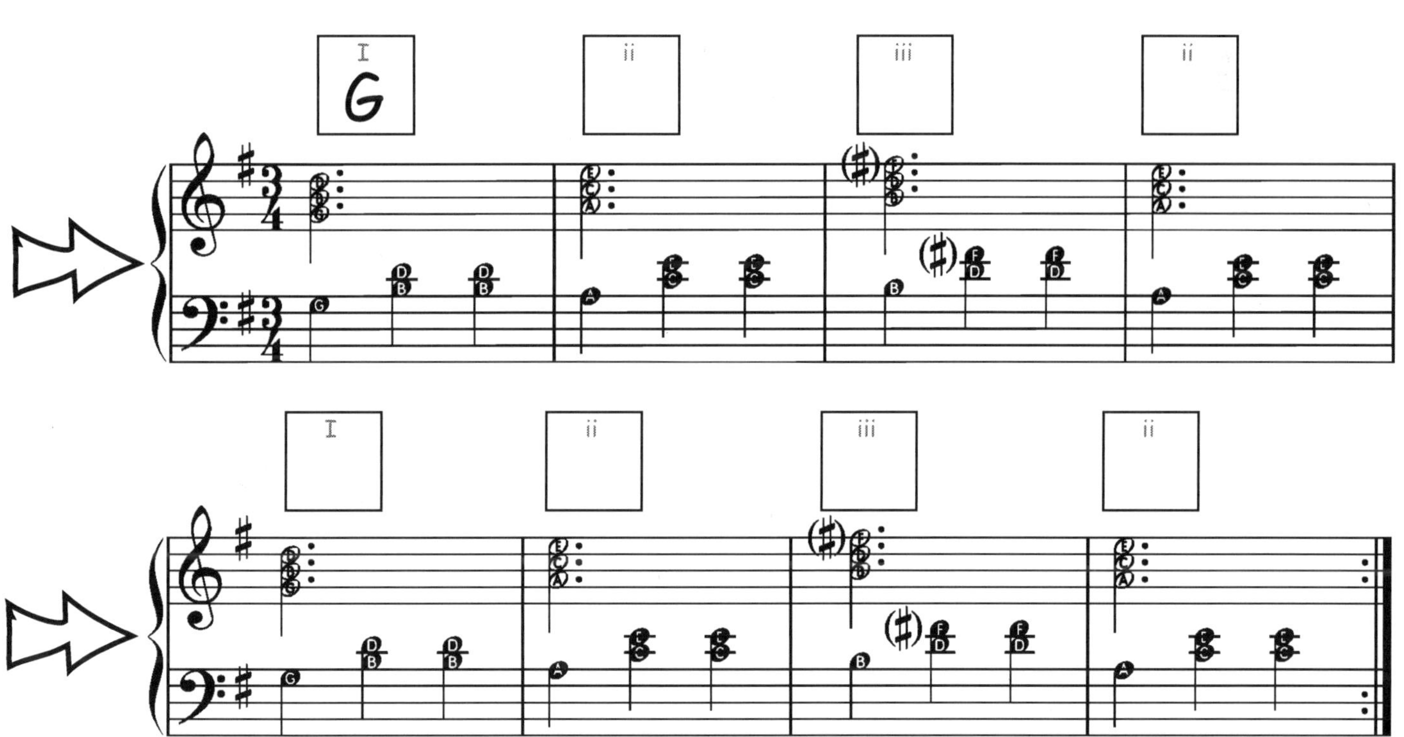

OOM-PAH OOM-PAH

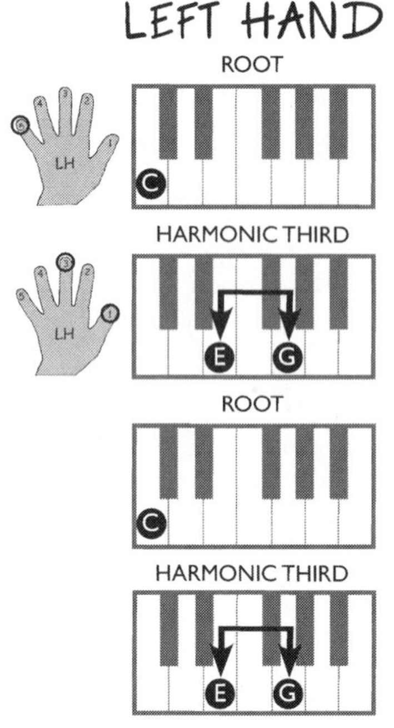

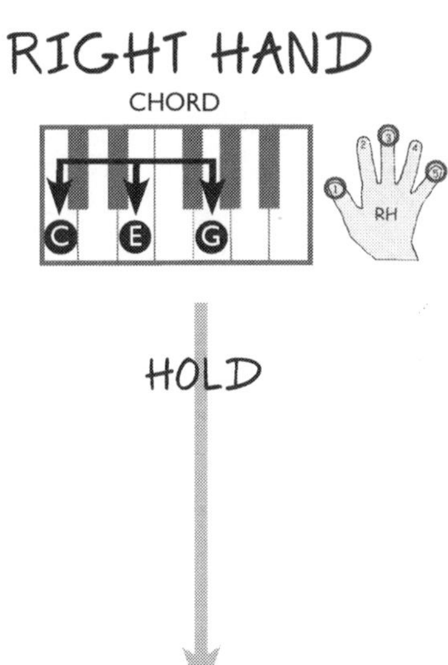

- Left hand plays the root, followed by a harmonic third (with the 1 and 3 fingers), then root and harmonic third again.
- Practice that until smooth, and then try adding your right hand, playing a chord and holding for four beats while the left hand plays the root note.

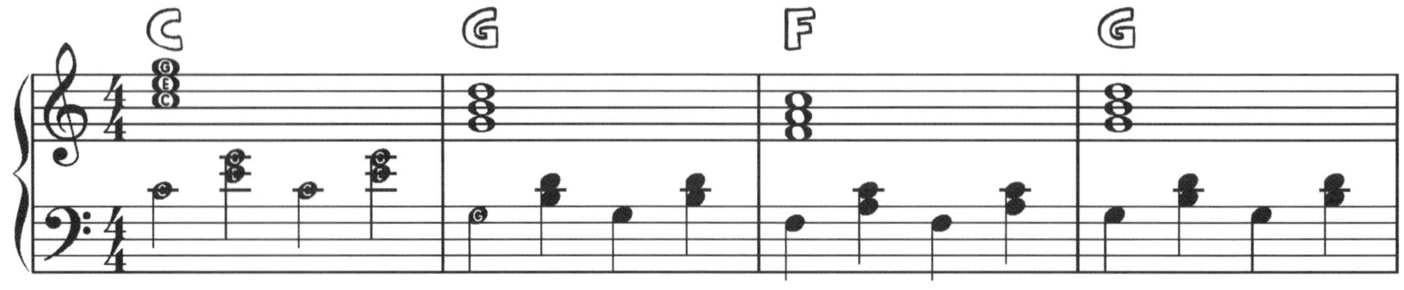

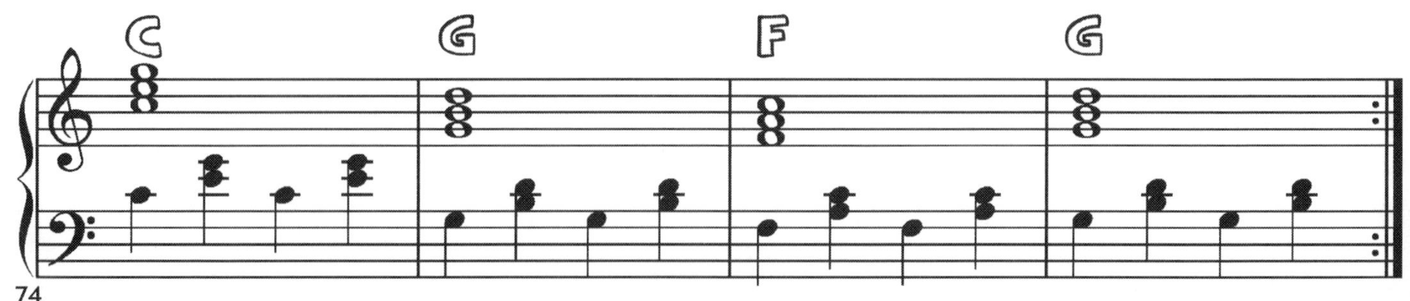

OOM-PAH DOO WOP

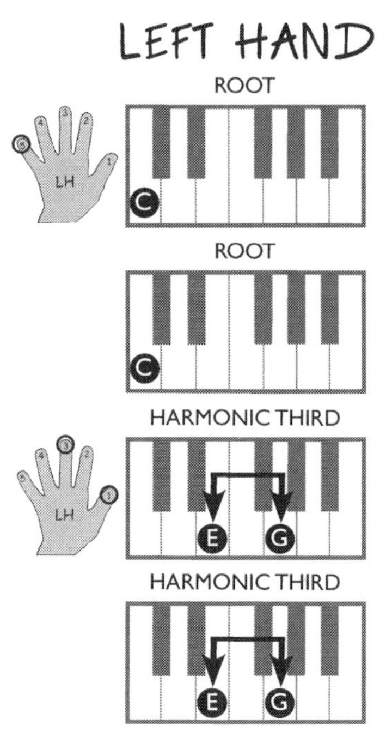

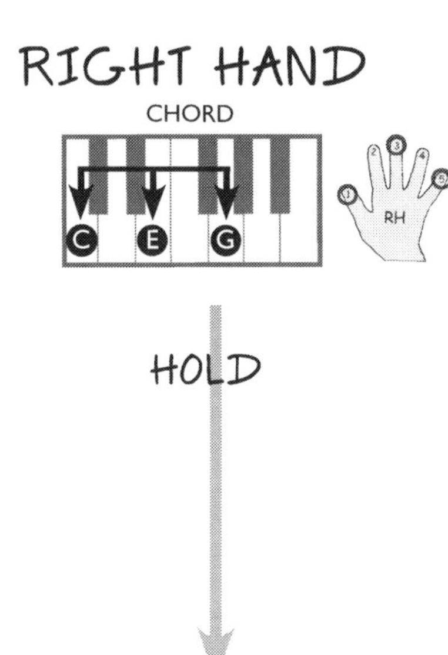

- Left hand plays the root note and then another root note.
- Next, it "bounces" to a harmonic third (with the 1 and 3 fingers) and repeats that harmonic third.
- Practice that until smooth, and then try adding your right hand, playing a chord when the left hand plays the root note and holding for four beats.

You can play this exercise as the accompaniment to the famous "Heart and Soul" duet.

#51. OOM-PAH DOO WOP

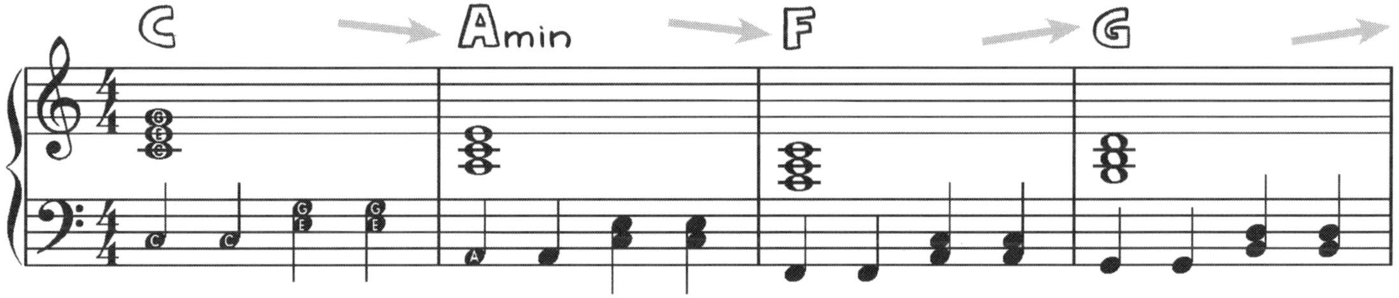

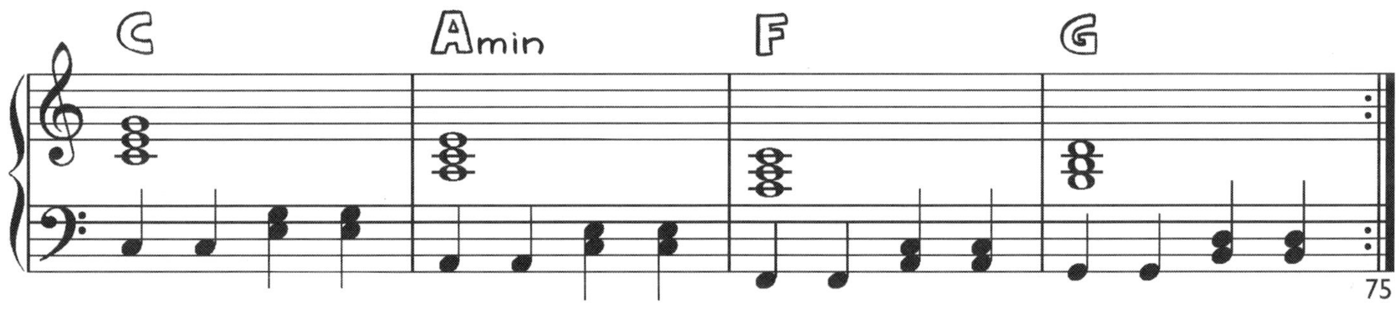

KLEZMERIZED

LEFT HAND RIGHT HAND

- On beat one, the left hand plays the root note.
- On beat two, the right hand plays the chord.
- On beat three, the left hand plays the fifth.
- On beat four, the right hand plays the chord again.
- Repeat the pattern.

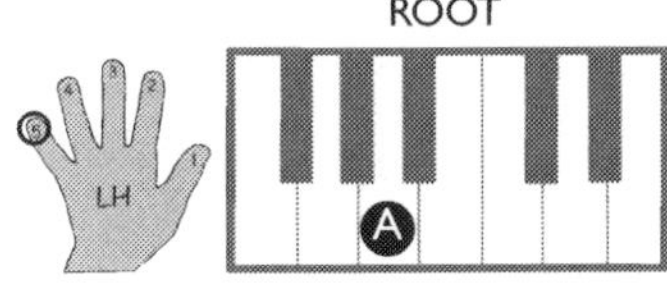

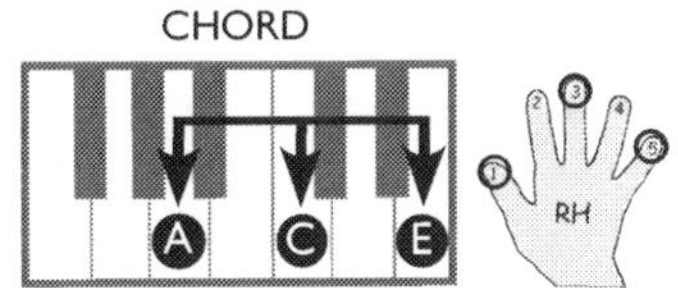
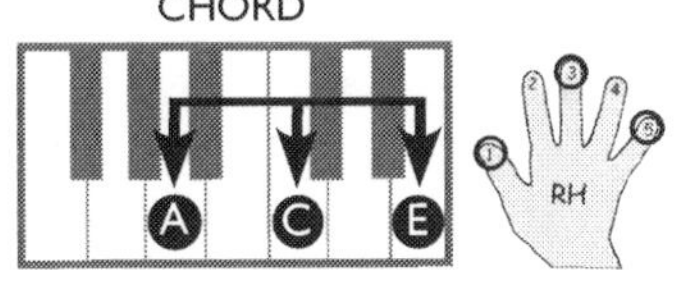

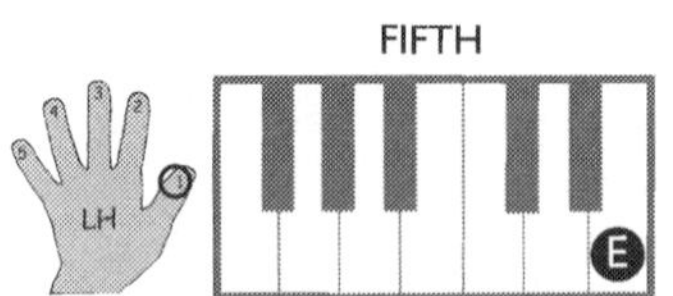

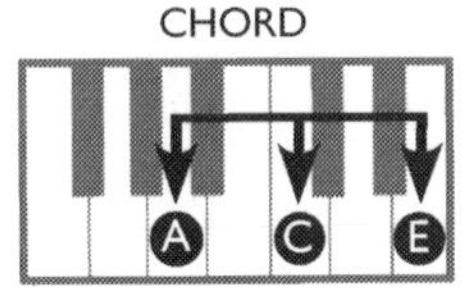

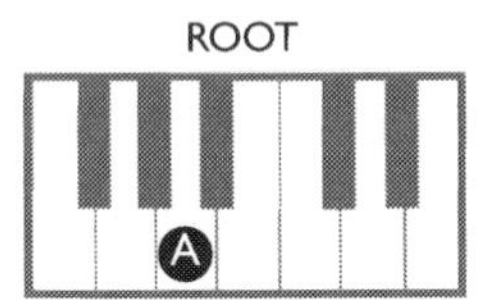

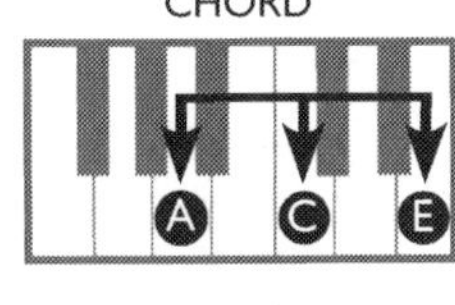

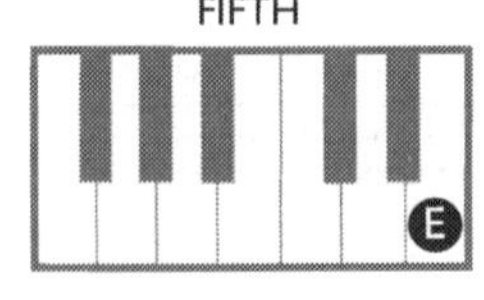

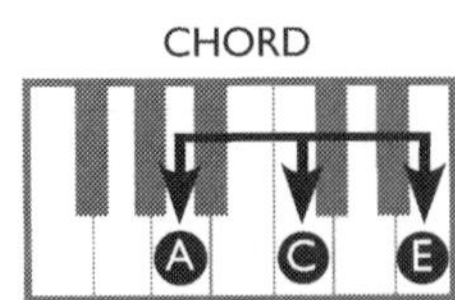

PRACTICE IN A POSITION UNTIL SMOOTH

#52. KLEZMERIZED

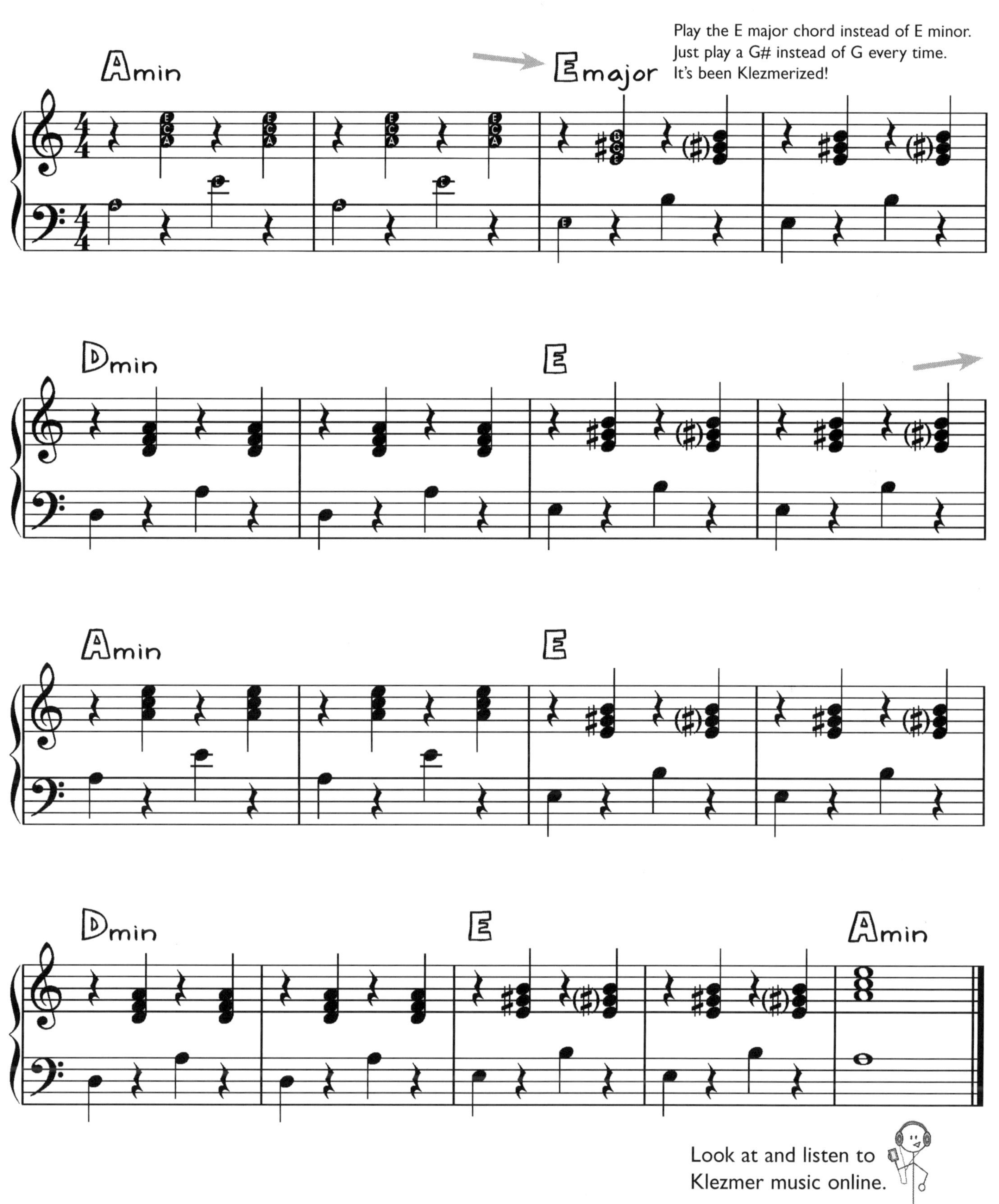

Look at and listen to Klezmer music online.

OOM-PAH BAND, KLEZMER STYLE

#53. STYLE 1

Left hand plays a bottom-middle-top-middle pattern while the right hand plays a chord.

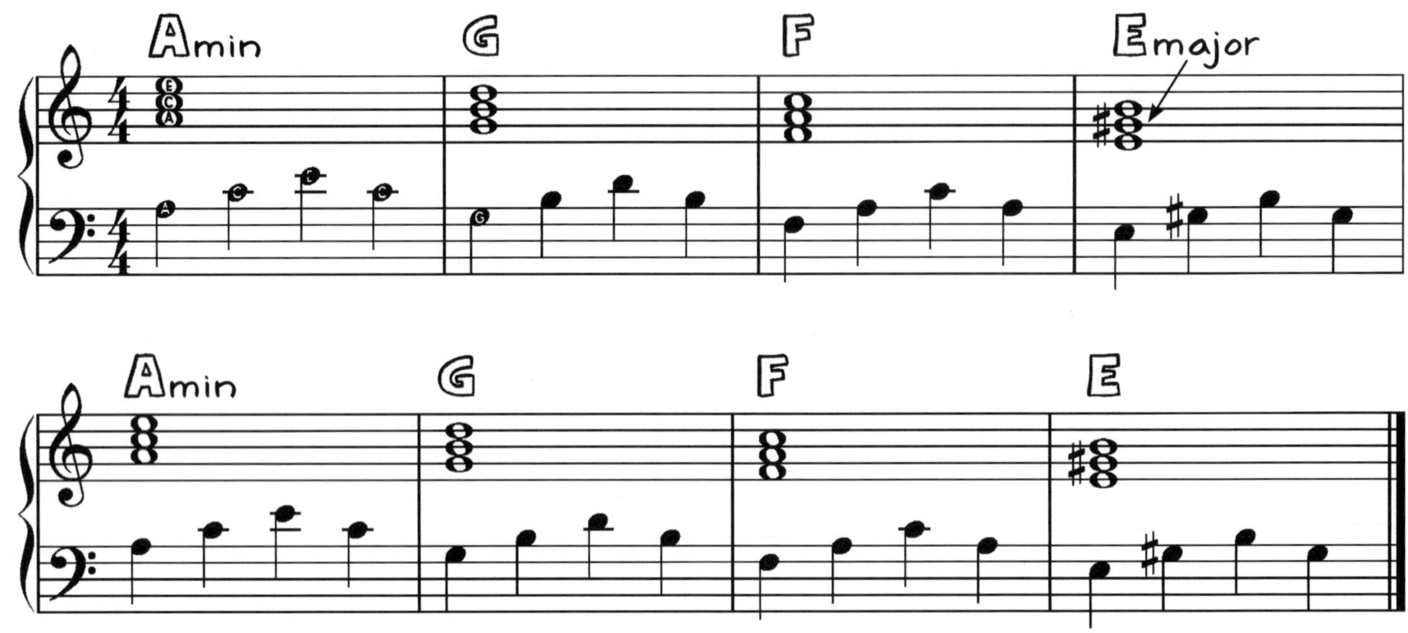

#54. STYLE 2

Left hand plays an oom-pah oom-pah pattern while the right hand plays a chord.

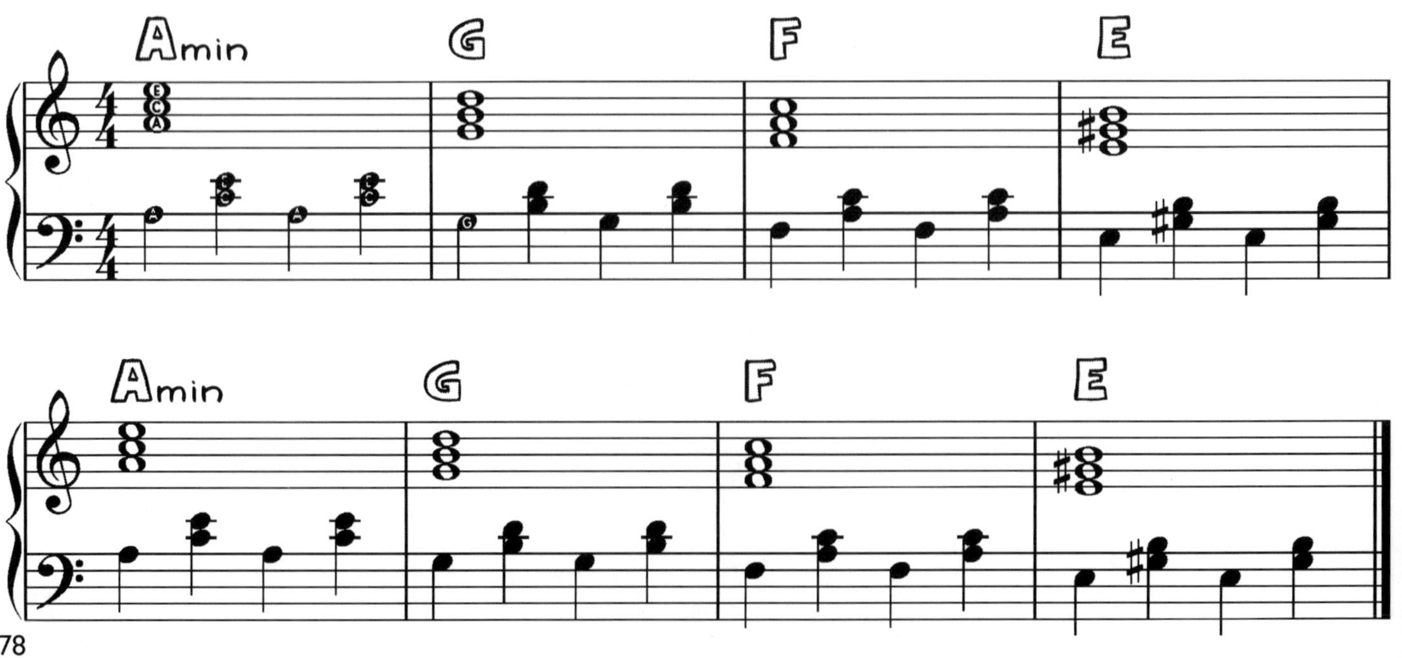

#55. STYLE 3

The left hand plays the root, the right hand plays a chord, the left hand plays the fifth, and the right hand follows with the chord again.

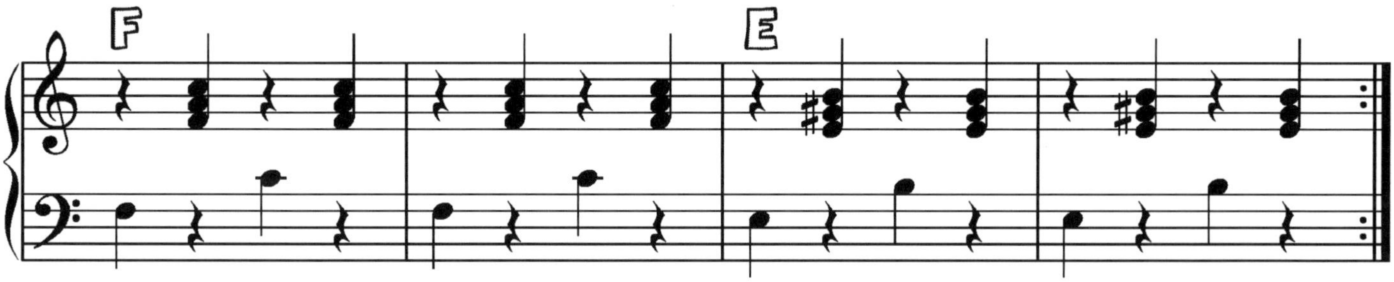

ADD EXPRESSION

Use the boxes below (or your own ideas) to add expression to these songs and others!

GRADUALLY SPEED UP

PLAY SUPER SLOWLY

PLAY SMOOTHLY

PLAY SOFTLY

PLAY FAST

PLAY STACCATO (CRISPLY)

PLAY LOUDLY

GRADUALLY SLOW DOWN

COMBINE ANY 2 OF THESE

EXPERIMENT

Create your own ways to play. For a blank game form, visit mwfunstuff.com/CCC

HOW DO YOU PLAY ALBERTI BASS?

Here, we'll practice playing the Alberti pattern in the left hand, while the right hand plays a chord.

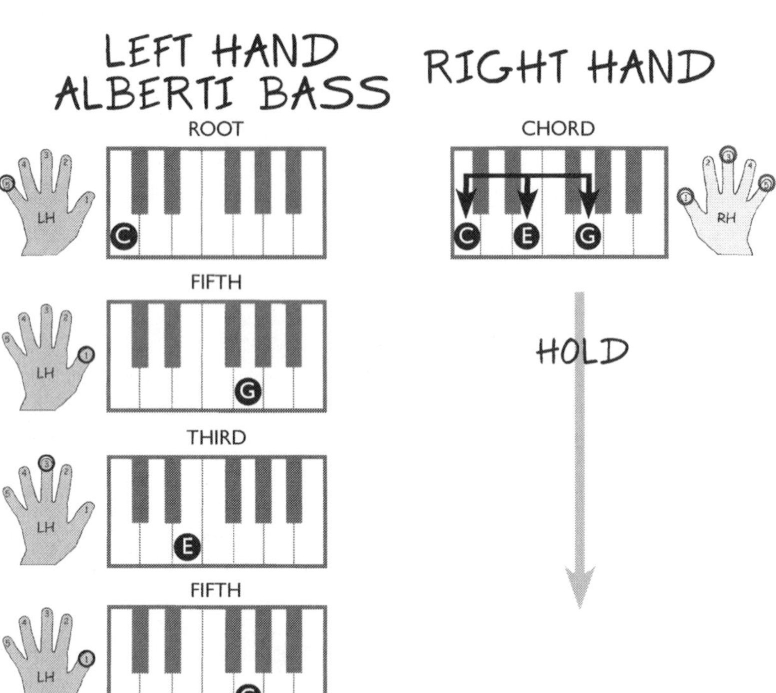

- On beat one, the left hand plays the root note.
- On beat two, the left hand plays the fifth.
- On beat three, the left hand plays the third.
- On beat four, the left hand plays the fifth again. That's the Alberti bass pattern!
- Practice that until smooth, and then try adding your right hand. For this exercise, your right hand will play a chord on beat one and hold for four beats.

PRACTICE IN C POSITION UNTIL SMOOTH

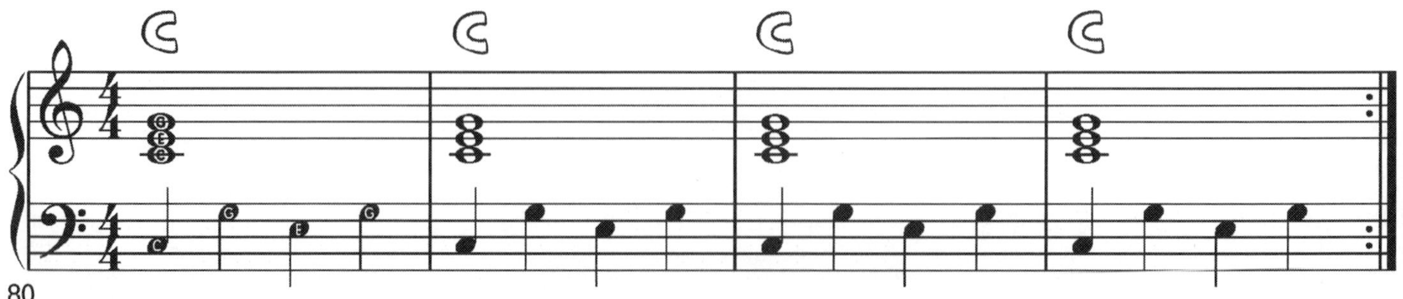

#56. ALBERTI SCALE

Go up the scale with your left hand playing the Alberti bass pattern and your right hand playing a chord.

C
Dmin
Emin
F
G
Amin
Bdim
C
C
Scale Down
Bdim
Amin
G
F
Emin
Dmin
C
C

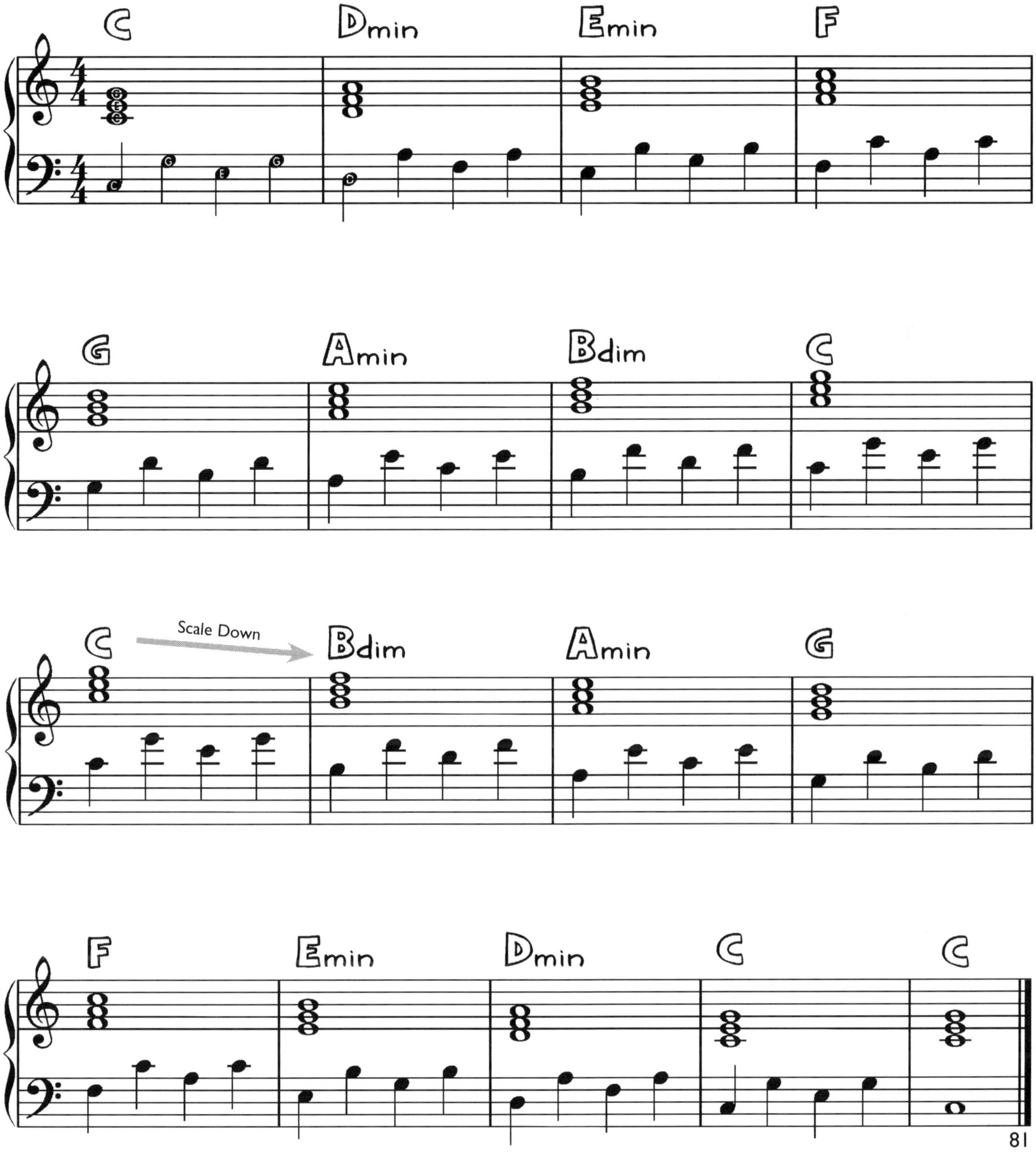

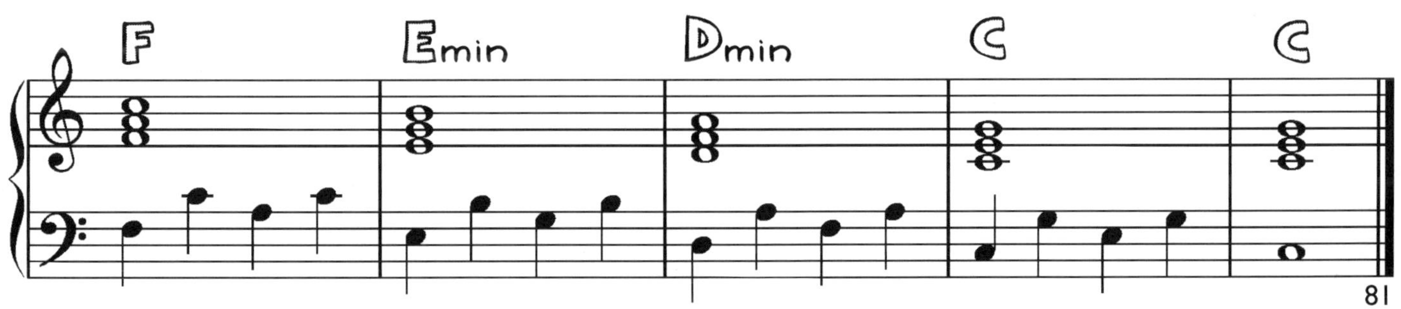

THE LEGEND OF ______________

#57. PART 1

The left hand plays the Alberti Bass pattern, while your right hand plays a chord.

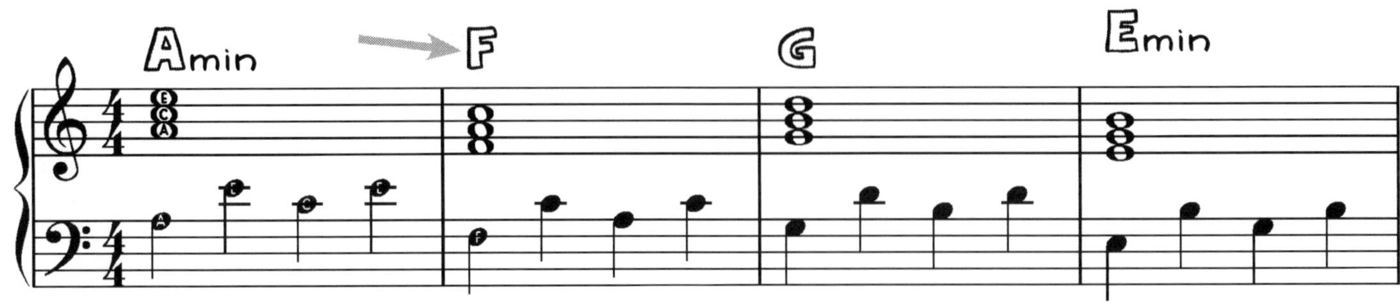

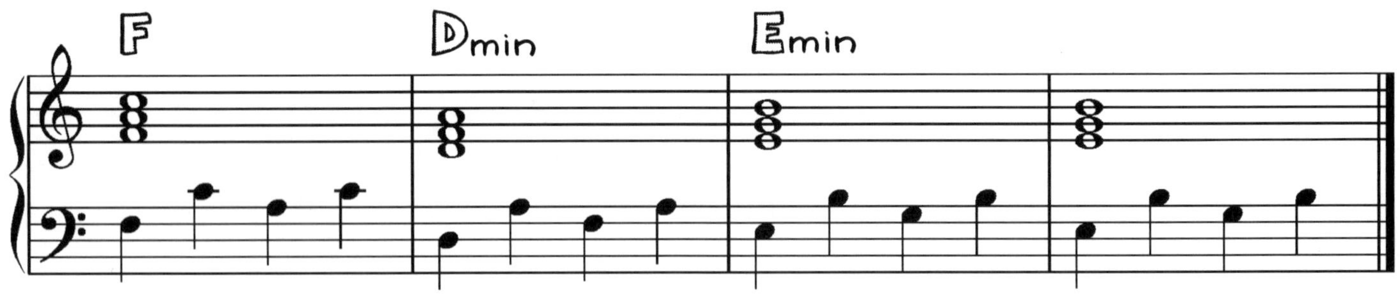

#58. PART 2

Both hands play the Alberti pattern to this enchanting progression.

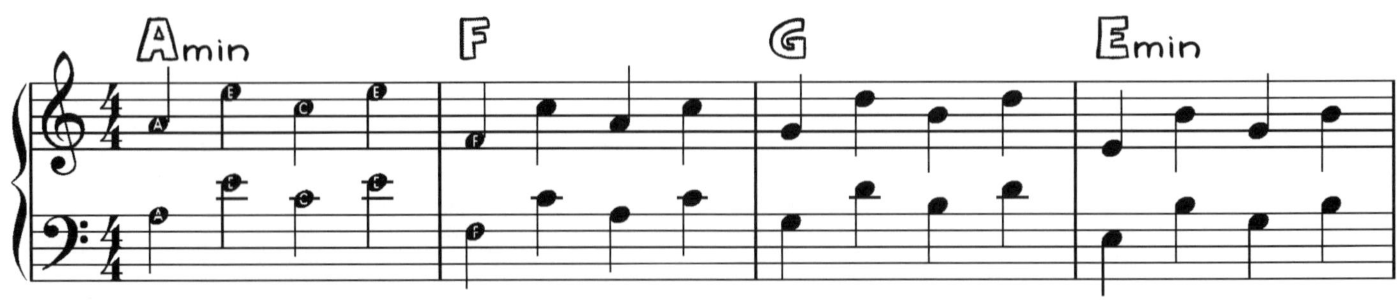

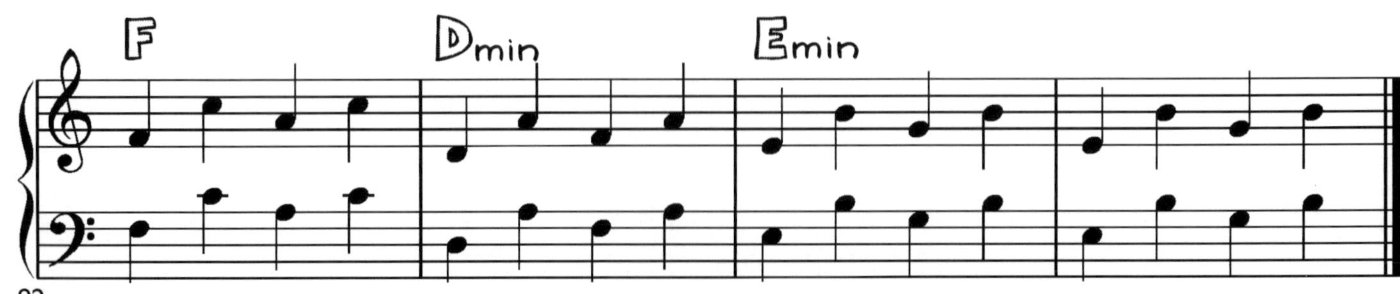

PACHELBEL MEETS ALBERTI

In these pieces, the most famous progression of all time (Pachelbel's Canon) meets one of the most famous classical patterns (Alberti Bass).

#59. VARIATION 1

Right hand plays the Alberti pattern while your left hand plays a chord.

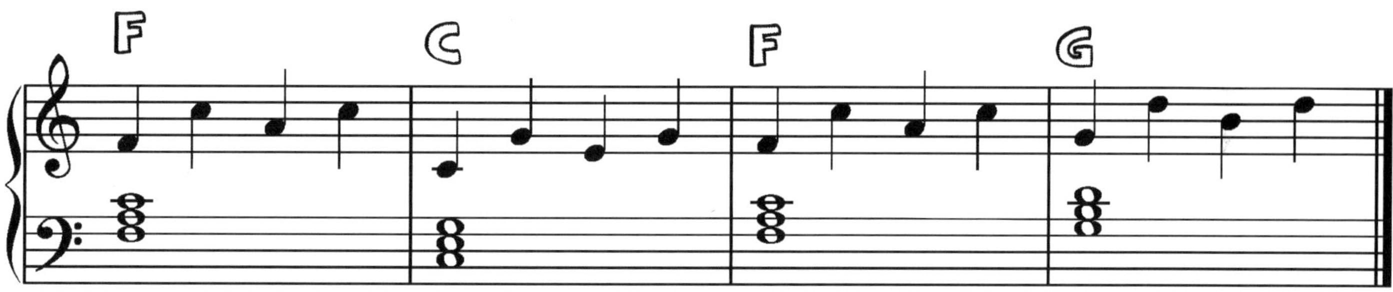

#60. VARIATION 2

Left hand plays the Alberti pattern while your right hand plays a harmonic third.

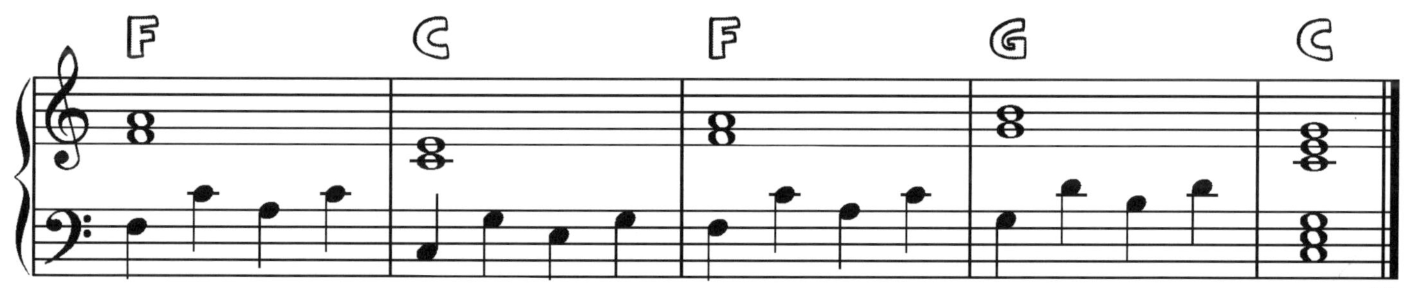

EXPLORE WITH STYLES

1. CHOOSE A STYLE

- [ ] ALBERTI

- [ ] OOM-PAH
- [ ] ANOTHER STYLE FROM THIS BOOK (crossover arpeggios, chords and more)

2. CHOOSE A CHORD PROGRESSION

- C Emin F G (I iii IV V)
- Amin F C G (vi IV I V)
- F G Emin F (IV V iii IV)
- C F G F (I IV V IV)
- Amin G F Emin (vi V IV iii)
- CREATE YOUR OWN!

3. CHOOSE A MOOD

- [ ] FLOWING
- [ ] CHEERFUL
- [ ] MYSTERIOUS
- [ ] MELANCHOLY
- [ ] JUMPY
- [ ] CHOOSE YOUR OWN!

AND PLAY!

Explore more! For a printable PDF of this activity, visit mwfunstuff.com/CCC

CHAPTER 9

LEAD SHEETS

By now, you can play chords and chord progressions, and come up with your own ideas using them. Here's another fun way you can use your chord knowledge: to play cover songs!

One of the rewards of knowing how to play chords is that it allows you to play your favorite songs by your favorite artists. When you play a song that was written and performed by someone else, it's called a "cover song." The chord progressions for many of these can be found online, or as part of printed sheet music. Now that you can identify chord symbols and play chords, all of these songs are open to you.

HOW DO YOU PLAY A LEAD SHEET?

STEP 1: PRACTICE PLAYING JUST THE CHORDS WITH YOUR LEFT HAND:

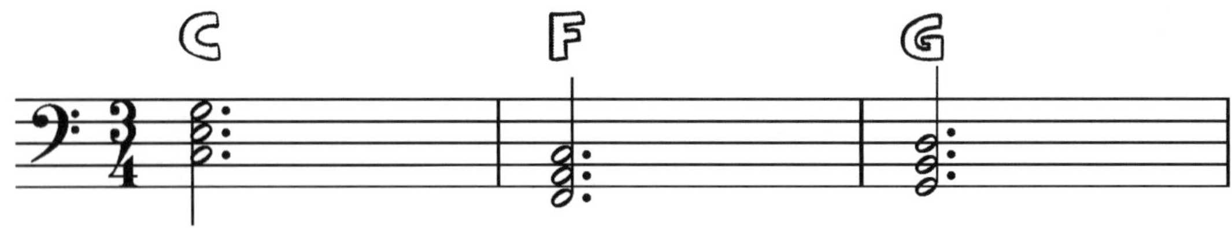

STEP 2: PRACTICE SINGING THE MELODY OR PLAYING THE MELODY WITH YOUR RIGHT HAND.

Super challenge: try singing and playing at the same time!

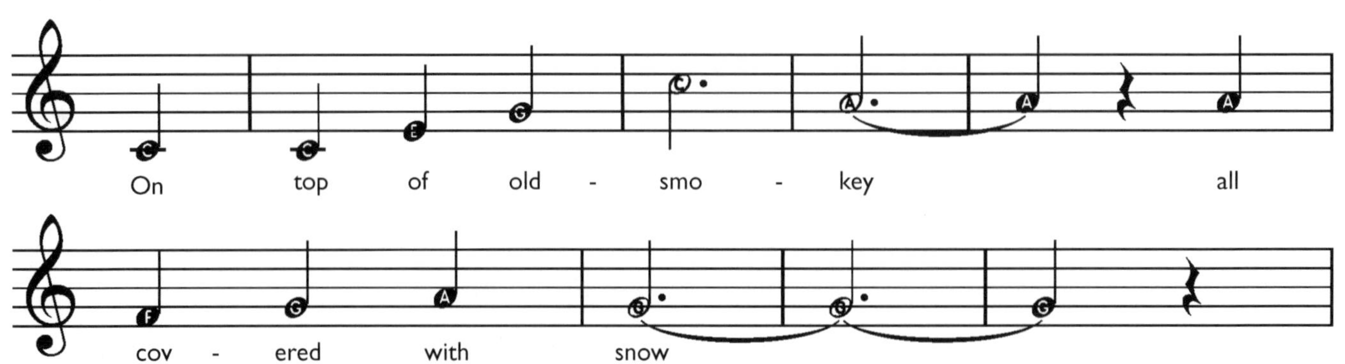

STEP 3: PUT IT TOGETHER!

With your left hand, play the chords at the place in the song where you would play the note or sing the word directly below it. If a measure doesn't have a new chord symbol written above it, you should keep playing the most recent chord. (I'll remind you at those spots to make it easier for now!) At the same time, sing the melody, or play it with your right hand (or both!).

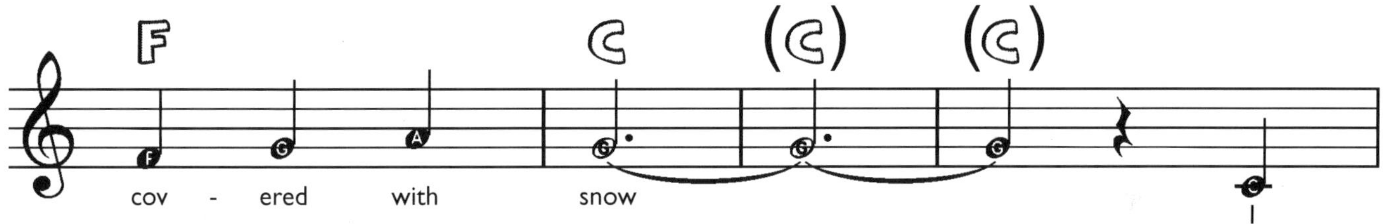

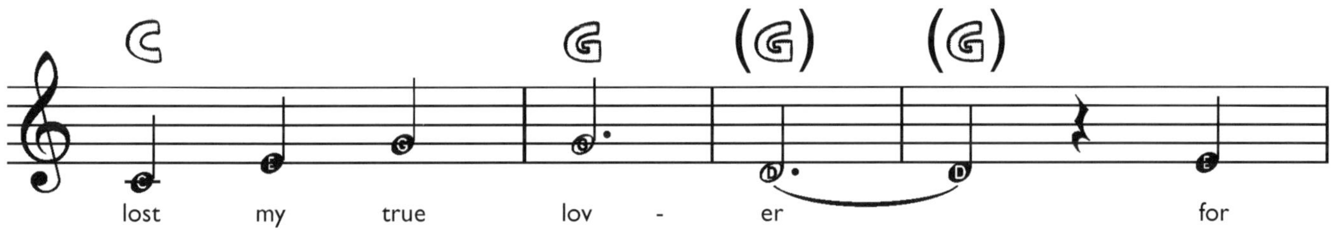

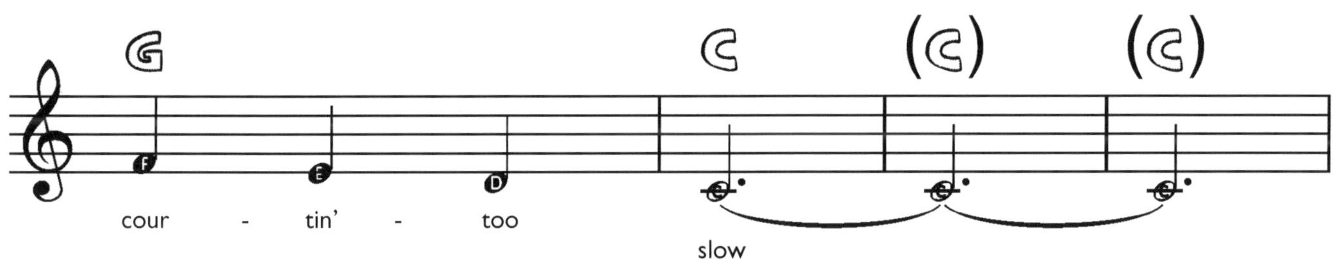

COVER SONGS: ONLINE TOOLS

STEP 1: SEARCH FOR THE SONG TITLE + THE WORD "CHORDS"

STEP 2: WHAT YOU FIND WILL LOOK LIKE THIS:

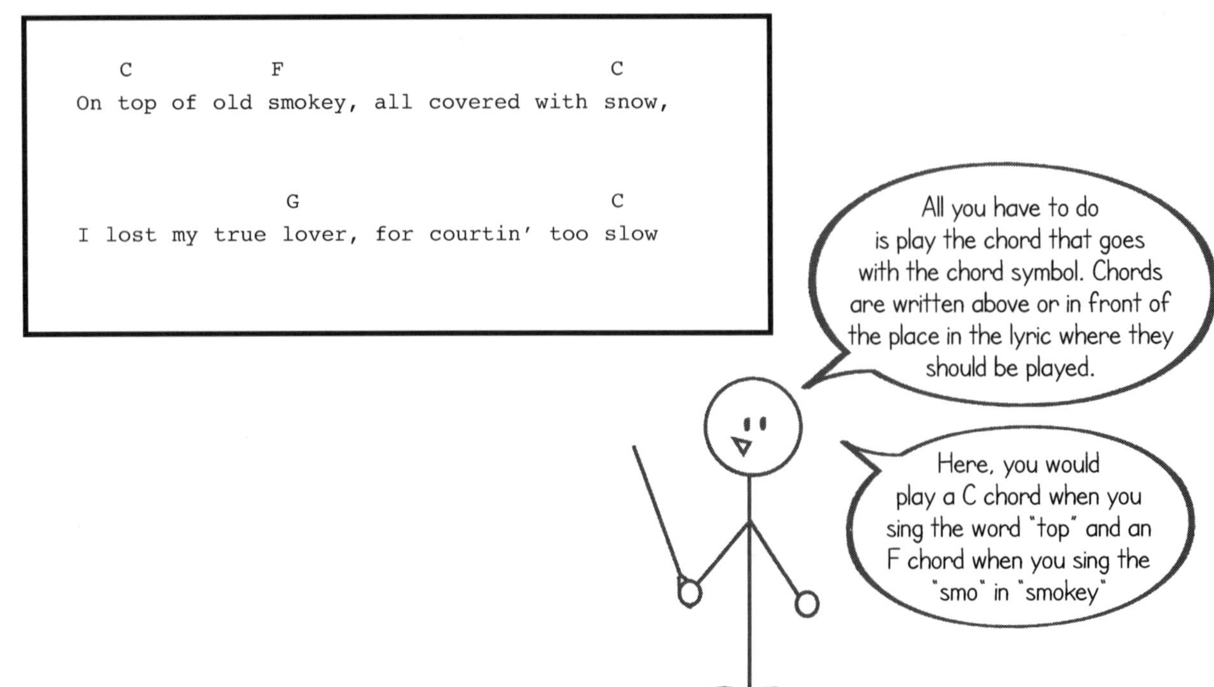

```
   C          F                        C
On top of old smokey, all covered with snow,


              G                        C
I lost my true lover, for courtin' too slow
```

It's important to remember that you've learned the basic ingredients of a chord: the root, third (major or minor) and fifth. The chord progressions you find online may have some fancier chords, with extra ingredients (sevenths, diminished and augmented chords, etc.). Luckily, you should still be able to play most of your favorite songs, which won't have too many complicated chords. When you do encounter a "7" chord, you can omit the "7" (for now that is – once you learn seventh chords in the next book, you'll be able to add them and appreciate the texture and color they bring to chords).

FOR EXAMPLE:

```
   C          F                        C
On top of old smokey, all covered with snow,
               G7                      C
I lost my true lover, for courtin' too slow
```

CAN BE PLAYED AS:

```
   C          F                        C
On top of old smokey, all covered with snow,
               G                       C
I lost my true lover, for courtin' too slow
```

Just make sure you pay attention to major and minor chords – which you should always play as written. Often, minor chords will be marked with a lowercase "m," like this:

```
C     G7         C
Home, home on the range
          Am           D7       G7
Where the deer and the antelope play
```

In this case, you can play the G7 chords as G chords, and the D7 chord as D. Just remember that A should be minor and D should be major!

PLAYING IN DIFFERENT KEYS

In this book, we've played primarily in the key of C (using the C chord scale). That's because, with no sharps or flats, it's simplest. When you find the chords to cover songs, though, they will be in a variety of keys. To play in these keys, simply use a chord scale to familiarize yourself with the new chords. (You can also look up how to play them online.)

Here, let's imagine that you looked up the chords to "On Top Old Smokey," and they're in the key of G.

STEP 1: PRACTICE THE CHORDS

Let's look at the chord scale for the key of G. (Note: unless the key is specifically labeled "minor," it's implied that it's a major key. So, we're in the key of G major here.) Practice the chords that we'll be using for this song.

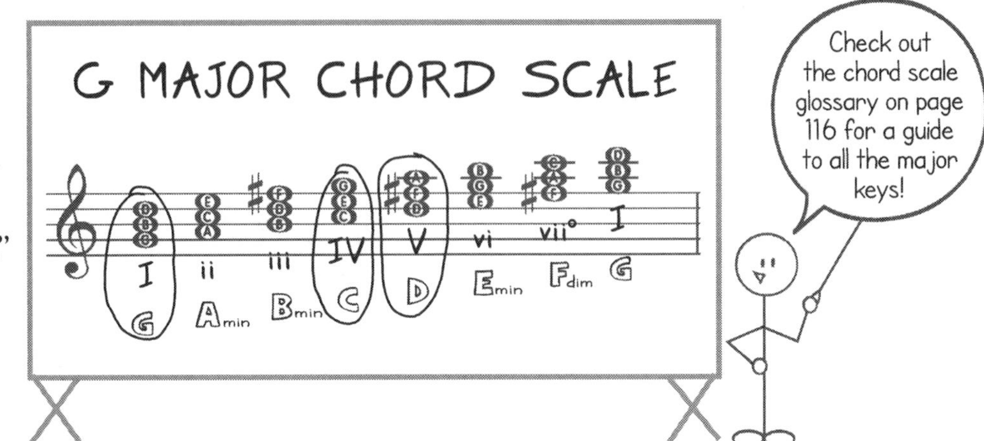

STEP 1: PUT IT TOGETHER

Here's what it would look like as a lead sheet. (Don't worry about playing the melody here. Just sing the melody and play the chords!)

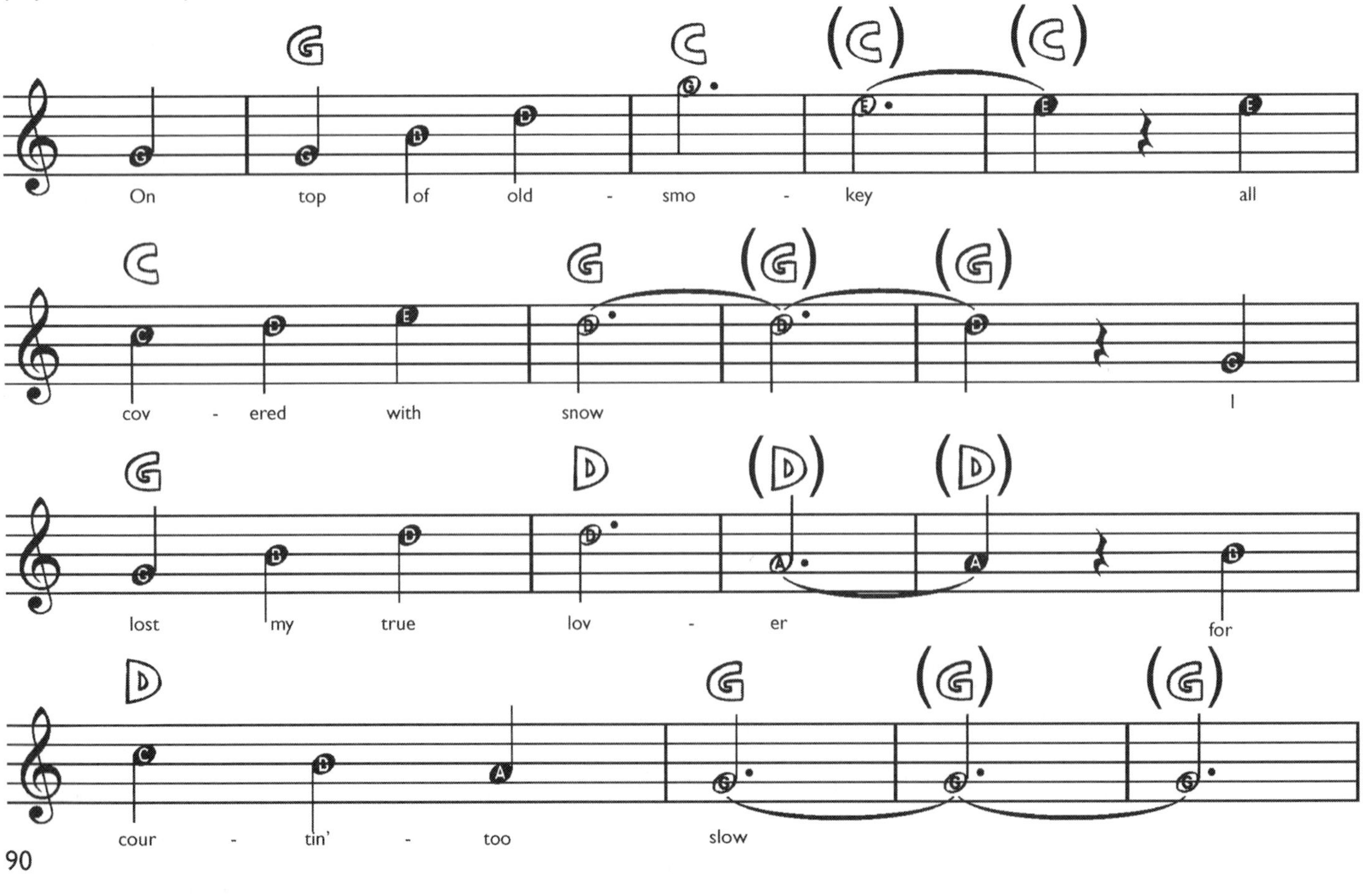

G C (C) (C)
On top of old - smo - key all

C G (G) (G)
cov - ered with snow I

G D (D) (D)
lost my true lov - er for

D G (G) (G)
cour - tin' - too slow

TRANSPOSING TO A NEW KEY

LETS TRANSPOSE FROM G MAJOR TO A MAJOR

STEP 1: WRITE IN THE CHORD NUMBER

Use the chord scale for the current key of G (you can look at the previous page) to write in the chord number.

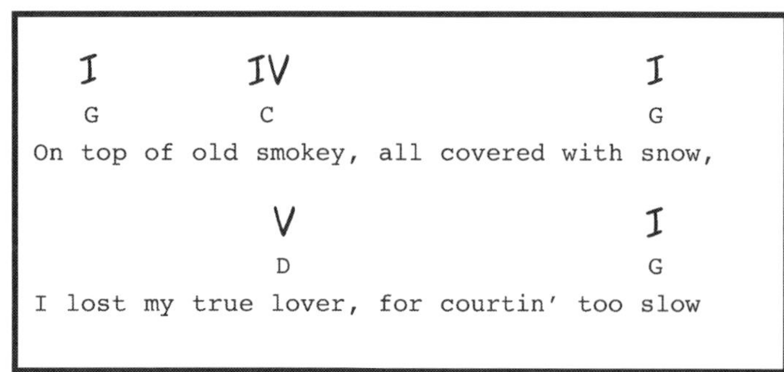

STEP 2: IDENTIFY THE CHORDS

Using the chord number, identify the corresponding chords in the new key (circled on the chord scale).

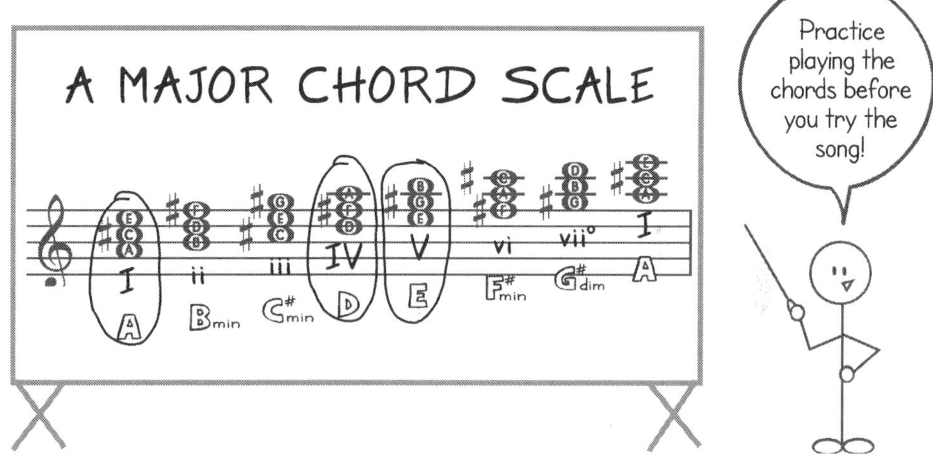

STEP 3: SWAP OUT THE CHORDS AND PLAY!

Write in the correct chord symbol for the new key of A in the box. Then try playing and singing. Hint: the chords in this song are all major chords. Watch out for sharps and flats!

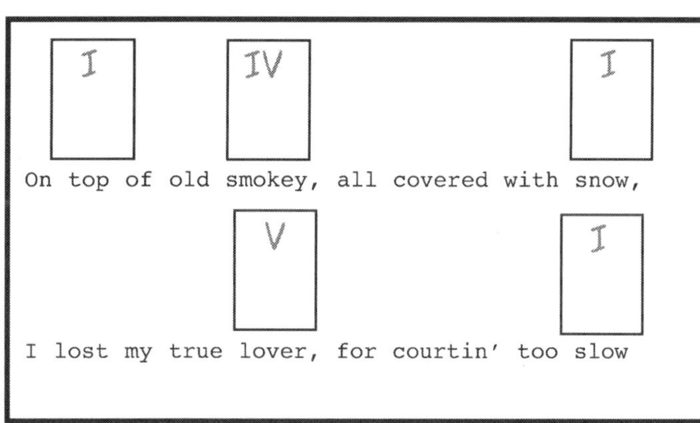

COVER SONG LIST

List the songs you'd like to learn and cover here!

CHAPTER 10

ROCKIN' RHYTHMS

Because you can play chord progressions and rhythmic patterns on the piano, you can compose for all types of instruments and ensembles – tubas and cellos, folk trios and orchestras, or bands and rock groups. Part of what makes your arrangements interesting is the rhythm or accompaniment pattern you choose. In this chapter, you'll learn some rhythmic patterns that will give you the ability to create tons of great songs.

BRING IN THE BASS

LEFT HAND RIGHT HAND

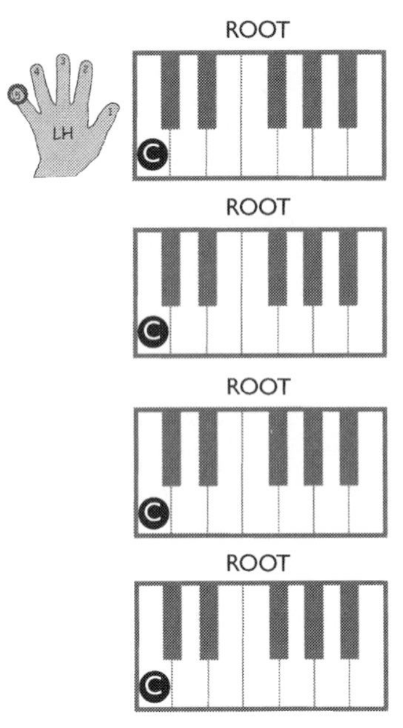

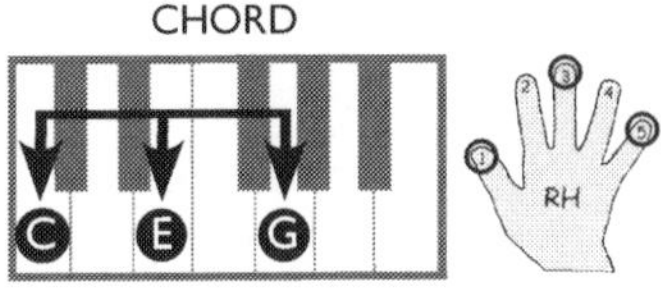

- Left hand plays quarter note root notes.
- Right hand plays a chord for four beats.

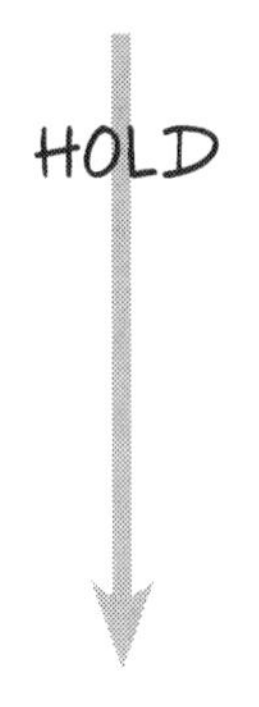

#61. FEEL THE BEAT

Left hand plays pulsing quarter notes while the right hand plays a chord.

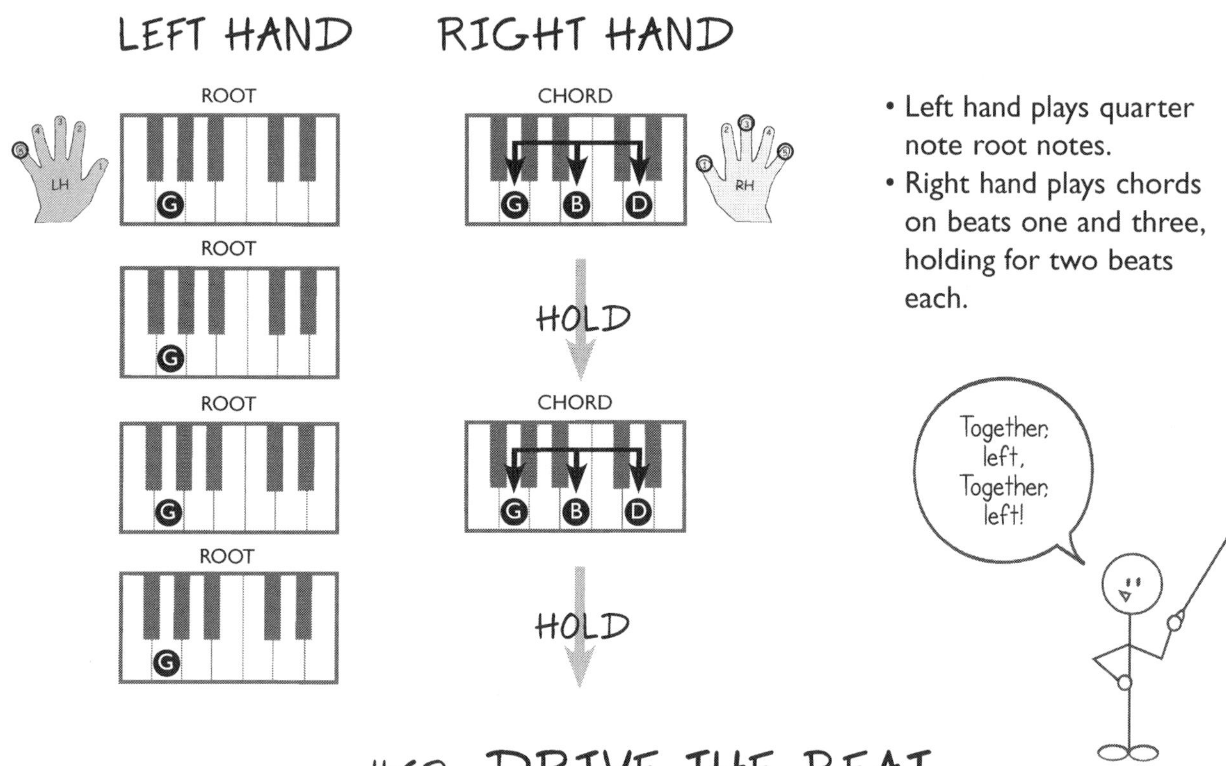

- Left hand plays quarter note root notes.
- Right hand plays chords on beats one and three, holding for two beats each.

#62. DRIVE THE BEAT

Left hand plays pulsing quarter notes while the right hand plays two half note chords per measure.

MOVE IT

LEFT HAND RIGHT HAND

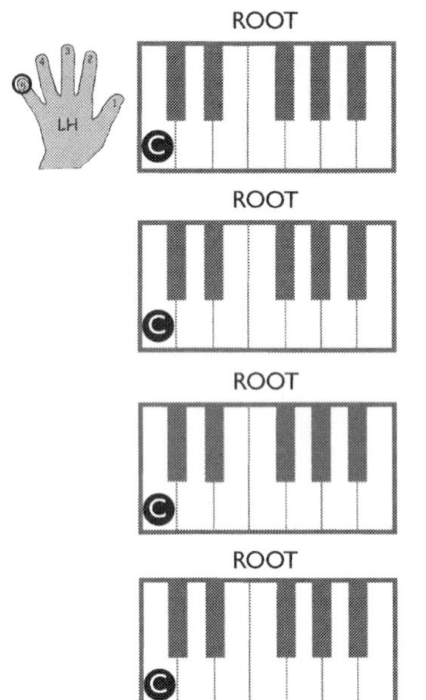

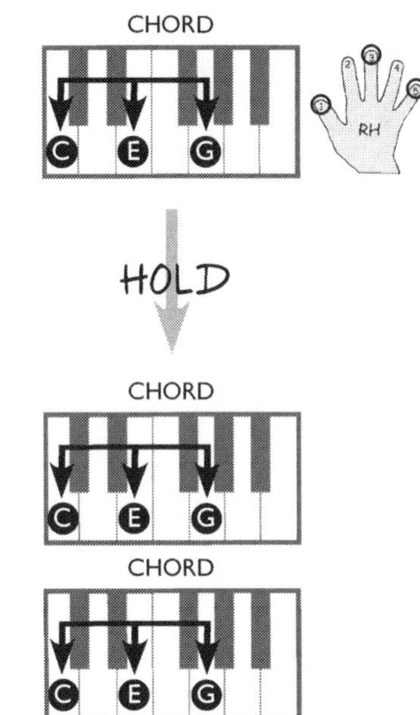

- Left hand plays quarter note root notes.
- Right hand plays a half note chord on beat one and quarter note chords on beats three and four.

#63. MOVE IT

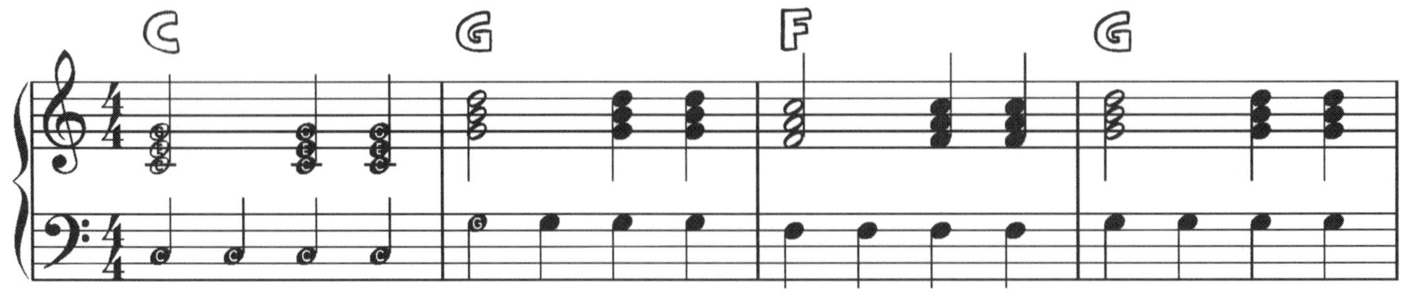

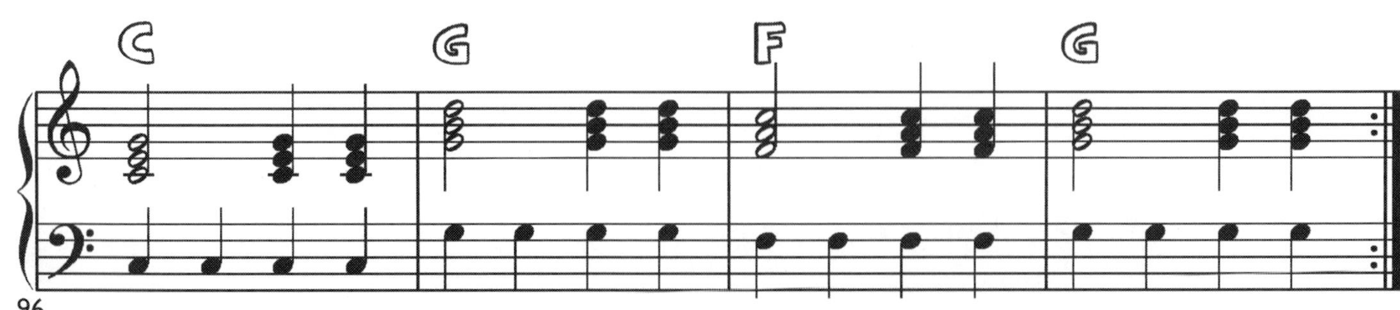

GROOVE IT

LEFT HAND RIGHT HAND

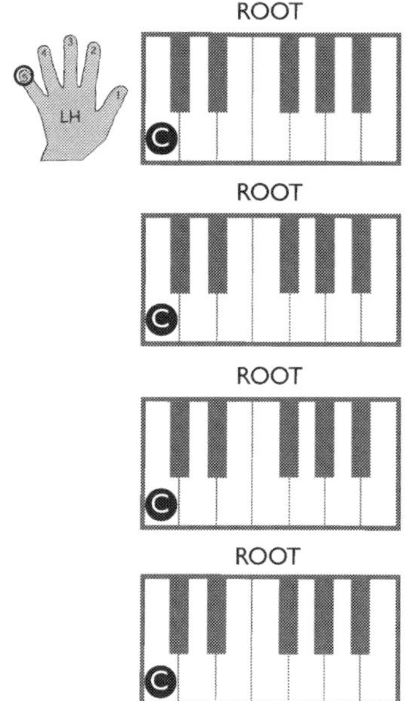

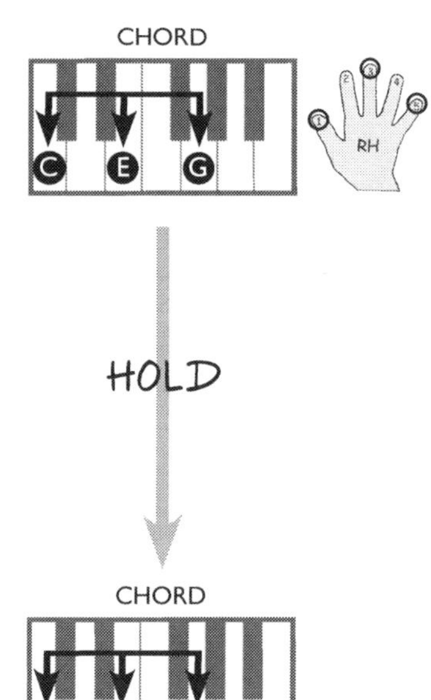

- Left hand plays quarter note root notes.
- Right hand plays a chord on beat one and holds for three beats, then plays another chord on beat four.

#64. GROOVE IT

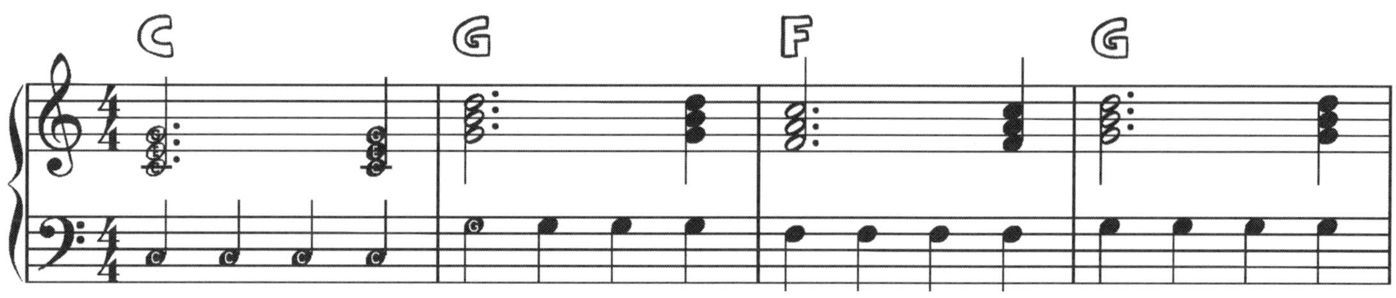

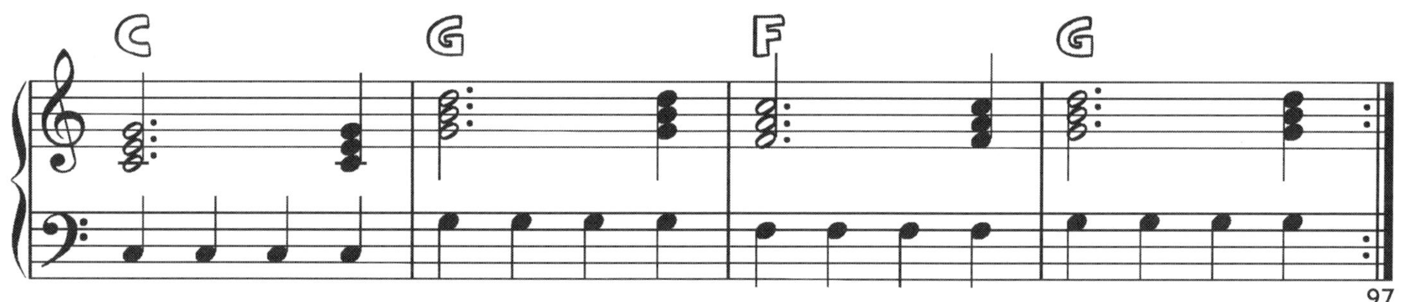

FACE THE FIFTHS

LEFT HAND RIGHT HAND

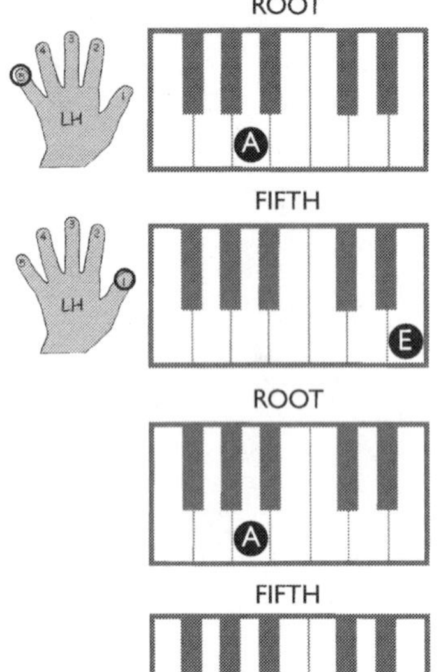

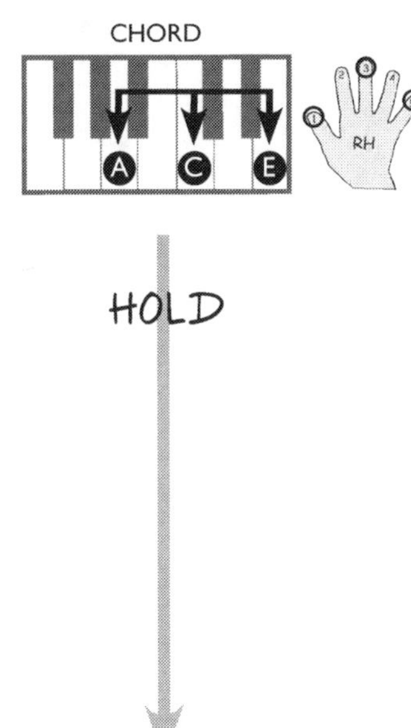

- Left hand plays the root, then the fifth, then another root and another fifth.
- Right hand plays a chord on beat one and holds for four beats.

#65. FACE THE FIFTHS

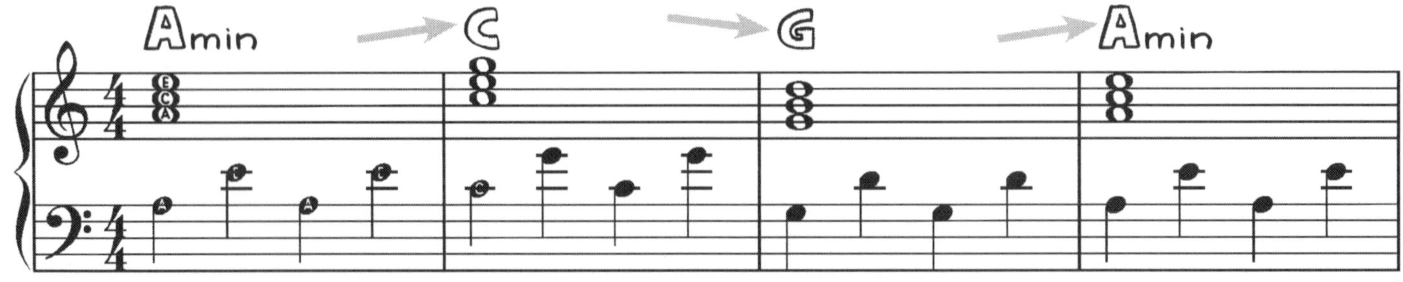

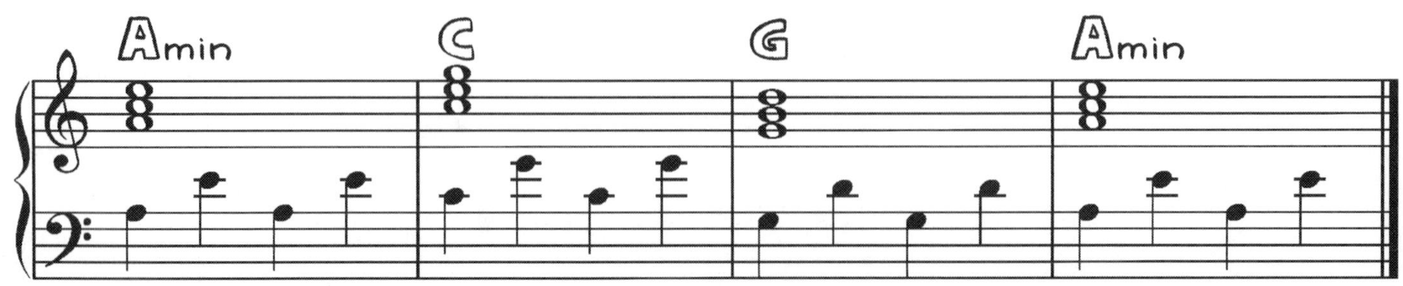

FIFTHS ROCK

LEFT HAND RIGHT HAND

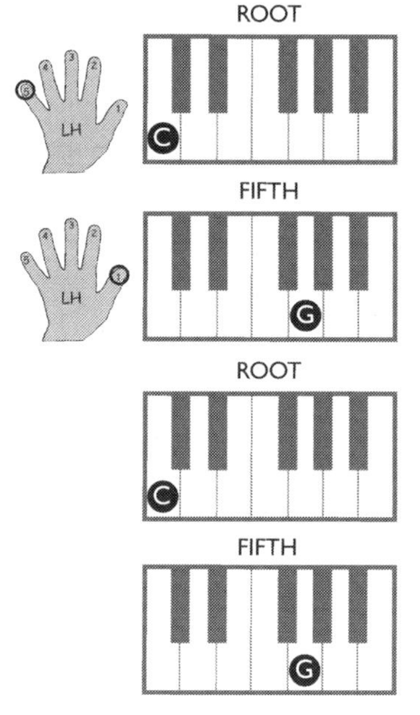

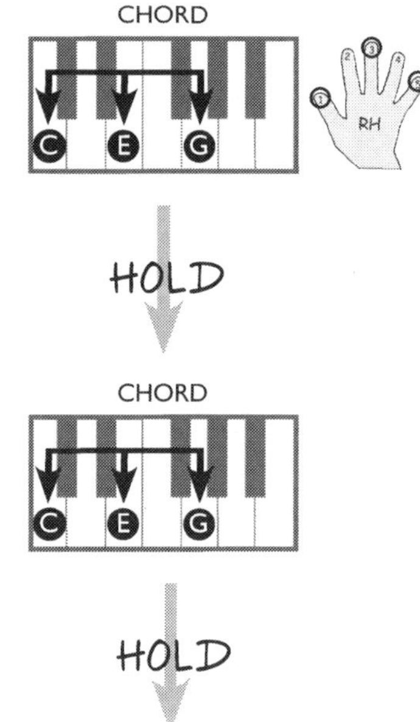

- Left hand plays the root, then the fifth, then another root and another fifth.
- Right hand plays a chord on beats one and three, holding for two beats each.

#66. FIFTHS ROCK

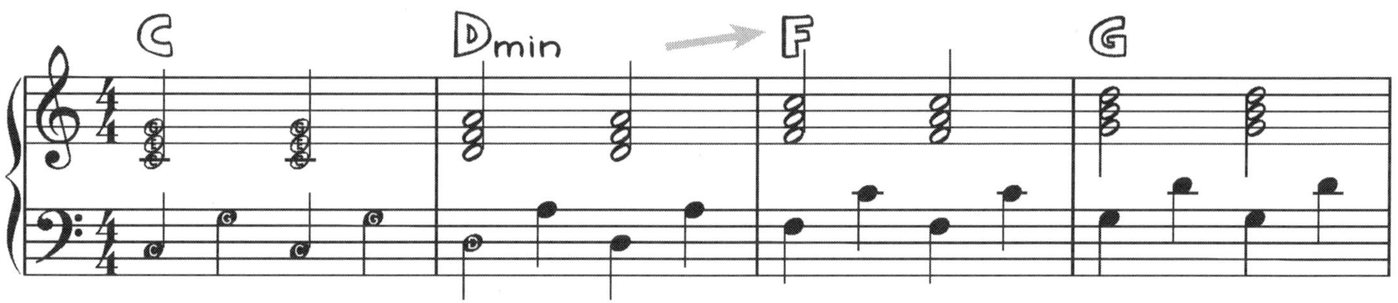

CHORD ROCK IN THREE KEYS

LEFT HAND

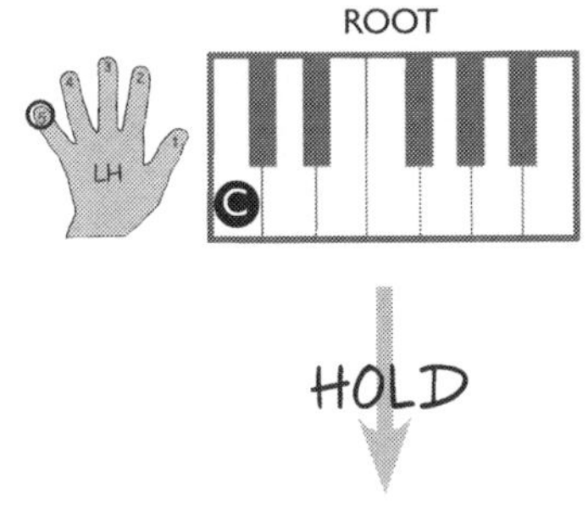

RIGHT HAND

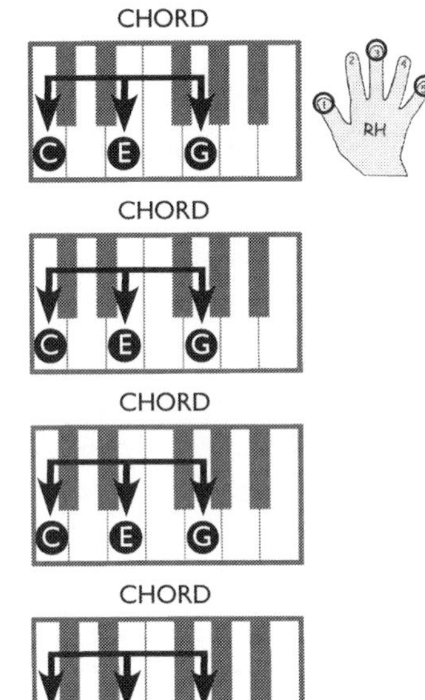

- Left hand plays the root and holds for four beats.
- Right hand plays a chord on beats one, two, three and four.

#67. CHORD ROCK IN C MAJOR

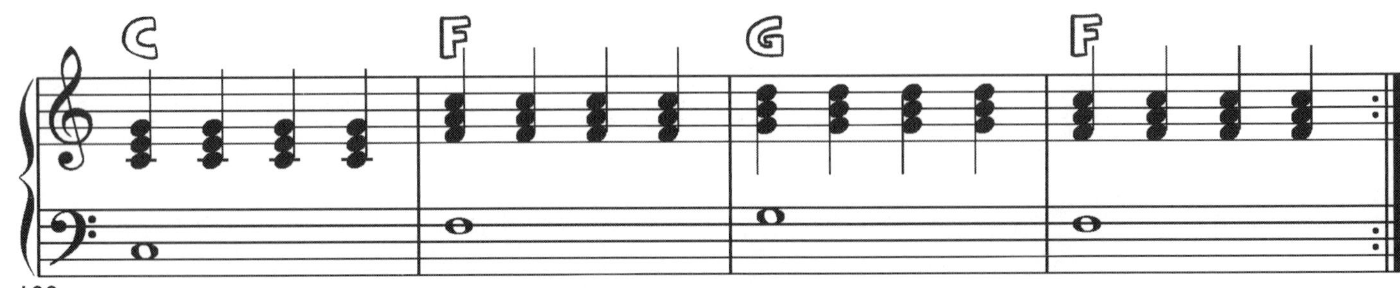

#68. CHORD ROCK IN G MAJOR

Prove your transposition skills by transposing "Chord Rock" to the key of G. Write in the new chord symbols and play.

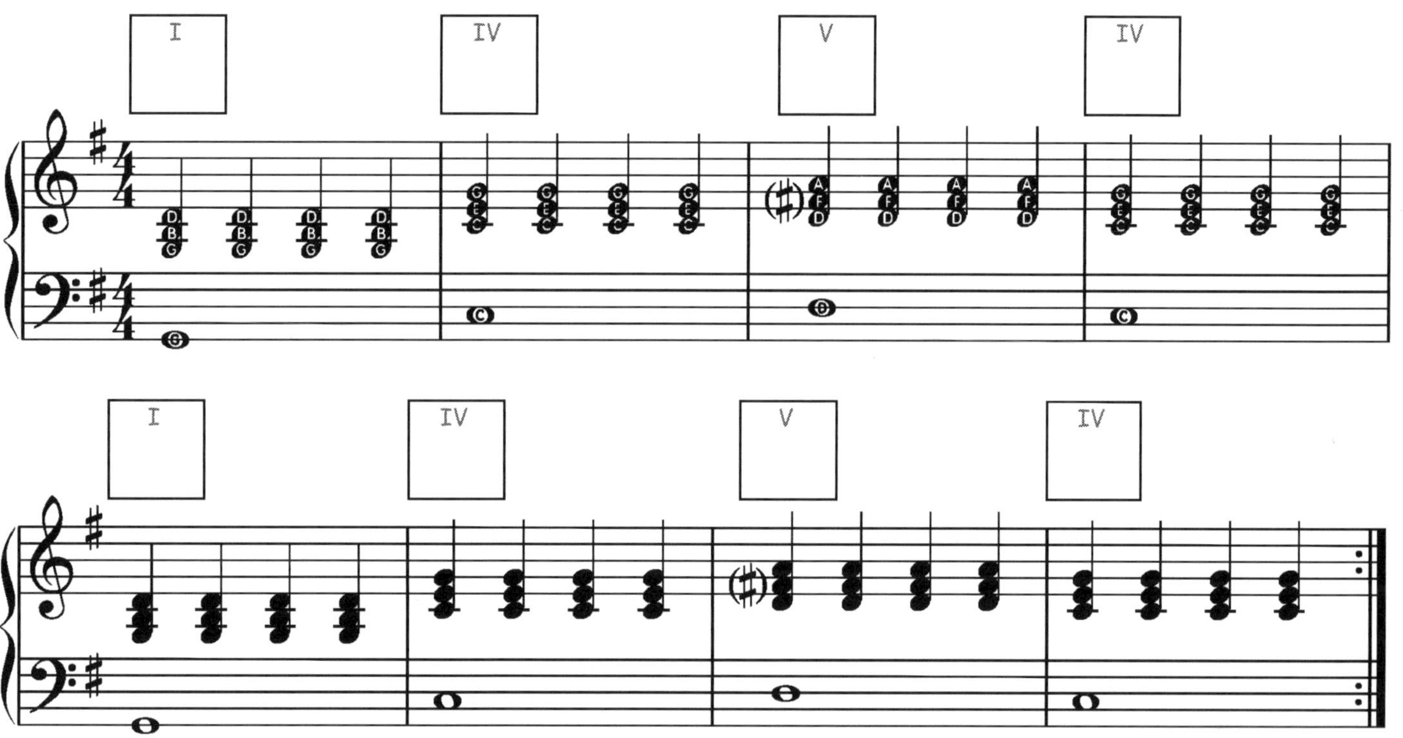

#69. CHORD ROCK IN D MAJOR

Now transpose "Chord Rock" to the key of D!

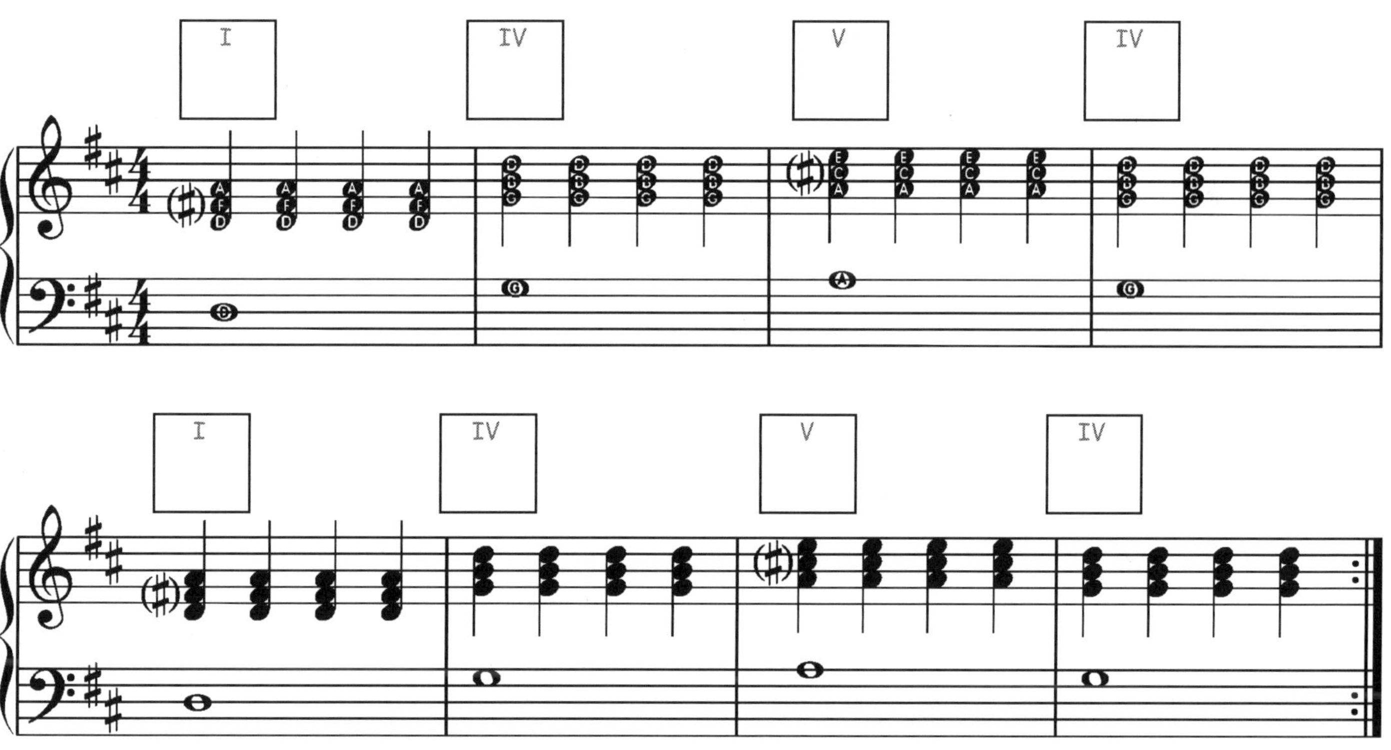

For a printable PDF of this activity, visit mwfunstuff.com/CCC

NOTES:

CHORDS & ARPEGGIOS
POWER CHORDS
INTERVALS
ARPEGGIO ACROBATICS
TIMELESS STYLES
ROCKIN' RHYTHMS
FOUR CHORD CONCERT
OPEN MIC
MAJOR & MINOR CHORDS
LEAD SHEETS
CHORD PROGRESSIONS
Congratulations! You've hit your tenth milestone on the course – Rockin' Rhythms. Next stop: the Four Chord Concert!

CHAPTER 11

EPIC FOUR CHORD CONCERT

EPIC CONCERT

Did you know that there's one chord progression that has been used in many mega-platinum hits?

Just four chords...

Tons of songs...

Now it's our turn.

Here is a hit songwriter secret (well, a secret that over 20 million people know): many hit songs were written with the same four chords, in the same progression. What are they? The chords are one, five, six and four – in the key of C, that's C, G, A minor and F.

You now have both the chops to perform like a rock star AND the secret of this powerful chord progression. The time has come for you to perform a concert medley of mega-platinum hits. Of course, to truly rock out, you'll need to sing along. Even better – write your own hit using this epic chord progression!

Find out more!
Search for: Four chord song (clean version) online.

FOUR CHORD CONCERT

Hit list of I V vi IV songs

- Can You Feel the Love Tonight?
- Hey Soul Sister
- Forever Young
- With or Without You
- Don't Stop Believing
- She Will Be Loved
- Love Story
- Halo
- I'm Yours
- Demons
- Someone Like You
- Paparazzi
- No Woman No Cry

And MANY MORE!

#70.

Play these different patterns over the same epic progression (C, G, Amin, F).

#71.

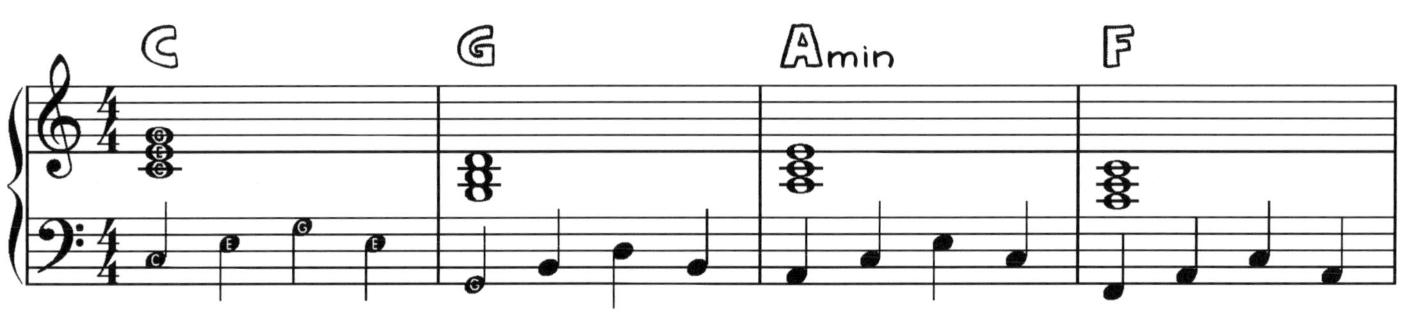
C
G
Amin
F

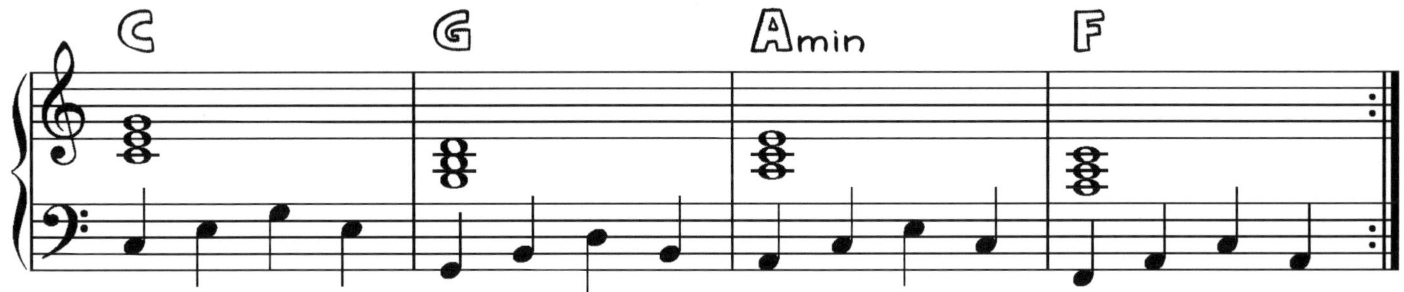
C
G
Amin
F

#72.

C
G
Amin
F

C
G
Amin
F

Try ending on a C chord.
ROCK ON!

This really is a rock star progression.
But it's not a real concert unless you sing along.
Try making these songs your own by adding lyrics.

#73.

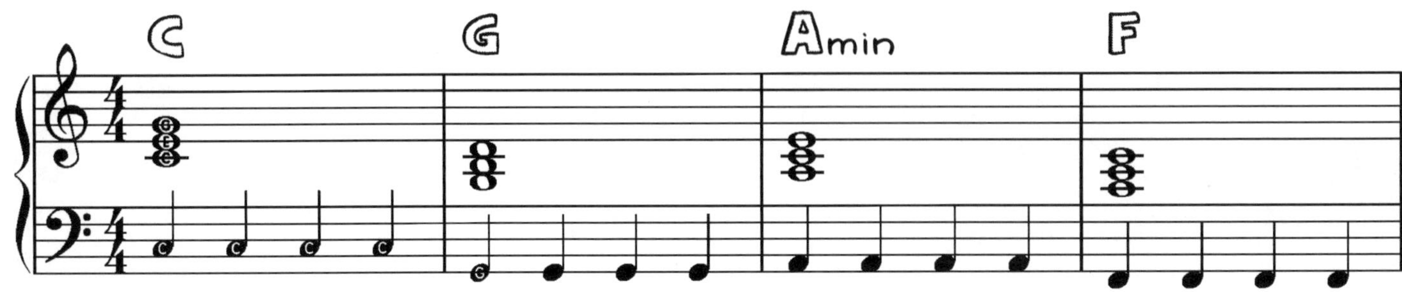
C
G
Amin
F

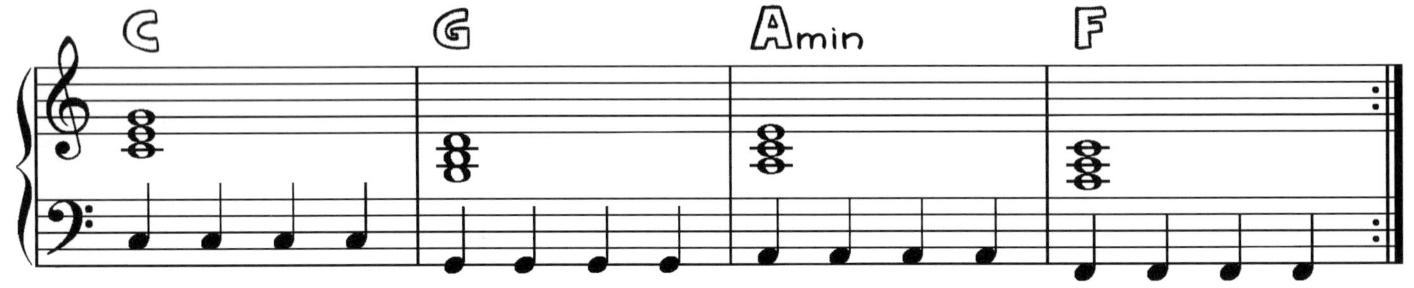
C
G
Amin
F

#74.

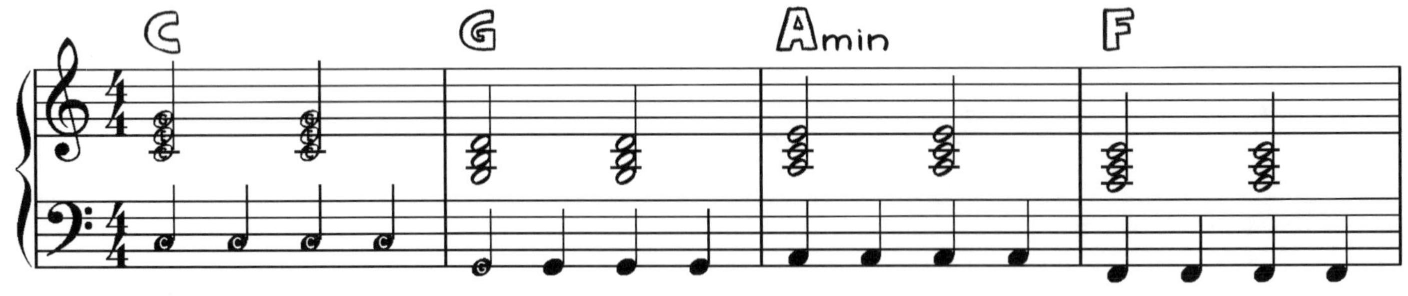
C
G
Amin
F

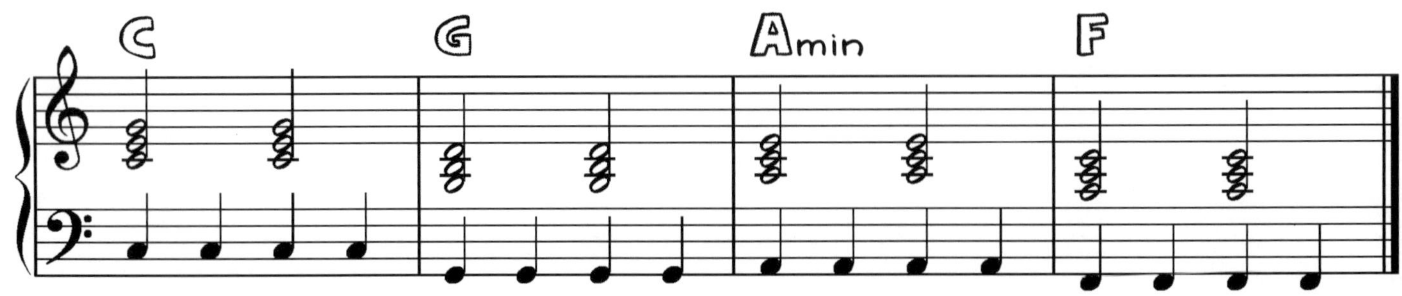
C
G
Amin
F

You really can make a whole concert with just this one powerful progression.
I can't believe it.
That's another song that uses this progression: Don't Stop Believing!

#75.

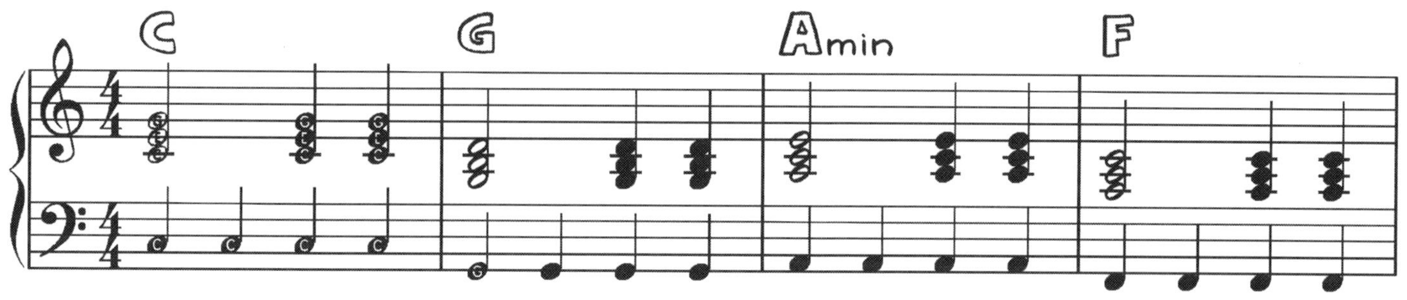
C
G
Amin
F

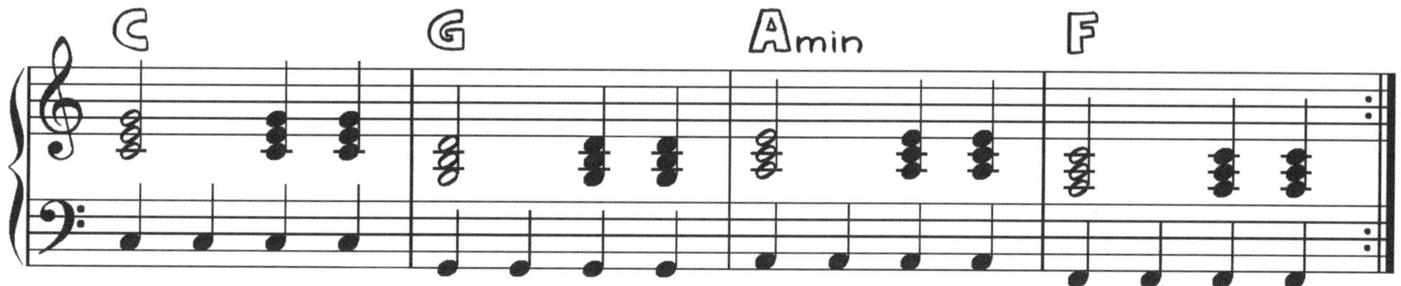
C
G
Amin
F

#76.

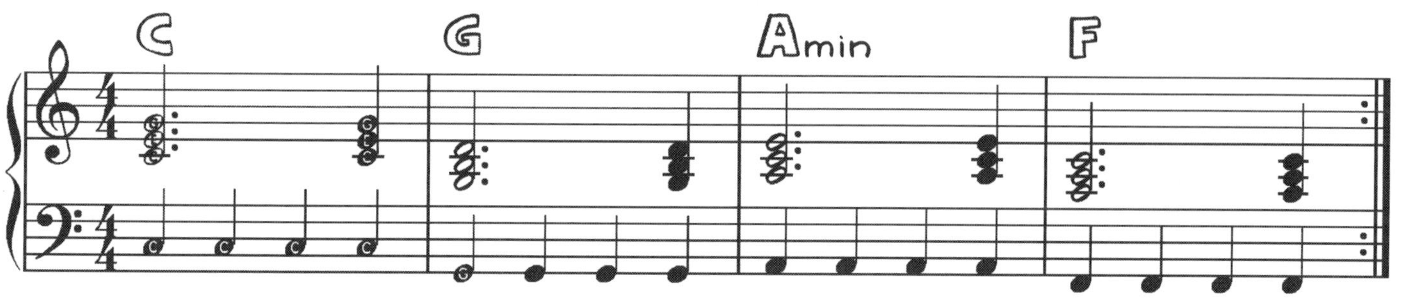
C
G
Amin
F

#77.

C
G
Amin
F

CREATE YOUR OWN LYRICS

Write your own lyrics here.

CHAPTER 12

OPEN MIC

You've gone from playing simple chords and arpeggios to playing timeless patterns and powerful progressions. It's time to put all of your skills together and take the stage.

In this "open mic" chapter, you'll create your own song by combining chord progressions and rhythm patterns. Come back to this activity again and again to write new songs, and who knows... perhaps you'll take your songs from this illustrated stage to a real one!

OPEN

CHOOSE A PROGRESSION

C F G F I IV V IV	C Dmin F G I ii IV V	Amin F G Emin vi IV V iii
G F Amin G V IV vi V	C Amin F G I vi IV V	C G F G I V IV V
Amin F C G vi IV I V	C Emin F G I iii IV V	Choose one from the book
Amin C G Amin vi I V vi	Dmin C G Amin ii I V vi	Create your own

MIC
CHOOSE A PATTERN
Choose one from the book
Create your own
Come back next week for a new song!

CREATE A SONG:

For printable staff paper, visit mwfunstuff.com/CCC

Keep creating! Come back to this chapter again and again.

UP AHEAD
LEAD SHEETS
OCTAVES
SYNCOPATION
SUS CHORDS
SEVENTH CHORDS
ROCKING CHORDS
CHORD VOICING
INVERSIONS
MERIDEE WINTERS
Now take your skills to the next level
In Chord Crash Course Book 2
CHORD CRASH COURSE BOOK 2

CHORD SCALE GLOSSARY

For a printable chord guide, visit mwfunstuff.com/CCC

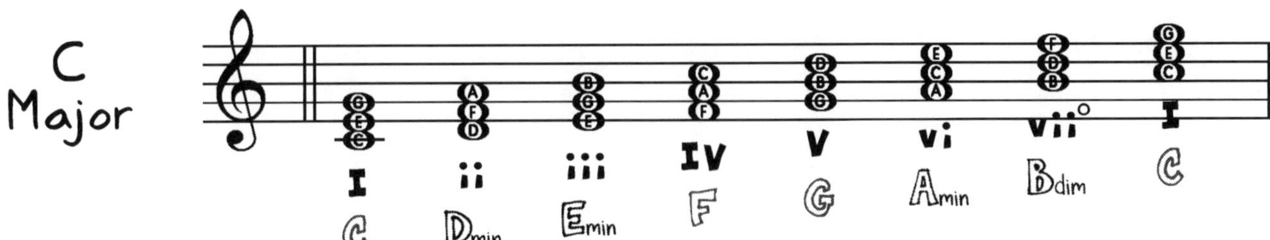

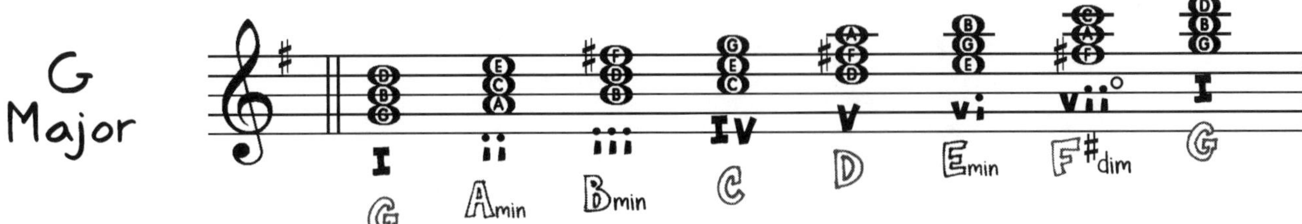

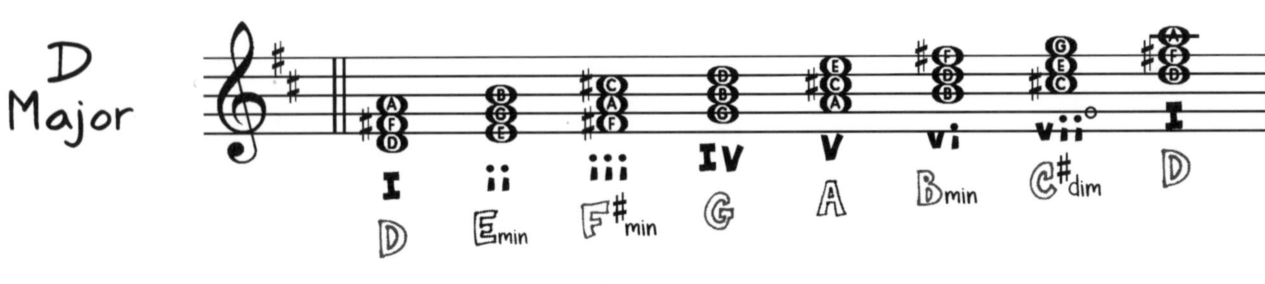

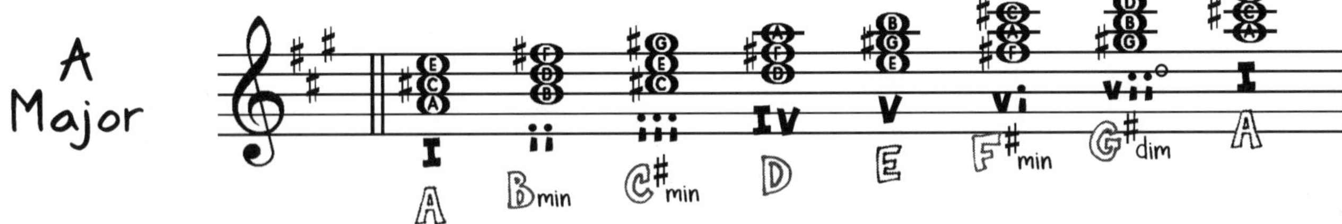

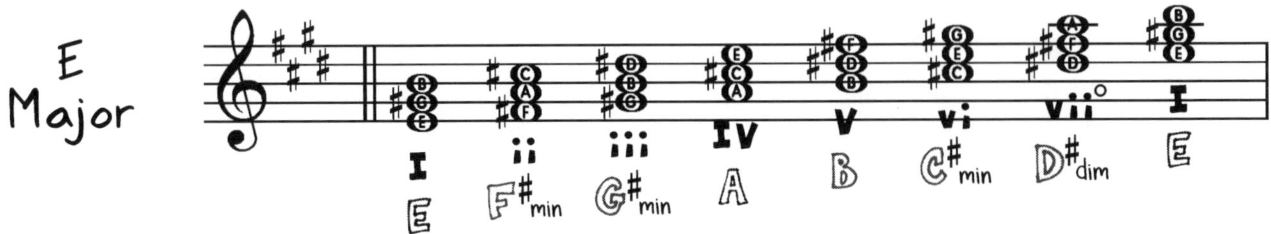

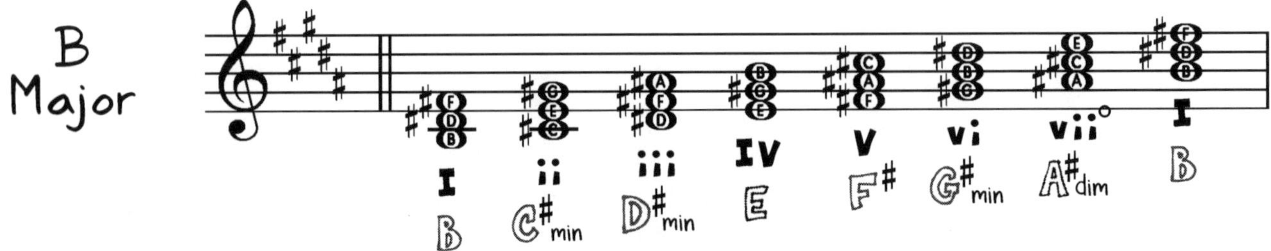

TOOL For a printable chord guide, visit mwfunstuff.com/CCC

SONG IDEAS

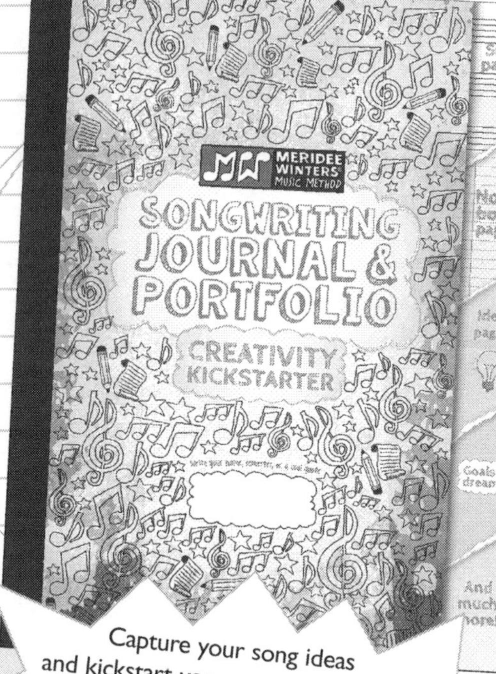

Capture your song ideas and kickstart your creativity with the Meridee Winters Songwriting Journal and Portfolio. With idea pages, staff paper, and space to write out goals and doodle, it is a great companion to the Chord Crash Course Series.

DOWNLOAD MORE SONGWRITING PAGES!

Visit mwfunstuff.com/ccc

DOODLES

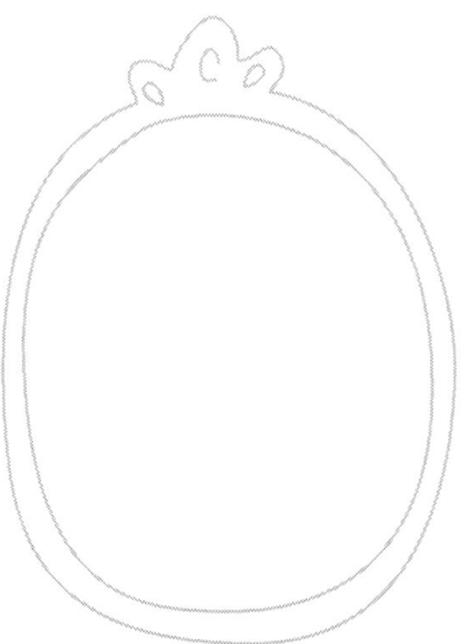

THE MERIDEE WINTERS MUSIC METHOD

Sparking brilliance with patterns, chords and games

Want to supercharge your progress with your instrument or find a tool to help you create music?
Find Meridee's globally-popular, trailblazing instructional books, innovative music games, online lesson info and more at merideewintersmusicmethod.com - or find us on Amazon.com!

EVIL VILLAINS

CHORD QUEST SERIES

Our brains are wired to excel at patterns. Finally, a kid's music book that teaches that way. (And sure has fun doing it.)

PORTALS & POWERS

What do you get when you take the great content and innovative teaching style from *Chord Crash Course*, but design and pace it for school aged kids? The *Chord Quest Powerful Piano Lessons* Series! Like its older counterpart, *Chord Quest* uses the power of patterns and shapes to have students playing great-sounding music from the very first lesson — without reading music. **Each book is its own quest where students learn universal patterns, earn powers and defeat villains like the Baron von Boring!**

PLUNKADILLO

SUPER START! MY FIRST PIANO PATTERNS

SPACE ANT

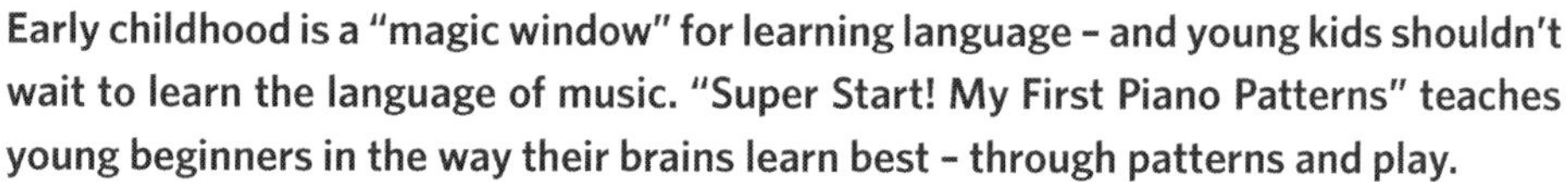

Early childhood is a "magic window" for learning language - and young kids shouldn't wait to learn the language of music. "Super Start! My First Piano Patterns" teaches young beginners in the way their brains learn best - through patterns and play.

Super Start! My First Piano Patterns contains 36 piano pattern songs, games and activities that will guarantee a fun and successful start to piano lessons. As students work their way across Planet Plunk they learn, play, improvise, explore and even encounter a few "Plunkadillos." By using patterns, simple diagrams and playful characters, students sound great from day one - without needing to read music. Songs gradually increase in skill throughout the book, culminating in a final chapter of youngster-friendly waltzes and classically-inspired pattern songs. **Sound great! Play by shape!**

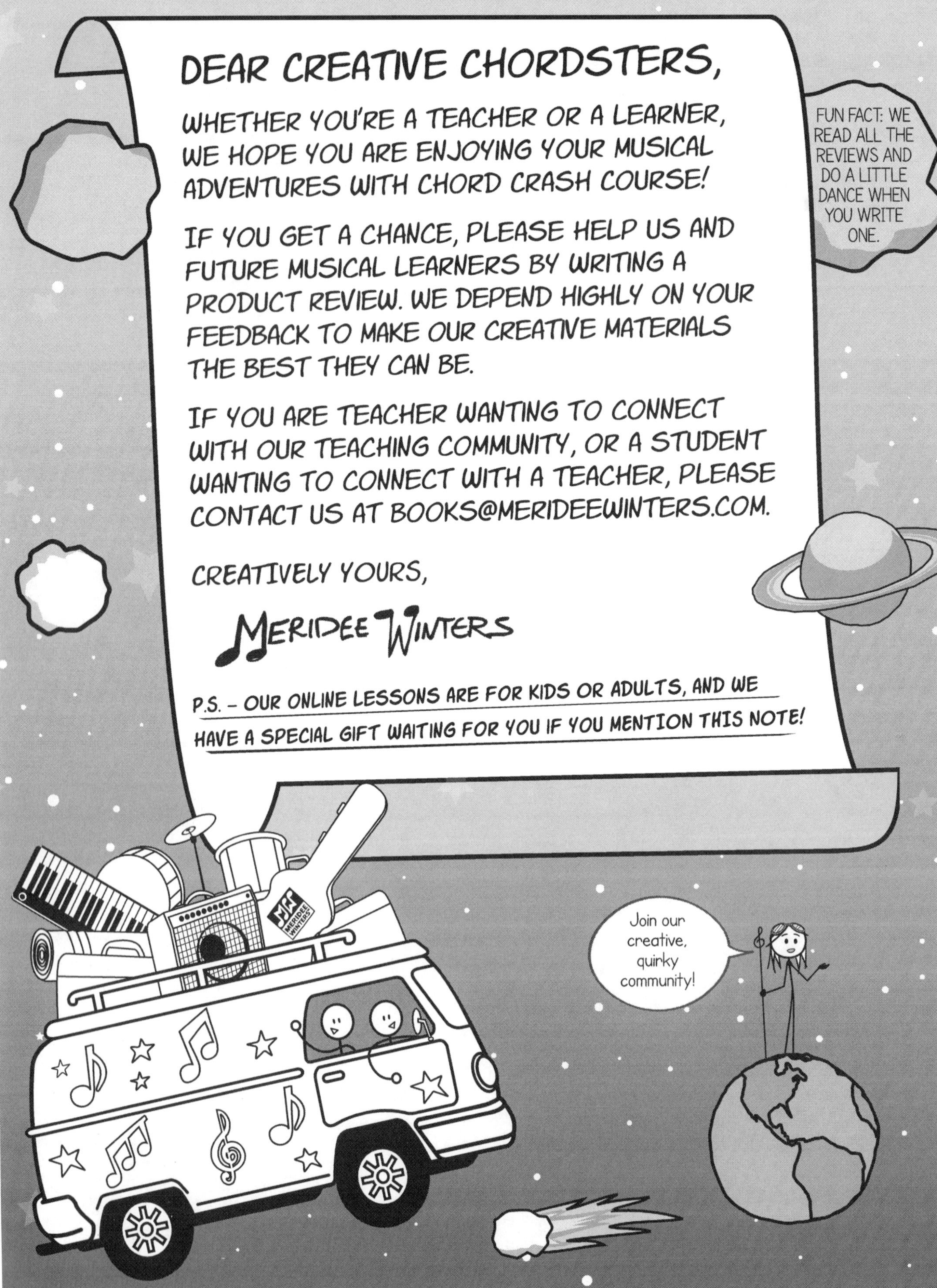
DEAR CREATIVE CHORDSTERS,
WHETHER YOU'RE A TEACHER OR A LEARNER, WE HOPE YOU ARE ENJOYING YOUR MUSICAL ADVENTURES WITH CHORD CRASH COURSE!
IF YOU GET A CHANCE, PLEASE HELP US AND FUTURE MUSICAL LEARNERS BY WRITING A PRODUCT REVIEW. WE DEPEND HIGHLY ON YOUR FEEDBACK TO MAKE OUR CREATIVE MATERIALS THE BEST THEY CAN BE.
IF YOU ARE TEACHER WANTING TO CONNECT WITH OUR TEACHING COMMUNITY, OR A STUDENT WANTING TO CONNECT WITH A TEACHER, PLEASE CONTACT US AT BOOKS@MERIDEEWINTERS.COM.
CREATIVELY YOURS,
MERIDEE WINTERS
P.S. – OUR ONLINE LESSONS ARE FOR KIDS OR ADULTS, AND WE HAVE A SPECIAL GIFT WAITING FOR YOU IF YOU MENTION THIS NOTE!
FUN FACT: WE READ ALL THE REVIEWS AND DO A LITTLE DANCE WHEN YOU WRITE ONE.
MERIDEE WINTERS
Join our creative, quirky community!

Made in United States
Orlando, FL
18 December 2024

56044435R00070